HABITUALLY EXCELLENT

THE 7 HABITS OF OPERATIONAL EXCELLENCE

HAROLD CHAPMAN

Habitually Excellent

The 7 Habits of Operational Excellence

ISBN: 978-1-66789-666-3

CONTENTS

ABOUT THE AUTHOR

A wise man once explained to me that all businesses have two wolves that live inside of them. These wolves are constantly battling each other. One wolf cares for the people within the business and sees the business as a means to provide livelihood and meaningful work to as many people as possible. Then there is another wolf that only cares about lining the pockets of the top leadership and owners and will do so at the expense of the people in the business. The latter wolf has a greed motive; not to be confused with a profit motive which is needed to keep a business in business and continue providing value to the many stakeholders in the business. When I asked the wise man which wolf would win, he told me, "Whichever one you feed!"

Hi, I am Harold Chapman. I hope you are feeding the right wolf in your business. I have devoted the last 28 years of my career constantly learning new ideas and coaching leaders in change management and in the application of operational excellence principles, concepts, practices, and tools. I haven't always called what I was practicing "operational excellence." Operational Excellence is the phraseology that I finally felt most comfortable using. I never considered what I was doing simply Lean, Six Sigma, Shainin, Modularity, or Theory of Constraints. It was more of a combination of all those disciplines depending on the problem in front of me. For the most part, it has been a blast, but occasionally I run across leaders that think their cup is already full (meaning they do not need to learn anymore, these leaders suffer from "Arrogance of the Learned"), and it is hard to pour into a cup that is already full. These are the same people who often suffer from NIH

(Not Invented Here) syndrome. My guess is you are neither of these types of leaders; otherwise, you would not be reading this book. Writing this book does not mean that I have arrived and know everything there is to know about operational excellence. I am sure I will look back on this book in a few years and think, "Wow! I didn't know how much I didn't know when I wrote that book." I personally embrace the times when I am proven wrong for that is the only time, I know that I have truly learned something new. My stance has always been once I am proven wrong, I am now less wrong about the world than I was before.

Before my time as a consultant (I never really liked being called a consultant due to the negative stigma, so I always consider myself a resultant), I spent 13 years at Bosch in various roles related to manufacturing. Bosch is one of the largest privately owned companies in the world and was (and may still be) the largest Tier 1 automotive supplier at the time. During my time as a coach at Bosch and outside of Bosch, I have had the pleasure of working with some of the smartest people and with some of the finest companies on the planet. The list of clients I have helped range from $10M to $80B in revenue per year. The company structures have ranged from Mom-and-Pop (one company was called MAP Industries where MAP literally stood for Mom And Pop) shops/startups, Multi-Generational-Family-Owned, to Global Industry Giants.

The types of industries served are listed below:

Oil and Gas	Automotive
Food	Toys
Pharmaceutical Packaging	Refrigeration
Medical Devices	Heavy Steel Fab
HVAC	Precision Machining
Military	Electronics
Paper Processing	Advanced Materials
Furniture	Injection Molding
Aerospace Components	Airplane Manufacture

The locations of these companies range from the US to Asia (Latitudinal) and Europe to Honduras (Longitudinal). With the wide range of industries and locations, I have and continue to utilize the thinking in this book coupled with a lot of blood, sweat, and tears, to generate hundreds of millions of dollars in savings; not simply cutting costs. The use of the word "savings" here is very intentional. There is a high price to reducing costs if not done the correct way. The problem with cutting cost is the cost being cut had a purpose and if that purpose is still present or will be present again in the future you will have created a void in the business. Never in my career have I (nor will I ever) approached a client with the goal of cutting costs (especially headcount). Headhunting in the name of cost-cutting is disrespectful to the people in the business. That is the worst way to approach improvement or change; more on that later.

There will be times when we reduce the need for headcount, but we do not lay those people off. Below is my philosophy on dealing with the additional headcount:

- Reduce Overtime to Zero
- Help with Continuous Improvement in other areas.

- Increase the rate of problem-solving.
- Do not backfill attrition.
- Grow the business, so they will be needed.
- Insource work that had been previously outsourced.

Note: *While it may be a good idea to outsource expertise that the business may not have (or may not ever want to have), it is never a good idea to outsource simply for the sake of reducing associates.*

I grew up in a small-town south of Greenville, SC (halfway between Atlanta GA and Charlotte NC). We lived on the Pelzer Mill Hill when I was born and soon after moved to the Williamston Mill Hill. A mill hill is a collection of cheap houses built around a cotton mill. The worker's houses were spec houses with a living room, kitchen, and a couple of bedrooms. They didn't have indoor plumbing at first, so everyone had outhouses. When sewage lines were run, there was a lean-to (still a trademark of a mill hill house to this day) added to each house that had a bathroom and often a back porch where a washer was located. Dryers were not affordable in the beginning, so everyone used clothes lines. The people that worked in the mill lived on the mill hill. Both of my parents were mill workers for most of their lives. My dad was a loom fixer (he eventually left in the 80's to start his own business), and my mom was a weaver. She worked in the mill until the day they closed it. She then moved to metal working and that is the job she had when she retired.

When I was 7, we moved to the "country." My dad had saved up some money and bought 12 acres between Belton, SC and Williamston, SC. We did not have much, but we had plenty of lands to run around on and play. It was on that land that we eventually built our own house. We gave our house in Williamston to my uncle, so six of us lived in a two-bedroom single wide, while building the house in the country. I thought that house would never be finished. We finally got the house to the point where it was inhabitable and moved in, but we never had central air conditioning and it was never really finished. That same house today sets way off the road and only a chimney and foundation blocks remain. We drank well water, had 5 (3 VHF, 2 UHF) channels on the TV (which I was the remote for most of the time), raised the windows when it was hot, and burnt wood when it was cold. On extremely cold mornings before school, we may even turn on the electric oven and leave the oven door open. I would not know what having central air conditioning was like until I was an adult and out on my own.

We were poor, but we did not know it. I didn't realize I was poor until High School. There were times when I wore sandals with soles made from old tires, and a fun weekend often included dumpster diving throughout the county. During one trip to dumpster dive, I remember a car pulled up and we were instructed by my dad to hide. A lady got out of a shiny new car with a pizza box, when she threw the box into the dumpster it startled me, but my scream seemed to have startled her even more. As we stood there awkwardly looking at each other, she said, "Son, there are some uneaten pieces in that box if you want them." Our family still laughs about that day. I thought dumpster diving was normal, and we would always find cool things that others would toss in the trash. It is true that one man's trash is another man's treasure.

As mentioned earlier, when my dad left the cotton mill in the early 80s, he started his own tree business. He and I built every piece of equipment used in that business. We would go look at a piece of equipment we needed, take some measurements, and then build an exact or better version. We built everything we needed, because my dad's motto was, "We have more time than money." Traveling the globe consulting can be very rewarding but it also consumes a lot of your time, so I find my problem to be just the opposite; I have more money than time.

This problem of having more money than time can lead to issues. An old man once explained to me that I should be very careful not to make life too easy for my kids. When I asked him why, he stated, "My grandfather walked everywhere he went, my dad always bought used cars, I have purchased several new cars, my children purchased luxury cars, but my grandkids were walking again." He explained that the following cycle plays out generation after generation if not broken:

TOUGH TIMES MAKE MEN STRONG,
STRONG MEN MAKE EASY TIMES; EASY TIMES MAKE MEN
WEAK, WEAK MEN MAKE TOUGH TIMES

Times were tough for me growing up. I worked very hard. My dad ensured that, but it was not for money; it was for room and board. While other kids were out playing games or hanging out with their friends, I was expected to work on whatever project we had going at the time. I resented it at the time, but I now know it formed the foundation for my mechanical knowledge. My dad and I did not get along at times, but he gave me skills that I still use to this day. My mom on the other hand is a Saint. She would serve as the mediator between my dad and me. We were both very strong-willed men, but she managed to keep the peace. I won the ovarian lottery when I was born to her. She taught me the importance of working hard regardless of how you feel. Afterall, she worked up until the day I was born and was back at work shortly after. She also taught me that sitting at home holding hands with a girl does not pay the bills.

Those tough times made me strong. Since we did not have money growing up, I vowed to out-work and out-learn everyone around me. Those were two things that I had complete control over. My first real job paid $2/hr. This job was at a pork-skin hut at a local flea market (The Anderson Jockey Lot) on the weekends. I worked there until I was fired by the owner for giving directions to a patron of the flea market. Back then, if anyone wanted to know where something was at the flea market, they knew to ask us, the food vendors. We spent our days cooking and selling to the other vendors, so we knew where everything was. That was the first and only time I have been fired. In hindsight, getting fired from the pork-skin hut was a blessing, since I went one mile down the road and got a job at a seafood restaurant, called Stanley's Seafood. The job at Stanley's required me to work during the week, so I had to ride the school bus there (I was only 13 years old) and my sister would pick me up late at night after closing time. I eventually was old enough to drive and bought an RX7 from Little Brown's Used cars. I paid $30/week for that car, and it was sharp. I would spend the next five years at Stanley's. I was mentored by the owner, Robert Stanley, and I cherish that time both for the mentoring and the friendships made. I made some friends there that I still cherish to this day.

After an altercation with my dad, I moved out of my parent's house when I was 13. I spent time living with my older sister and anyone else that would let me crash in their house. There were some nights where I would simply find an old dirt road and sleep in my car.

I graduated high school when I was 16 years old and spent the next two years helping Robert manage the restaurant. There was a time in my life when I thought I would be a restaurateur. However, when I got my first taste of manufacturing, I was hooked. The idea of having a rhythm (what I later learned to be takt) in what you were doing connected with me. The restaurant business was very non-rhythmic.

During my senior year in high school, I began working multiple jobs. Back then you could get a work permit and work in factories if you were under 18. I worked some nights at a local textile mill. The work was easy, and the money was good. I would also be working at the restaurant when not working at the textile mill. Right before Christmas one year, the textile company had a huge layoff, and I was affected. The bad part was when they called back after the new year to ask me to come back. My response was, "Not a Chance." I do not want anything to do with a company that will lay people off in that manner. At age 18, I was able to work at another factory called Autecs. My cousin Billy Chapman was already working there and told me the right channels to follow to get hired. Autecs was a joint venture between Bosch and Unisia JECS Corp from Japan. My main goal was to use this job at Autecs as an inroad to Bosch. As I was growing up, I knew people that had been in the Bosch Apprenticeship Program. I saw what working at

Bosch had done for one of my friends. His family was poor like mine, but he was able to pull himself out of being poor by working at Bosch and getting into the apprenticeship. My goal when I learned of the apprenticeship was to get in it. My first step was to work at Autecs and be the best "whatever" they had ever seen. It turns out my first job was running a machine that put four screws (at the same time) in a mass air flow meter housing. ***Disclaimer: This was before my understanding of flow had been developed, so do not judge me.*** I could run eight hours' worth of product in four hours. I would then set the, what I now know to be WIP, to the side, what I now know to be my customer (the next process) and vanish. I did not do this so I could simply go goof off. I had discovered who the maintenance technicians and engineers were, and I wanted to learn more about what they did. I asked them if I could shadow them, and that is exactly what I did every day. I learned a lot by shadowing these folks. I am not sure they knew what impact they were having on me at the time, but they laid the foundations for what would become my love affair with manufacturing.

I became a dad around this time. I am not sure Dyllon will ever realize that his arrival was perfect timing for me. I needed that little guy in my life to slow me down. Life was moving fast and all the things that go along with a fast life had gotten a hold of me, but when he came along, I had to grow up fast. I knew that I was not going to be with his mom, but I wanted him to be with me, so I fought to get him, and I eventually won custody. In those days it was unheard of for a dad to get custody.

"Unflinching, unremitting work will accomplish anything."
—*Thomas Edison*

Eventually, my hard work paid off and I got a job at Bosch. My first job was in the department that manufactured Oxygen Sensors for the automotive market. In fact, when I was at that site, all the products were automotive. Not sure if that is still the case. I quickly discovered there was another area on the site that paid more money. I asked and was told that you must take a test to work in that area. Of course, my next question was, "When can I take the test?" I took the test and passed. I then started working in a building called 104 (aka The Country Club, since it was so clean and quiet) and an area called The Cleanroom. This area was the coolest.

The technology in this area was beyond anything I had ever seen. My next step was to see what it would take to get into the apprenticeship program. The program had been paused for a few years, but they had restarted it the year before, so I missed the first year spot. My goal was to be in the apprenticeship in the second year after the restart. I found out who was over the apprenticeship program and approached her. Her name was Carrie Wasson, and she did not know me at the time, but eventually we became great friends. I will never forget her first advice to me. I was not as clean cut as I am today. Back then I was a long haired, earring wearing, crotch-rocket riding, cigarette smoking, 19-year-old. It turns out I did not look the part of a professional back then. Who knew? She looked at me and said, "If you cut your hair and take those earrings out, you might go places." The next day, I was back in front of her with short hair and no earrings asking, "What's the next step?" My reasoning for making the change so quickly was based on two important things I had learned growing up. Those two things are iron sharpens iron, and only a fool rejects correction. Carrie was my iron and source of correction early on at Bosch.

Even at this young age, I realized the value of going down to go up. I had to take a pay cut to enter the apprenticeship, but that was a step down that I was willing to take. That step down has paid huge dividends. I entered the apprenticeship in the second year after the restart. The time spent in the apprenticeship was one of the coolest experiences of my life. I was able to work, learn machine tools, and go to school at the same time. Bosch worked closely with two local schools to fill our calendars with learning opportunities. I would spend time at Tri-County Tech, Clemson, the Bosch Toolroom, and the Bosch Electronics Lab. In my spare time, I would work as much overtime as possible at the plant. I had plenty of people around me to help me raise my son, and other than him, I had few responsibilities and plenty of time to spare. I wish I had all the money I blew back then.

After I graduated from college, I spent a very short stint back in building 104 in the Cleanroom on 3rd shift doing maintenance. I am glad it was a short stint since working 3rd shift hours almost killed me. I do not know how people do that for the long-term. I was on the 3rd shift for 8 months. One great thing came out of that time on the 3rd shift, which was me meeting my future wife (Lori). Our first date was at the Cracker Barrel after work one morning. We now have four children (Dyllon, Kelsey, Kensley, and Prestyn) and five grandsons (Gabe, Lucas, Cash, Grayson, and Malachi). Dyllon is a lot like my dad and can fix anything, Kelsey taught me how delicate a girl can be, Kensley taught me how tough a girl can be, and Prestyn is the most compassionate of the group. Prestyn is often the voice of reason when things are escalating. I am very proud of my children and have enjoyed raising them with Lori. Lori and I will be celebrating 24 years of marriage this year. It all started when I was her maintenance technician at Bosch. I jokingly tell people that she had the best running machine in the plant. There is some truth to that.

I was settled into the 3rd shift maintenance routine and had not considered management at that point in my career, but an off-shift group leader (Janet Jones, a great lady) approached me and stated that she thought I should apply for a shift coordinator (supervisor) position. I decided to apply, and I eventually got the job. I later learned that I was not the reporting manager's top pick, but the interview process was set up in a manner that prevented one person's opinion from over-riding the group's opinion. That was one of the many things I learned at Bosch; always create a solid process and then trust the process. I spent the next few years moving up the ranks in leadership and eventually landed in Engineering.

Engineering was the ultimate for me. I love leading people, but people are not like machines. My engineering mind loved the discipline of programs and robots. You tell them what to do and it happens over and over without question. Later in my career as a consultant, this love of engineering and equipment got me the moniker of Machine Whisperer at many of my clients. I have not found a process that I cannot improve, and I cherish the opportunity to prove that point.

My engineering career at Bosch gave me a chance to combine all my skills up to that point. If the program or robot is not running, I would simply lean on the skills I learned in maintenance. All machines can be broken down into their simplest forms (wires, frame, motors, sensors, controls, etc.) at which time the machine, no matter how complicated, becomes very simple. If I had to implement a new complex process that involved people, I would simply lean on the skills I learned in management (including the skills I gained from my time with Robert at Stanley's Seafood). I was having a blast and saving Bosch tons of money in the process. I took a very brief hiatus from the Bosch Anderson plant to Knoxville, TN to work at a plant that Bosch eventually bought but was back in Anderson within eight months. It was my idea to move to Knoxville that first time, but it turned out my wife did not really want to live in Knoxville, TN which explains the short time before moving back to Anderson. The move back to SC was a hard decision for me, but it was the right thing to do for my family. That was in the early 2000's. We later moved back to Knoxville and lived there for 8 years. It was her decision to move the second time; lesson learned. I have learned that when I honor my wife good things happen.

Upon arriving back at Bosch after our 8 months in TN, my new position was great. I was traveling to Germany on a regular basis and even considered moving there for a multi-year assignment. However, the assignment did not pan out, and I was getting bored. One of my fears in life was I didn't want to sit back and simply count the years; I wanted to make my years count. At that time, I had been moonlighting with some small capital automation projects and I had an offer to go work with a consulting firm. The combination of these two items made it appealing to leave Bosch, so that is what I did. Concerning leaving Bosch, it was very important to me to finish strong, and I never wanted to burn a bridge that I may need in the future.

This approach had already paid off when I had to ask if I could come back to Bosch when I was in Knoxville the first time. Knowing Lori wasn't happy, I called the plant to let them know I was interested in returning, and I had a job offer with a raise and a relocation package by lunch time that same day.

I will always look back on my time at Bosch with fondness. Bosch is one of the best companies for which one could ever hope to work. On the day I got my hiring notice from Bosch, I felt like I had won the lottery. Those were some of the most impactful years of my life. If anyone is looking for a great company for which to work, I highly recommend Bosch. Out of respect for the past and current leaders at Bosch, there will never be a negative word about Bosch come out of my mouth.

The years since Bosch, have been a blast as well. The boredom I felt at Bosch, has never returned. In my current role, I must prove myself every time I show up at a client. There is no resting on one's laurels in the consulting business. You either perform or you do not eat. The length of engagement for a consultancy with any given client ranges from weeks to years. I have been blessed to have clients that I have been consulting with for over 16 years (My first engagement was before I left Bosch, and he is still a client. I would use my vacation days at Bosch to consult. To this day, I am not sure he knew he was my first consulting engagement.). For me, another welcomed challenge of being a consultant is you must constantly learn. An example of this is when a client asks if I can do a workshop on a book they just read. My answer is always yes. I then go home and read the book and study everything I can on that topic to enable me to WOW them with the workshop. My philosophy is, if your client knows more than you know about operational excellence and change management, then they do not need you.

As far as education, I have a General Engineering Degree (Electrical, Mechanical, Controls, and Industrial). This degree was developed by Bosch to close a skill gap they had at the time in manufacturing. They did not need solely mechanical, electrical, control, or industrial skills in separate individuals. They needed multi-skilled engineers that could design and maintain the complex processes that were needed to manufacture the state-of-the-art products that were (and I assume are still) coming out of Germany. In addition to my degree in General Engineering, I have also studied at Wharton School of Business, Harvard Business School, Rochester Institute of Technology, and the University of Kentucky. However, most of my learning has come from working shoulder to shoulder with my clients and fingertip close to their processes. I never formally pursued an MBA, but I guess you could say that I got my MBA from the school of hard knocks.

There are many companies, books, seminars, and people that have shaped my thinking over the years. As mentioned before, some of the most profound impacts in my career I attribute to Bosch and all the fine people that sewed into my life during my many years there, and some even after I left. For these people, I am forever grateful. After leaving Bosch, I have been on a journey of my own helping other businesses improve as well as starting new businesses, coming up with new innovations, and realizing that part of innovation is an evolutionary iterative process that if followed will always generate new ideas and products. These experiences have further developed the critical skills I developed during my time at Bosch. I am honored that I have been given the opportunity to do what I do, and I stand on the shoulders of the giants of the industry that have come before me.

Many thanks to my wife for putting up with the extreme depths of ignorance I have toward how to be a good husband and father. She has been patiently coaching me in that regard for many years now. She has also endured the many years of my constant travel and made every place we moved a welcoming home to our four children. When we first met, I was a single dad with only a bag of clothes, a KIA Sophia, and a mattress to my name. Some guys wonder if a woman is after them for their money or not. I am 100% sure that was not the case with Lori since neither of us had any money when we met. We have come a long way together, and I look forward to what the future holds for us.

I am honored to have had so many business leaders trust me with their teams. I love what I do. Which is a good thing, because one cannot do this kind of work if they do not love it, and I hope that my love for it shows when I am with my clients. I also hope it shows in this book as you read it. Consulting is not for everyone, but for those who want a variety of work, travel to cool places, and meet lots of new people across varied industries, I highly recommend it. It has been and continues to be a wild ride. A special thanks to all of those I have met along the way, you have impacted me as much as I would like to think I have impacted you!!!!

PREFACE

"An Investment in Knowledge Pays the Best Interest"
—Ben Franklin

Warning: I am especially hard on leadership throughout this book, as I believe leaders have a huge responsibility to protect the livelihoods of those who are under their leadership. I also believe that there are no bad teams, only bad leaders. I have seen too many times where a poor leader has caused many people to lose their jobs. In my opinion, this happens due to the leader's inability to run the business. Some reading this book may think I am being hateful; the truth will sound like hate to those that hate the truth. I can assure you it is in the spirit of being brutally honest that I am writing this book. Anyone who knows me, knows that I have the heart of a teacher, and there is nothing more important (in the business world) to me than developing stronger leaders. My goal for every leader is for them to have a standard of habitually excellent behavior that becomes a matter of conscience. If you do what you have always done, you will get what you have always gotten, so the change must start with you.

Ha·bit·u·al·ly /hə ˈbiCH(o͞o)əlē/ - by way of habit; customarily.

Ex·cel·lent /ˈeks(ə)lənt/ - extremely good, outstanding.

To be extremely good, outstanding, by way of habit. How cool would that be both personally and professionally? Life isn't easy. Life as a leader is even more challenging. There should be a sign in the maternity ward that states, "Welcome to Life; Results May Vary." That is true, and we in large part can control those results. Having good habits is important in all aspects of life. If you look at any great business, you will see at the heart of that business, a leader or group of leaders that have habits that allow them and their business to be excellent. A famous case in point are the Rockefellers. John D.

Rockefeller, at one point the wealthiest man alive, had ten habits that led to his success. Those ten habits are below:

1. The executive team is healthy and aligned.

2. Everyone is aligned with the #1 thing that needs to be accomplished this quarter to move the company forward.

3. Communication rhythm is established, and information moves through the organization accurately and quickly.

4. Every facet of the organization has a person assigned with accountability for ensuring goals are met.

5. Ongoing employee input is collected to identify obstacles and opportunities.

6. Reporting and analysis of customer feedback data is as frequent and as accurate as financial data.

7. Core Values and Purpose are 'alive' in the organization.

8. Employees can articulate the key components of the company's strategy.

9. All employees can answer quantitatively whether they had a good day.

10. The company's plans and performance are visible to everyone.

These habits were penned many decades ago, but they are timeless and universal and can be applied today to any enterprise. They served as the foundation of Rockefeller's business for many years. The fact that he distilled them and led by example made them effective. Everyone has habits (good and bad) whether they think they do or not. What are your habits?

> "People don't decide their future. They decide their habits and their habits decide their futures." — *F.M. Alexander*

Great habits must be based in principle, and I firmly believe that anyone or any company can be excellent if they consistently apply themselves in a principled way. Afterall, success doesn't come from what you do occasionally;

it comes from what you do consistently. Too often ambition and passion get in the way of principle centered habits. I propose that we should never put passion ahead of principles, for if you win, you will lose. The correct principles must be formed into habits that become a part of the person or persons (when speaking of an enterprise) daily practice. You may ask what habits one must have to ensure they are excellent today and into the future. In this book I will discuss the need for habits, the habits themselves, and the journey to become Habitually Excellent for any enterprise. I would hope that every enterprise has the goal of becoming world-class or even breaking through the current world-class barrier and defining the new world-class.

"We can't solve a problem with the same thinking we had when we created it." — *Albert Einstein*

I am often asked what the best approach is to improve a business. My answer is always, "The approach that works is the best approach." Followed by, "We will start with what we know now, iterate and adjust until we find the right approach." Afterall, all models are flawed, but some are useful. It is my hope that you find something useful in what I have written here. The thinking outlined in this book will naturally lead one to world-class and even beyond.

"You can't see what you don't understand. But what you think you already understand, you'll fail to notice." —*Richard Powers*

However, before we begin the journey, we must first understand what it will take and agree to even take the journey. This understanding must come before ever implementing the tools. Some companies see the tools of improvement during a tour somewhere or read about them in an article and blindly implement them in their business. The problem with this approach is the tools they are implementing were to solve a problem at the other company. They may not have the same problem, or it may not be the biggest problem. This approach can lead to improvement, but not the long-lasting culture change that will be needed to endure the journey and support those improvements. The culture you have today (good or bad) is the culture you have earned. If we want to improve the culture, we must change the leader's thinking. The change in thinking will change the leader's expectations and that will change the culture for the better. We must constantly strive for a culture of excellence. My focus in this book is mainly on developing the mindset and habits behind becoming Habitually Excellent. This is NOT a tool book.

> "Life, as I see it, is not a location, but a journey. Even the man who feels himself "settled" is not settled; he is probably sagging back. Everything is in flux and was meant to be. Life Flows. We may live at the same number of the street, but it is never the same man that lives there." — *Henry Ford*

Implementing tools will not build a culture. Our goal is to create a better culture. This process of transitioning a culture is very delicate and must be protected from those wishing it harm. In his book "Accountability: The Key to Driving a High-Performance Culture," Greg Bustin describes what he refers to as culture crashers:

The Sugar Coater: Willing to address 90% of what needs to be addressed, but avoids, downplays, or glosses over the difficult 10% that can drive positive change. Unwilling or unable to talk about tough issues that must be addressed to improve organizational or individual performance.

The Control Freak: Doesn't trust anyone or anything so cannot let go and, as a result, is always doing someone else's job… except their own. The same person will erect barriers to colleague's initiatives.

The Monday Morning Quarterback: Armed with 20/20 hindsight, this second guesser says little of substance before a decision is made, and then spouts off afterward about what should have been done differently.

The Gossip: Spreads rumors and loves to dissect problems while rarely suggesting a solution. Avoids speaking to people who are the subject of the rants as well as to people with the power or capability to solve or improve issues.

The Dictator (aka Emperor with no clothes): Known to banish people from plum assignments and key meetings, those who answer hard questions truthfully. Also, regularly shoots messengers who surface problems.

The Know-It-All: As the unofficial expert on everything, this person has rarely had an idea that was not the best solution. Tone deaf to other possibilities.

The Fire Fighter: Rushes in to save the day but cannot or will not prevent the problem from recurring. Potentially could light fires to play the hero.

The Cover-up Artist: Dodges responsibility by deflecting blame to others. First in line, however, to take credit, regardless of whether they were responsible for success.

The Joker: Loves to poke fun at principles, policies, projects, and people. Everything is funny to this one, except themselves, which they take far too seriously. The Joker's deadlier cousin is **The Assassin,** who is more vicious in their ruthless approach to dispatching anyone or anything not to their liking.

The Quitter: Surrenders at the first sign of difficulty. Is tired of the fight, but not the paycheck. These individuals can often retire in place.

The Sandbagger: Protects budgets, goals, and deadlines with plenty of cushion to ensure underwhelming results. Has never seen a stretch goal they could not reduce.

The Empire-Builder: More interested in how many people report to them than developing talent, fixing problems, and getting results.

While Greg does not touch on this, it is also important to ensure the leader's leadership style is not leading to any of these culture crashing behaviors. For example, A person may resort to "sugar coating" behavior on a team led by someone who uses fear and authority to intimidate. Afterall, accountability goes in both directions, so a deeper look at the situation may be prudent. Our goal is to build a solid culture focused on improvement, so be on the lookout for these individuals in your organization. Consider this the social engineering work that must be done. Every organization has at least a few culture crashers. It is your job as the leader to deal with them; not ignore them. Should you choose not to deal with them, you are creating what I call management debt. Management debt is accumulated any time the leader does not make the right decision or takes the easy way out. The debt builds over time and will eventually come due with extreme interest penalties. By the way, these kinds of debt always come due in the worst timing. Instead of looking for an easy way out, look for a way through the issue you are facing.

During an interview with an incubator group, one of the CEOs of an older and highly successful start-up that came out of the incubator, was asked, "What is your biggest regret in leading a start-up?" His response was, "Not dealing with poor leadership early in the start-up. By the time I got around to dealing with the leadership issue, that leader had already hired ten other people that were just like them: not a good member of the team. Now I have eleven people to deal with instead of one." This is a perfect example of management debt accumulating interest. In this case, the CEO did deal with the issue, but in many cases, the top leader will not deal with it and simply let the mediocrity spread. If you are wanting a meritocracy-based, not mediocrity-based, enterprise, poor leadership cannot be tolerated. This long-suffering when it comes to dealing with poor leaders baffles me. We will burn through a lot of good people by not dealing with poor leaders. One should never underestimate the damage of a poor leader or the benefit of a good leader. It is magical to see the impact of the "right" leadership adjustments.

I witnessed another example of management debt at a $35B US based company. At the morning meeting we were discussing the fact that we were running out of bins to put our production parts into. When asked where all the bins were going, we were told that there are thousands of parts that need to be scrapped. These parts were stored in the bins that we needed. However, we can't scrap them due to the cost impact per the plant manager. This scrap had built up over years; long before the plant manager arrived. Instead of scrapping the parts, they are going to keep the parts and continue to handle them and count them as inventory which is adding more cost to those parts that should be out of the system. Some of these parts were raw metal which means we could get pure metal reclamation cost back (positive cashflow). Eventually, there will be a leader that has the nerve to deal with the issue. That leader would need to be high enough in the organization to be able to do the right thing without getting fired. I can tell you the plant manager at that site would have lost his job if he would have scrapped all that material without support from the top, and I assure you he didn't have support from the top in this case. This was a case of "Looking Good" for the market, instead of "Being Good" for the business.

In his book, "The Motive," Patrick Lencioni describes two types of leadership:

1. Reward Centered Leadership – the belief that being the leader is a reward for hard work.; therefore, the experience of being the leader should be pleasant and enjoyable, free to choose what they work on and avoid anything mundane, unpleasant, or uncomfortable.

2. Responsibility Centered Leadership: the belief that being a leader is a responsibility; therefore, the experience of leading should be difficult and challenging (though certainly not without elements of personal gratification).

Complete a quick personal assessment to determine in which group you would fall? Responsibility Centered Leadership is what it is going to take to do the work that lies ahead of you. If you are not there, you need to seriously consider your current situation and whether you want to begin the journey or continue in your role. Leadership is not a license to do less; it is a responsibility to do more.

When I think about the role of leadership and the sacrifice it entails, I am reminded of a story that was shared with me many years ago. A gentleman and his wife had traveled to a village in Africa as missionaries. As with most tribes, this tribe was living without many amenities that we take for granted. Their method for drawing water was to send these very strong men down into the wells. They would bring up the water on their backs. During one of their visits, one of these men had fallen back into the well and broken both of his legs. Everyone in the village had tried to free him from his watery grave, but no one was strong enough. The villagers summoned the Chief from his well-appointed tent. He appeared on the scene robed in fine garments and wearing a large headdress. As the Chief looked in the well at his fallen villager, a tear rolled down his cheek and he began to disrobe. He removed his headdress and proceeded down into the well. A few minutes later he rose from the well with the large man on his back. The gentleman telling the story was in awe that the Chief of the village had the strength and will to go into the well and save a villager. Well, that is what we as leaders are called to do sometimes. We must go down in the well and rescue our businesses and teams and give them hope that the best is yet to come. As leaders, we must be the ultimate hope-givers.

"Without hope in the future, there is no power in the present." — John Maxwell

Thank you for taking the time to read this book. I know you are very busy, and I am honored that you would spend your valuable time reading something I have created. With utmost respect, I would ask that you not move forward in your journey unless you are ALL IN. There will be many trips to the well for you. It will not be easy.

"If it were easy, it would already be done." — Aaron Styles

You must do what others will not to achieve what others cannot. There is no room for false starts. If you allow false starts to occur, your team will begin to think "false in one false in all" and lose trust in you. You must ensure that once you start, you can keep the momentum. Many challenges face you each day. You must be competitive despite: Labor costs in low wage countries, inflation and dollar valuation, piece price reductions built into purchasing contracts, increasing product variations, decreasing time to market expectations, increasing costs to do business (e.g.- fuel and steel surcharges, healthcare costs, etc.). These are challenging today and will get even more challenging as the years go by.

"Let your actions reflect your hopes; not your fears."
— Nelson Mandela

Getting over these challenges will be tough. Some leadership teams have got in their heads that implementing this new mindset will lead to quick results. These same leaders often exit the improvement initiative before the results flow through to the bottom line.

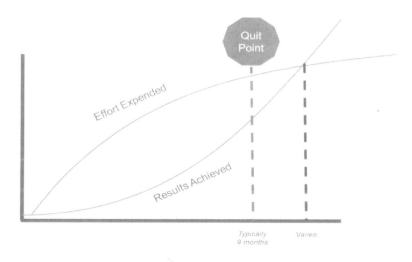

"Your journey isn't over when you mess up. It is over when you give up." — Unknown

This is a long journey, and it WILL NOT be easy. Some companies start the journey only to pull off at a rest stop and do tool implementation. The road to success is dotted with many tempting rest areas and parking lots.

I assume by reading this book, you want to be successful, so let us start with the difference between successful and unsuccessful people:

Successful People...	Unsuccessful People...
Focus on Being Taught	Focus on Being Entertained
Recognize and Develop	Neglect to Criticize (Apathy)
Embrace Change	Fear Change
Forgive	Hold Grudge
Talk About Ideas	Talk About People
Constantly Learn	Already Knows Everything
Accepts Responsibility	Blames Others
Has a Sense of Gratitude	Has Sense of Entitlement
Sets Goals	Has No Direction

How many of the unsuccessful items apply to you? Your goal should be to have zero.

The journey will require you to constantly look at the system that drives the processes. I have always been a believer in Thomas Edison's adage of "Genius is 1% inspiration and 99% perspiration." As you know, leadership is hard work. Part of our problem today is that hard work pays off in the future, but laziness pays off today. It is true that above average ambition with average intelligence will beat above average intelligence with average ambition every time. If you can find both in yourself and others, there will be no limits to what you can achieve in a free market economy. Remember, do today what others will not do so you can do tomorrow what they cannot do. Do hard things!

To be a good leader, you will often be physically and mentally drained at the end of each day. You will be physically drained because you have been on the beat talking to the people that make your business run, and mentally because you have been putting the brain power into making a great company that will be around for generations to come. It is also mentally exhausting to be an active listener. However, you must always be actively listening to ensure what is being said is correct and supports the direction of the company. If you allow wrong thinking to be expressed in your presence, it becomes the new standard of thinking. Leadership is challenging, and leading change is action oriented. It is easier to act yourself into a new way of thinking than to think yourself into a new way of acting. Action always leads to insight; but insight doesn't always lead to action.

> "Opportunity is missed by most people, because it is dressed in overalls and looks like work." — *Thomas Edison*

As I stated before, many leaders are tempted to jump straight to tool implementation to get quick wins. I want to impress upon you the importance of the Journey. The journey is long. It is lonely at times, but it is the only way to instill true Habitually Excellent behaviors and world-class systems in your organization. Your time spent in the GEMBA (Gemba is a Japanese word used to describe where the work is done, or the customer is served) will increase significantly while you ensure things are being done and results are achieved.

> "When you are out at the Gemba do something to help them. If you do, people will come to expect that you can help them and will look forward to seeing you again on the Gemba."
> — *Taiichi Ohno, the father of the Toyota Production System.*

As the leader, you must send the message that every leader's responsibility in your organization is to ensure Standards are Maintained, Continuous Improvement is embedded, and Innovation is pursued and adopted at the right time. As you embark on this journey, I am sure you will lose members of your team since they do not want the pressure. However, you will also see others unexpectedly rise to the challenge. When you have a Habitually

Excellent staff that is needed to be world-class, each one of them should be capable of being a world-class consultant for their function.

I will be using the word "value" a lot in this book, since providing value is the main purpose of any business. All businesses exist to add value in some form or another. If the business is not adding value, then why does the business exist? The example I have used in the past (borrowed from Will Franks) is a shirt. If you ask someone how much they would pay for some raw cotton, dye, buttons, and thread, you may get an answer like a couple of dollars. However, if you show them a finely crafted shirt made from those raw materials, you will get a much higher number. I personally pay close to $35 for a nice dress shirt. The difference between the two costs is that value has been added by converting the raw materials into a finished product (shirt in this case) with a desirable design and high-quality level. If the customer were willing to buy the raw materials and produce the shirt themselves, the shirt company would not have a business. Lucky for the business in this example, people do not want to make their own shirts. The challenge then is for the business to manage its resources in a manner to make a profit from the delta in raw materials cost, the cost to convert those raw materials into a shirt, and the price the customer is willing to pay. The same is true for your business.

I am certain that you are resource poor, so you must always ask yourself and your teams, "What problem are you trying to solve?" If there is no clear answer or the activity is not providing value to the customer (internal or external), we must wonder why we are doing the activity. As a business, everything we do must either make us money today or set us up to make money in the future.

> "You must engage the people in your organizations to improve the work that they do in accordance with company expectations and goals!!" — *Unknown*

Growing up in the rural part of South Carolina, I often visited a sawmill nearby. We heated with wood, so getting scraps from the sawmill was much easier than dropping trees, sawing them up, dragging them out of the back side of our property, and finally splitting the logs to fit the stove. During one of my trips to the sawmill, I asked the owner of the sawmill why a singular handle on the sawmill was painted bright green. This stood out to me since the rest of the sawmill was dingy, but this handle was pristine and bright green. His response to me was, "Son, that is the money-handle." Not fully grasping what he meant, I asked, "Why do you call it the money-handle?" His response was, "If that handle isn't being pulled, I am not making money." As I watched him afterwards, I noticed that he kept his eye on that handle and would respond when it was not being pulled. This handle was how he gauged if value was being added or wasted time was being created. What in your business is your money-handle? How often is it being pulled? Using this concept, I often conduct studies and show companies tons of opportunities in their business.

The money-handle is often tied to a piece of equipment in the business, but we cannot overlook the human assets within the business. I would argue that the human asset is the most valuable asset within any business. If you are prepared to shift your mindset in how you and your leaders manage the human assets within your company, AWESOME, you should continue reading this book. A lot of the approach given here is based on leveraging the human asset. Don't worry if you have not focused here in the past and forget the fact that you may have been totally wrong in your past approach. Though no one can go back and make a brand-new start, anyone can start from now and make a brand-new ending. Afterall, what happened yesterday is history, what happens tomorrow is a mystery, but what we do today can make a difference. Some people will not have the motivation to change. Many people have tried to explain the factors that drive an organization's motivation to change or not to change.

I personally like how David Gleicher et al attempted to assess an organization's readiness for change and created the following formula:

Resistance < Frustration*Vision*Path

Where:

Resistance (Organizational Memory) = The measured resistance of the organization to needed cultural, organizational, and technical change. This is at all levels but is heavily weighted with management (front line, middle, senior, and executive).

Frustration = The current dissatisfaction with the status quo measured at all levels but heavily weighted at the process operator levels. It has always interested me that the operators are often the most frustrated.

Vision = The measured existence of both a compelling plan along with its level of dissemination throughout the organization.

Path = The measured existence of the strategic and tactical plan to move us further along the path toward our vision.

In short, the frustration with status quo coupled with a vision and a clear path forward, must be greater than the current resistance (organizational memory) for change to occur. As an author and consultant, I can help with the Vision and Path. However, only you and your leadership team can deal with the level of resistance and frustration. Only you and your team can create the burning platform. Leadership in this case is the means to get us to the end (The Vision).

Do not start this journey if you do not think you can finish. We do not want to show people what 'can be' then take it away. They are better off not knowing and not having than to know and not have. I was reminded of the importance of this approach during one of my first trips to Honduras. During this trip, I visited a landfill. There were small children running around the landfill. The landfill was where their parent(s) would take them to look through the trash to find items for recycling that they could sell at the end of the day. The kids would do this instead of going to school. The kids there were very happy, since they did not know what they did not have. They are perfectly content with their current situation, so I did not do anything special that could not be sustained by the local teams in Honduras. I hope that over the years, what is possible for these people will increase and be sustained.

The local orphanage was being sponsored by the company I was helping, so we were doing our part to help. This was the main reason I was willing to help my client without charging my daily rate. With the support of my client, the orphanage was able to give the parent(s) the money the child would make collecting trash in exchange for letting the child attend school. We also created jobs for the local adults. We realized that a dollar earned goes farther than a dollar given. The jobs also gave them a sense of purpose, which is priceless.

A couple of years back while on a check-in visit with my client in Honduras, I had lunch with gentlemen named Raphello Minelli. Raphello is the President of a very successful wood business in Italy. The business is family owned and is in its 4th generation. Most family-owned businesses do not make it to the 4th generation. When I asked about why the business was a success and made it to the 4th generation, Raphello responded with a question. He asked me if I knew what the longest surviving business was and why it was successful. While I was contemplating my response, He stated that it was the Catholic Church, and the reason was because there is only one Pope. His conclusion was a business must have one Pope to survive and that was the motto of their business. He was the Pope for his business. You will have to be the Pope for your business.

The buck stops with you. You must stand for something, or you will fall for anything. I hope that something that you stand for is found within this book. As I mentioned before, the reward comes with time, but the work comes now. If you are too lazy to plow, do not expect a harvest. Top Leaders should be plowing the soil for other leaders to plant the seeds. You may even plow soil that you will never see produce fruit. The next generation will see the fruit instead, and you must be OK with this. It is the top leader's job to push the new expectations and the practitioner's job to respond to the pull that is created. Nothing is more frustrating than to simply get authorization to participate in change rather than active support in the change from the top leadership.

Make no mistake that the CEO (or top officer at the site) sets the tone for the company. We must have leaders that serve as the thermostats for the business instead of the thermometers of the business. Let me explain what I mean. The thermometer is a simple device that does one thing: react to external factors. As the temperature in an area rises, the thermometer rises. As the temperature in the same area cools off, the thermometer falls. A thermometer does not do much else. The reading just rises and falls as the environment around the device changes. A leader acting like a thermometer can also be referred to as tofu, since they adopt the flavor of whatever is next to them. Compare the thermometer to the thermostat. While the thermometer reacts to the temperature, the thermostat regulates the environment. It does not matter if it is raining, if there is a blizzard, or a record heat wave... the thermostat carries on in a predictable way. Leaders must be the thermostat. If you think that you can change the company by implementing tools and not changing how you and your leaders lead, then you should find the nearest fire or trash can and give this book another purpose. If you are ready to make lasting change, let us get on with it!

> "If you want something you have never had, you are going to have to do something that you have never done."
> — Thomas Jefferson

The layout of the book starts with the need to change and leading change. I then transition to covering the habits that I believe will allow one to be Habitually Excellent. Once the habits have been thoroughly discussed, I discuss how to staff and lead the journey.

The complete list of habits is:

- Acting Long-term
- Valuing the Customer
- Embracing the Total System
- Focusing on the Process
- Obsessing Over Quality
- Capturing Organizational Learning
- Respecting People

In Chapter 1, "Change", I focus on the need to change and the different elements of change that will need to be considered. Many companies want to simply focus on the technical changes that need to occur. However, there are two other complementary elements that must be considered to ensure lasting change. Those elements are: Organizational and Cultural. Without including these two additional elements in your change strategy, you will only see quick wins in the technical change with a quick recession back to the old way of doing business as leaders shift their focus to another area.

In Chapter 2, "Leading Change", I cover the paradigms that exist in many businesses and the type of leadership it will take to overcome those paradigms. Afterall, we don't see things as they are, we see things as we are. I also review the things that should matter most to the leader and how the leader can ensure those things are done on a routine basis at the leader's level and the levels below. I conclude this chapter with some of the common pitfalls faced by leaders during the change process.

In Chapter 3, "Habit 1: Acting Long-term", I dive into the first of seven habits that allow one to become Habitually Excellent. In this chapter, I contrast the difference between short-term and long-term thinking. I also cover Organizational and Personal Time Management as it relates to improving the business for the long-term.

In Chapter 4, "Habit 2: Valuing the Customer", I discuss the importance of both the internal and external customers to the business. Most companies are only focused on the end customer, but there is a lot to be learned by focusing on each step in the process as if it were the customer of the previous step in the process. I also discuss some concepts that will help support-groups better align to the needs of the value creation part of the business.

In Chapter 5, "Habit 3: Embracing the Total System", I compare the difference between having a functional view vs. a system view. A functional view will always lead to siloed thinking in the business and anytime there are silos the business suffers. I cover ways the team can ensure better alignment in the creation and execution of their strategy.

In Chapter 6, "Habit 4: Focusing on the Process", I discuss the importance of having a process regardless of what you are doing. If you are providing a service, designing a product, manufacturing a product, distributing, or all the above, you must have a standardized way of doing it, and everyone should follow that standardized way.

In Chapter 7, "Habit 5: Obsessing Over Quality", I explain the importance of having a quality product and/or service that is produced from a quality process. I also discuss the importance of leaders being where the work is done and what questions should be asked while there.

In Chapter 8, "Habit 6: Capturing Organizational Learning", I share the importance of learning within the enterprise and the importance of capturing that learning to ensure the organization's learnings do not leave as people retire or move on to other opportunities.

In Chapter 9, "Habit 7: Respecting People", I cover the importance of our team. As a leader, we must take care of People, Product, and Profit (in that order). When it comes to our team it is important that we see together, learn together, and solve together.

In Chapter 10, "Get the Top Team Right", I discuss the importance of getting the right leaders on your team. One should never underestimate the value of good leadership or the damage that can be created by poor leadership.

In Chapter 11, "The Journey", I walk through beginning, planning, and leading the journey. I also cover that there are times when you will need outside help, an outside set of eyes. I refer to this outside help as trusted advisors and consultants.

In the Conclusion, I give some final thoughts, define what being Habitually Excellent is as a system, and give a summary of the approach that I use when faced with improving a business.

At the end of each chapter, I recommend you take some time to reflect, preferably with your team, by asking the following questions:

1. Are we progressing on the actions from our last discussion?
2. What was the key learning from the current chapter?
3. As a team, what do we do well as it relates to the key learning?
4. As a team, what do we NOT do well as it relates to the key learning?
5. What do we need to Start, Stop, or Continue doing as a team to improve going forward as it relates to the key learning?

I will repeat the questions at the end of each chapter as a reminder. My hope is each reader will take the time to discuss these questions with their extended team. It would be a shame to not have this new understanding shared with a broader audience within the enterprise. If you are reading this and are not at the top of the organization, I encourage you to try the ideas in the book on your own in your area of responsibility. Some people may say what you are trying is stupid. However, if it is stupid and it works; it was not stupid. I am a firm believer in asking for forgiveness rather than asking for permission. If what you are doing can be defended, you should do it. Most leaders would rather reign in a mustang than have to kick a mule. Stay at the edge of authority and they will rein you in if needed. If what you are doing is for the betterment of the company and you still get fired, you did not belong there anyway.

At the end of each habit, I will outline what one should expect from the leader regarding their thinking and behavior and then give the leader some reflection questions. These questions are for the individual leader. However, it may be good to discuss them as a group for accountability purposes.

At the end of the book, I provide a recommended reading list of books that have served me well in my journey. I hope they will serve to further enforce the teachings in this book.

Thanks again for taking the time to read this book, and it is my hope that it will add value to you and your team.

CHAPTER 1

CHANGE

"Change everything but your wife and children."
— *Lee Kun-hee former Samsung CEO*

NEMAWASHI

I have worked with several people that were part of the startup of the Toyota plant in Georgetown Kentucky. One story told to me had to do with the language difference. During his first day of orientation, a friend of mine was grouped with both American and Japanese teammates for a review of the plant's evacuation procedure. The instructor went on for what seemed 5 minutes in English on what to do in case of a fire or tornado. Then the instructor said like 3 words in Japanese to which the Japanese teammates acknowledged quickly. My friend stated that he was amazed that 5 minutes of English could be summarized by 3 Japanese words. Japanese must be the most efficient language on the planet. He then turned to one of the interpreters and asked, "What did he say in Japanese?" The interpreter responded, "The instructor simply stated that they should follow the Americans."

The Japanese language may not be efficient enough to convert 5 minutes of English into 3 words, but a lot of the learning I have received over the years is based on Japanese language and management. One of my mentors, Paul Thompson, worked directly with Toyota leadership when Toyota decided to partner with GM to build the NUMMI plant in Fremont, CA. Paul mentored under a Japanese guy by the name of Uchikawa, and Uchikawa worked directly for Taiichi Ohno. Paul had a very pure understanding of the Toyota Product System. Paul and I spent a few years together in Mexico, and I would find myself mesmerized by the difference between the Japanese approach to business and the Western approach to business. This time with Paul coupled with the improvements I helped drive at Bosch with support from Toyota proved to me that the Japanese approach was the best approach. However, I have noticed that Americans do not take kindly to the overuse of Japanese words. I have removed most of the Japanese words from my writings and teachings. However, it is not always possible to simply translate a word from one language to another and retain all the nuances of meaning associated with the word in its original language. Can you imagine explaining "raining cats and dogs' ' to foreigners?

Nemawashi is a word that is not easily translated from Japanese to English – if all the nuances and applications of its use are to be understood and applied.

A literal translation of Nemawashi is "going around the roots", from 根 *(ne, root) and* 回す *(mawasu, to go around [something]).*

It is a term originating from farming, with literal implications for agriculture and planting: digging around the roots of a tree, to prepare it for transplant; the idea is that before a farmer plants a rice seedling, he should prepare the roots to go into the soil, so that the seedling has the best chance of survival; a term taken from bonsai culture, in which, whenever a miniature tree is repotted, its roots are carefully pruned and positioned in such a way as to determine the tree's future shape; roots carefully wrapped together so that they will go on living again later. Even the size of the pot used to plant the bonsai will determine its future size. There are some parallels that can be drawn here concerning where we place ourselves and our teams, but that isn't the purpose of this explanation.

The focus of Nemawashi is on the actions taken to prepare the plant and its roots, and not on the preparation of the soil.

Drawing upon their agricultural legacy, the Toyota people began to use, and then more formally practice, Nemawashi as a process to facilitate (i.e., to make easier) making decisions and acting on those decisions. Afterall, two of the most dangerous things within a company are indecision and inaction. Nemawashi became: a process which determines that agreement is sought before a formal meeting in order to avoid any direct confrontation; consensus building through prior consultation with all concerned; an informal process of quietly laying the foundation for some proposed change or project, by talking to the people concerned, gathering support and feedback, and so forth; involves a cautious feeling-out of all the people legitimately concerned with an issue; groundwork to enlist support or to secure informal consent from the people concerned prior to a formal decision.

Nemawashi as a process of facilitation focuses on the "roots of the plant"; that is, the idea or proposal being put forward. The informal, background, prior consultation, and cautious feeling-out conversations and discussions are intended to assure that the idea will "grow" successfully when it is accepted and applied. Through Nemawashi facilitation, the idea evolves to one that will be successful.

The intent of Nemawashi facilitation is not to "prepare the soil"; that is, the intent is not to "work" the people who will be involved with the idea and its implementation so they will accept the idea. Rather, the idea or proposal is developed and refined through the process of Nemawashi to allow it to be successful.

Nemawashi, as effectively practiced, facilitates decision making by applying the "go slow to go fast" approach. Nemawashi is not a meeting - it is the activity that takes place prior to the meeting: necessary to secure informal consent and enlist support prior to decision-making; agreement is sought before a formal meeting; agreements have been reached and the final meeting is a formality; enlist support or to secure informal consent from the people concerned prior to a formal decision. A meeting would be used for all parties to reach a decision to jointly, and publicly, affirm that decision – with only limited discussion required in the meeting, with everything necessary for the idea, or decision, to successfully "take root" already accomplished.

Before you begin implementing what you read in this book, you will need to prepare many soils. Let the learning begin!

WHY CHANGE?

There will always be change. Some change will be evolutionary while other change will be more revolutionary. As leaders, we must ensure both types of change are for the better. Change for the sake of change is a waste of our time and resources. Real change is hard, and it takes time. The good thing is if you are persistent, you will get the change you desire, and if you are consistent, you will sustain it. Just ensure you have an idea of what you will do when you get what you are persistently pursuing. You don't want to be the old dog that finally caught the car and didn't know what to do with it.

"The more I practice, the luckier I get." — *Arnold Palmer*

Things do not improve by chance; they improve by change, and you must be the chief change agent. If left untouched, entropy ensures all things will return to nature, dirt. Entropy is not what it used to be (pardon my attempt at grammatical humor). Think of physical things left unattended to. They will eventually get reclaimed by nature. The same is true for businesses that fail to maintain and improve. Things do not change for the better naturally, there must be an impetus for change. That impetus is leadership in good times and survival instinct in bad times. We should prefer the former. We would prefer to have a business that is always strong and ready to take advantage of opportunities. It is harder to grow a business if you are in a defensive posture. When some companies fail and see their competitors succeed, they blame it on luck. I personally do not believe in luck. What I have seen is, the harder I work the luckier I appear to be. I believe in being attentive enough to recognize an opportunity and being prepared enough to take advantage of it. People like to think that when there is pressure, they, the team, and the business will rise to the occasion. However, what happens is we typically fall to the highest level of preparation. So be prepared!!

> "In times of peace, prepare for war."
> — *Publius Flavius Vegetius Renatus*

Your business may be doing well today, but what happens if a major shift in the economy occurs. Will you be able to survive? Or maybe your business is not doing well, and you want to save it and all the jobs and families those jobs represent.

Some companies struggle to determine where they are in the change process. A great tool used to make this determination is referred to as the Change House. Originally developed in the early 1970's by Claes F Janssen, its original or proper name is The Four Rooms of Change or the 4-Room Apartment. I often use this house to explain to clients that they may be stranded in the wrong room of the house. They may even be out on the "Sun Lounge."

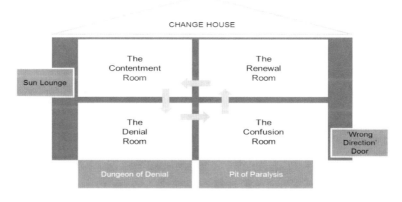

Source: Paul Kirkbride, The Change House, Claes Janssen, The Four Rooms of Change

Once you realize in which room your company is, you have a choice to move to another room. Below I discuss the transitions from room to room:

From Contentment to Denial

- Provide data / stories on how well other companies are doing.
- Provide a symbolic shock / burning platform.
- Meet the customers.
- Spread discontent!
- Challenge the Business.

Note: In western society we are steeped in the idea that we should always be positive, so Spreading Discontent and Challenging the Business may seem awkward. However, it is often necessary.

From Denial to Confusion

- Continue outside benchmarking.
- Expose most of the employees to the problem.
- Avoid providing solutions, but
- Support those looking for solutions.

From Confusion to Renewal

- Provide a vision and a direction.
- Sell solutions, do not tell!
- Focus on the first steps.
- Set demanding goals.
- Achieve closure on past events.
- Reward new behavior

> "Efforts and courage are not enough without purpose and direction" — *John F. Kennedy*

Prevent moving back from Renewal to Contentment

- Keep providing feedback.
- Keep refining the new strategy.

- Find the next S-Curve (more on this later)
- Link success to targets, objectives, and goals
- Constantly question all the things you are doing, never be satisfied with the status quo.
- Focus on being Habitually Excellent.

The process of determining one's room will help the team drive the needed change to ultimately get and stay in the "Renewal Room." If you stay in the contentment room, your competition will certainly overtake you in the marketplace. Always be thinking "Good, Better, Best. Do not rest on your good. Make your good, better and your better best." We must keep reminding ourselves that we are farther from where we need to be than from where we have been.

> "Opportunities are never lost because someone will always take the ones you miss." — *Andy Rooney*

ELEMENTS OF CHANGE

When attempting to drive change within an enterprise, we must consider what changes are needed on a technical, cultural, and organizational level. Experience has shown me that most executives embrace technical change. Those same executives fight organizational and cultural change since it would require active engagement on their part. I have been a part of many change initiatives that were stopped dead in their tracks when it came time to change the cultural and organizational parts of the business.

Once we have laid a strong bedrock of values (our promise to our employees), created a mission (our promise to our customers), shared a vision (what we want to be when we grow up), and developed a strategy (our internal response to outside factors), we can then plan the change needed to achieve all the above. As mentioned before, that change will impact the technical, organizational, and cultural aspects of our enterprise.

"Diversity Is Good As Long As It Isn't Diversity In Values."
— Unknown

The Venn diagram below shows the interaction between the individual elements required to successfully drive change. We will cover each of the elements and the interactions on the following pages.

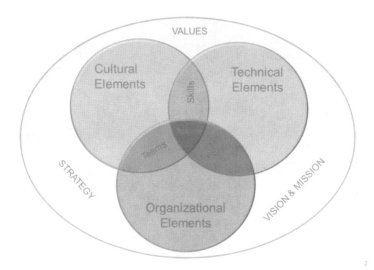

Technical (the science of things) aspects of the enterprise are things like:

- Process Orientation / Process Focused
- Expertise/Capability
- Skills Set
- Process Development
- Tools
- Methods
- Product Design / Development / Introduction
- Plant / Office / Warehouse Layout

Organizational (how we are arranged to get the work done) aspects of the enterprise are things like:

- Value Stream Thinking (mine the gap between processes)
- Physical Environment
- Org Structure and Proper Span of Support
- Matrix Organization
- Functions
- Internal Politics (how things really get done)
- Initiative Organization
- Initiative Management
- Policies and Procedures
- Compensation

Consider Organizational as the way we are organized to get the work done that must be done to meet the desired target condition. There is no one right organization, the organization must be designed to fit the work to be done. No more, and no less.

Cultural (The Invisible Hand) aspects of the enterprise are things like:

- Non-blaming/Non-judgmental behavior
- Principle centered habits
- Trust
- Leadership
- Relationships
- Paradigm changes
- People development
- People engagement

When it comes to culture, we must realize that there are some contradictions that leaders face. Some cultural contradictions for leaders are:

Be a team player **BUT,** focus on your job.

Take risks **BUT**, don´t fail.

Think out of the box **BUT**, follow procedures.

Tell me the truth **BUT**, don´t bring me problems.

Value employees **BUT**, fire average performers.

Help customers **BUT**, spend less time with them.

Work more hours **BUT**, mind your home life.

At times, the leader may feel like they are caught in the middle, and they are. Great leaders know how to manage both up and down the organizational chart as well as align the culture to get the results needed.

"To be able to succeed spectacularly you must be willing to fail spectacularly." — *Biz Stone*

Many companies fail to recognize the impact a culture can have on any given strategy. If you are implementing a strategy and you haven't assessed the impact the culture will have on that strategy, you are about to make a huge mistake. Peter Drucker, the famous management effectiveness author, speaker, and guru stated, "Culture eats strategy for breakfast." A natural follow up to that quote is, "Same goes for objectives." There is a lot of truth to these statements. The culture you have is the culture you created, so if it is to be changed, you must make it happen. Culture is like the spirit in the walls of a business. Culture is hard to explain, but you can feel it. To change a culture takes time; it will not be fast. My guess is it took a long time to create the current culture, so it cannot be changed overnight. A new culture cannot simply be painted on, culture is more like patina and forms over years. An attempt to paint on a culture will flake off under pressure or the weather of the storm. I believe great leaders that are not satisfied with their current culture want to change it. But they do not! Why is this? I believe, and have confirmed this, that they do not focus on culture because it is too hard and takes too long to change. We live in a society where we need instant gratification, so working on something that may take years or even an entire career is not palatable to most leaders. This coupled with the fact that leaders change jobs every two years makes the problem even worse. I propose we leaders time to inculcate principle-based habits into the organization before moving them on to different businesses.

> "The man who grasps principles can successfully select his own methods. The man who tries methods, ignoring principles, is sure to have trouble." — *Ralph Waldo Emerson*

Doing this, inculcating, will take a ton of time and the top leader must be prepared to spend that time. Your time will be spent modeling the behaviors you want to see in others and setting the expectation that those behaviors be followed. Kimberly Evans from Relations Research reminds us to keep in mind that performance must be a bilateral accountability, and that performance must be evaluated all times and in both directions. You do not want your associates working for you because they must or because you have put "golden handcuffs" on them. You want them working for you because they want to. There is a balance between the needs of the employee and the needs of the business. Employees should be asking, "Do I add unnecessary risk to the organization? Do I consume more resources than others?" The business should be asking, "Why should these employees work for us?"

Let your yes mean yes, and your no mean no. If you do not model behavior of a leader that is worthy to be followed, then I recommend you start with you. Ralph Waldo Emerson summed it up well with his statement, "What you do speaks so loudly, that I cannot hear what you say." You can bet your team is mentally tabulating your "Say:Do" ratio. They are looking to see what percentage of the time what you say matches what you do. That number must be 100%.

It is easy to set expectations; it is hard to ensure they are being met on a consistent basis. You will not get what you do not ask for, so ask for what you want from each person on your team. You will need to be involved in every performance evaluation at your staff level plus one level down from your staff. You will need to ensure promotions and succession planning aligns with the new habits. We cannot let the espoused (what we say we do) habits be out of sync with the theory in use (what we do). As in many things in life, in leadership, you don't have to be extreme; you just need to be consistent. If you as a leader cannot be consistent in your approach, you will lose trust with the team.

> "The is nothing more difficult to take in hand, more perilous to conduct, or more uncertain in its success than to take the lead in the introduction in a new order of things, because the innovator has for enemies, all of those who have done well under the old conditions, and luke—warm defenders in those who will do well under the new." — *Niccolo Machiavelli*

Will everyone in your organization be on board? No! You will have those in your organization that will try to fly under the radar to see how long this "new" change lasts. They are trying to hold their breath longer than you. Do not let them win! Bring your SCUBA tanks!

While understanding Technical, Organizational, and Cultural aspects individually is important, there are also overlaps between these aspects that must also be understood.

Those overlaps are:

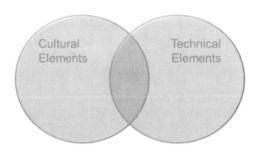

At the overlap of **Cultural** and **Technical**, we have the following:

- Institutional Knowledge (not tribal knowledge)

- Learning (at all levels)

- Problem Solving (not only by managers or engineers)

- Quality (built in quality, not simply inspected in quality)

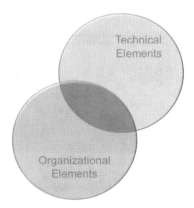

At the overlap of **Technical** and **Organizational**, we have the following:

- Shared Objectives

- Timeframe (not too short; not too long)

- Metrics (that matter)

- Functional Excellence (in serving the value-added flow)

- Goals/ Targets (that are shared and understood)

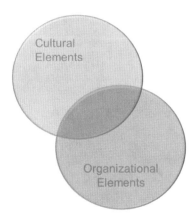

At the overlap of **Cultural** and **Organizational**, we have the following:

- Teams (not heroes)
- Collaboration (not one of us is better than all of us)
- Mutual Ownership and Accountability
- Functional Alignment (No Silos)

The results of ensuring all these aspects are addressed during the change initiative will be Goal Achievement in the following areas:

- Business (Profitability, Cash Flow, Market Share)
- Process (Lead Time, Process Reliability, Resource Reliability/ Flexibility)
- Task (Cycle time, changeover time, first time quality)
- Organizational Learning
- Sustainment of efforts (little to no entropy, negentropy)
- Standardization (best way we know today)

Should you decide to drive significant change within your organization, do not fall victim to not including all the elements of change covered in this section. If you do not include all the elements, you can expect short term improvements that will not be sustained.

ICEBERGS

Another way to look at these elements is in the form of an iceberg. The idea of using icebergs to diagnose the deeper issues within an organization has been around for many years. However, adapting the Technical, Organizational, and Cultural elements into the iceberg was developed by one of my clients, a well-known snack cake company. This team, led by the CEO and a seasoned OpEx leader on his staff, dove into what some would call the soft side of improvement. However, the CEO and OpEx leader understood very early on that the soft side (thinking, reflecting, learning) is indeed the hard side. He and his team went to work on developing their version of an operating system that any company would envy. For my part, I was simply blessed to have been a part of their journey and made some dear friends along the way. Below is a graphic of the iceberg concept:

In the consulting business, one of the main roles I must play is facilitator. In this role, I do not necessarily have to have any content knowledge. In most cases, not having content knowledge is an advantage. I only need to have a process to help the team discuss their own content. The Iceberg is one of those processes. I am only going to cover the basics here, since one could write a complete book on the use of icebergs and how to use icebergs to engage teams in deeper conversations. As a consultant, I am always amazed at how much knowledge is in the room when we can get the team talking openly. I am equally amazed at how some people think certain things are common knowledge when that is not the case. I always tell them that common knowledge/sense is not that common anymore. This tool is one of those tools (coupled with a skilled facilitator) that allows open dialog to happen, every-single-time. Like I said earlier, one could write a book on this topic, however, I am only going to briefly cover the application of the iceberg as it relates to becoming Habitually Excellence.

The idea is to start at the top of the iceberg with what we can see happening. In some cases, companies will simply correct that problem and move to the next problem. The issue here is that if we correct the same problem repeatedly, we have what is called an adaptive problem. If you treat an adaptive problem in the same manner as a technical problem, you will stay very busy playing whack-a-mole.

The only way to deal with an adaptive problem is to go deeper. If the leadership in the room has provided a psychologically safe environment, the iceberg helps us go deeper by asking the following questions:

What **Problem** are we trying to solve (what we see)?

What **Technically** is driving the problem? Then,

What **Organizationally** leads to this technical problem? Then,

What about our **Culture** allowed us to develop said Organizational issue? Then,

For each person in the room:

What am I **Personally** doing (my habits, my mental models) to impact the Culture that allowed this Organizational Issue to arise?

We have concluded the diagnosis once we have reached the base of the iceberg. Everyone has personally reflected on how they impact the issue, so now we can go up the other side. This is the innovation/improvement cycle.

Only when we get to the root of the problem (base of the iceberg), can we really affect change. Once the root is understood, we can then go back up the other side of the iceberg and innovate a new solution to improve the cultural, organizational, and technical aspects of the problem. I believe change happens one conversation at a time and this tool provides an avenue to have a deep conversation. By doing this as a team on a regular basis we can gain shared consciousness around the deeper issues driving the business.

As we go up the other side of the iceberg, we ask the following questions:

What is the new **Mental Model/Thinking** for leadership? Then,

What **Organizational** changes need to be made with this thinking? Then,

What **Technical** changes need to be made based on the new organizational (governance) change?

Another benefit of using a tool like the iceberg is it helps us understand the visible, invisible, personal, and collective aspects of our culture. The Individual-Invisible are the paradigms that people bring with them to the team. These are shaped long before we know that person. These form the basis of their habits and mental models. It is also possible for the same person to have a different paradigm depending on their frame of mind. This concept is partly why you can see the same movie or read the same book multiple times and get something new each time. Your experience has changed since the last time you watched the movie or read the book. Barring the parts that you simply missed due to being distracted, your frame of mind is different each time you watched/read it. The Individual-Visible are the behaviors that we see from people. These behaviors are very much affected by one's paradigms (individual-invisible). If we are not satisfied with someone's behaviors, we must deal with the paradigms, not the behaviors directly. The dealing with core beliefs can take time and is often referred to as double-loop learning. Double-loop learning is a concept and process that involves helping people to think more deeply about their own assumptions and beliefs. The concept of Double Loop Learning was created by Chris Argyris, a leading organizational scholar. The Collective-Invisible is what is being played out in our culture (the invisible hand, the spirit in the walls). The culture is the interaction of all the Individual-Visible (behaviors) from the entire team working together. This collection then starts building new paradigms that further support the cycle. The Collective-Visible is the performance of the business or team driven by the underlying culture. With this understanding, we can now see that our work begins much deeper than most leaders are willing to go.

Dealing with paradigms is probably the hardest work since paradigms are held as core beliefs. When we introduce change that works against that core belief the new evidence cannot be accepted by the individual. This creates a feeling that is extremely uncomfortable, called Cognitive Dissonance. In some cases, it is so important for the individual to protect the core belief, they will rationalize, ignore, and even deny anything that does not fit that core belief. Understanding how to implement change is not easy. I have heard intellectually lazy (not willing to put in the mental work) people refer to this level of understanding as the "Unknown and Unknowable." However, I disagree. If you are willing to put in the time to learn about and not judge your team, you will know what others may consider unknowable. The key here is to start with the assumption that most people have pure motives and want the company to succeed.

> Leaders who do not listen will eventually be surrounded by people who have nothing to say. — *Andy Stanley*

As I stated before, the iceberg is an excellent tool to deal with adaptive problems. I have completed lots of these with teams over the years, and it fascinates me at the depth of discussions it provokes.

To further explain the iceberg concept, I will give an example. In the food industry, a large portion of the waste goes out the door in cartons of the product in the form of overweight, not internal wastes as you would expect. The customer is paying for net weight, and anything above that is overweight and considered over-processing in the Lean Manufacturing world. There are federal regulations governing the net weight limits (underweight), and there is only front-line leadership governing the overweight issue. You can guess which one gets the best treatment, which is completely understandable. As a matter of business ethics, we want to feed the customer, not fleece the customer. Regulations tell you what the law requires, ethics tell you what your values require. However, the food industry is a very competitive space, so cost does matter. In this case, we were making snack cakes. The basic snack cake consists of the cake, crème in the middle, and coating, in that order. If you have a process that is out of control concerning weights, your last chance to fix the product weight is with the coating. It turns out that the coating is also your most expensive component. The iceberg below was targeting this problem:

What **Problem** are we trying to solve (what we see)?

Operators are tampering with the process.

What **Technically** is driving the problem?

The weights of the product are varying, so the operator is trying to keep the process in control.

What **Organizational/Governance** issue leads to this technical problem? Then,

The product is always overweight driving ingredient cost variance since we penalize low weights and not high weights.

What about our **Culture** allowed us to develop said Organizational issue? Then,

We do not value components weights; we value end of line carton weights. This shows a lack of understanding that the correct components weights will add up to the correct carton weight.

For each person in the room, what am I **Personally** doing (my habits, my mental models) to impact the Culture that allowed this Organizational Issue to arise?

This is only from one of the leaders in the room: As the leader, I ask about and monitor the number of cartons and the average weight of the cartons. I never look at the component weights.

What is the new **Mental Model/Thinking** for leadership?

Process Capability (CpK) at the component level is more valuable than simply focusing on output.

What **Organizational** changes need to be made with this thinking?

Our future measures align with the quality (includes capability) of the process over the amount of output from the process.

What **Technical** changes need to be made based on the new organizational change?

Conduct formal Statistical Process Control (SPC) training and measure process capability (CpK) as a key performance indicator.

A more advanced use of the tool would have the team reflect at each question to determine what habit (referring to the 7 habits of Habitually Excellent) was violated (on the diagnosis side) or reinforced (on the innovation side). The problem I see most often is the team will try to complete the iceberg in reverse. They will see a problem, find the technical cause, address that cause, and may or may not implement organizational (governance) changes. This typically results in them having to solve the problem again in the future, since they did not deal with the underlying issues.

As the leader, you must be the change that you want to see in others, so be sure you are engaged in all aspects of the change initiative. Everyone is watching you to see how you are dealing with the change before they decide to get involved. Be careful how you lead!

End of Chapter GROUP Reflection Questions:

1. What was the key learning from the current chapter?

2. As a team, what do we do well as it relates to the key learning?

3. As a team, what do we NOT do well as it relates to the key learning?

4. What do we need to Start, Stop, or Continue doing as a team to improve going forward as it relates to the key learning?

CHAPTER 2

LEADING CHANGE

"Planned, purposeful abandonment of the old of the unrewarding is a prerequisite to successful pursuit of the new and highly promising." — *Peter Drucker*

We briefly touched on paradigms in the previous chapter, but I want to go a little deeper in this chapter. The people in our organizations are going to see what we are doing through many different lenses called paradigms. What are paradigms? I always ask this question during my initial visits with clients. Inevitably, someone says, "$0.20, a pair of dimes" which always gets a chuckle out of the group. I then go on to explain that paradigms are the way we see the world. Our paradigms are shaped by how we were raised, where we went to school, where we work, etc. If there are 30 people in the room then, we have 30 different paradigms. We could be looking at the exact same thing, and literally have all 30 people see it differently. A slightly embellished (for clarity of teaching) version of a scientific study of how paradigms are formed is below:

A group of scientists placed 5 monkeys in a cage and in the middle, a ladder with bananas on the top. The natural tendency of the monkeys is to go get the bananas. However, every time a monkey went up the ladder, the scientists soaked the rest (not the offending monkey) of the monkeys with cold water. After a while, every time a monkey went up the ladder, the others would beat up the one on the ladder. After some time, no monkey would dare to go up the ladder regardless of the natural temptation. Scientists then decided to substitute one of the monkeys. As one would expect, the first thing this new monkey did was to go up the ladder. At that point, the other monkeys would immediately beat him up. A second monkey was substituted and the same occurred. Even to the point where the first monkey participated in the beating for the second monkey. A third monkey was changed and the same (beating) was repeated. The fourth was substituted and the beating was repeated and finally the fifth monkey was replaced. What was left was a group of five monkeys that even though they had never received a cold shower, continued to beat up any monkey who attempted to climb the ladder. Everyone knows that monkeys cannot talk, but if it were possible to ask the monkeys why they would beat up all those who attempted to go up the ladder. I bet you the answer would be….

I don't know – that's how things are done around here.

Does that statement sound familiar? I have heard this comment thousands of times across many countries and industries. My challenge to you as the reader is to never accept this response. The person 'doing the spraying' may not even be at the company anymore. Everything will need to be questioned and challenged if the company expects to be Habitually Excellent. No sacred cows can remain un-tipped.

As we innovate in a new direction, we will find that there are different people that we will encounter along the way. The Diffusion of Innovation Theory is a helpful way to look at the different groups of people we will face and how to deal with them.

The graphic below shows the percentages of each group.

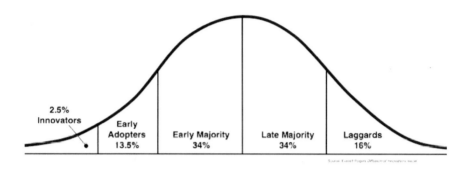

Innovators - These are people who want to be the first to try the new idea. This group is considered risk takers and come up with lots of new ideas. You will spend little of your time convincing this group of the change needed; they are ready to change now. These are the types of people that went against the adage, "You will never get fired for buying an IBM." during the early days of computers.

Early Adopters – These people are influential and are sought out for their opinions. They are typically in leadership roles and embrace change that is for the good. They often have already decided that change is needed, so when the idea is presented, they quickly get behind the idea. Your goal with this group is to educate; not convince.

Early Majority – These people are often followers in the organization, but they do adopt new ideas before the average person. They take a "wait and see" approach to change, but once they see it working, they are on board. Your goal with this group is to show them the results.

Late Majority – While the Early Majority may be on the fence, this group is firmly planted on the other side of the fence. They will only cross over when most of the others in the company have crossed over. Your goal with the group is to market the success of what others have embraced.

Laggards – These people are probably still using flip phones. They would also be using rotary phones if they still worked. They are very skeptical of change and are the hardest group to bring on board. Your goal with this group is to be patient and compassionate. Change scares them, so be careful how you lead them. They will eventually come around.

There is another group that is not covered in the Diffusion of Innovation Theory, but I think they are worth mentioning here.

Those who are passive and do not challenge the status quo (Laggards) are one thing, but there is another more dangerous group of people in the company that should be considered. I call these folks CAVE Men:

 Citizens

Against

Virtually

Everything

The paradigm, which is more actively exercised, held by these individuals is that everything is just fine the way it is. They have convinced themselves that we do not need to change. These same people also have a problem for every solution. In the words of Mike Rother, you often must tell these folks, "Don't tell me that it sucks, go use it, break it, and come back and tell me HOW it sucks. Then we'll adapt it relentlessly forward."

These CAVE men are the same people that say:

If it isn't broken, don't fix it.

This statement comes from those with a status quo mindset. In the past, if this was your mindset, you were sitting still like everyone else. However, in today's highly competitive business landscape, if you are not improving, you are moving backwards. The way I see it is you have 3 choices: You can passively sit by not making any decisions to improve and let your competition pass you, you can actively move backwards by making poor management decisions, or you can actively move forward by continuously improving the business. To do this, everyone's paradigm as it relates to improvement must change to:

If it isn't broken, improve it.

Henry Ford once stated, "I refuse to recognize that there are impossibilities. I cannot discover that anyone knows enough about anything on this earth to say what is and what is not possible." We cannot get new results with old thinking, and we must put in a lot of effort to overcome this psychological inertia to create the change desired. We don't have bad people; we have good people with bad thinking. Sometimes the least questioned assumptions are the most questionable. As leaders, we must challenge the thinking as well as unquestioned assumptions. We are also faced with two other groups of people; those that say their area cannot use continuous improvement (typically in support functions or service organizations), and they cannot use the continuous improvement approach because they do not make cars. They are different! I wish I had a dollar for every time I heard that statement.

"If you say you can't, you are right!" — Henry Ford

My response to the first group is that continuous improvement will improve every aspect of the business process. If you cannot define what you do as a process, then you do not know what you are doing. To the second group, I let them know that I am glad they do not make cars, and continue with, can you imagine having to coordinate over thirty thousand components into your product using your current processes. This is exactly what Toyota does, and they make a car every 52 seconds. Great process yields great results, and we should always know our process and continually improve it.

SOCRATIC LEADERSHIP

As we decide to create positive change within our enterprises, the focus must be on learning and teaching the habits that make enterprises highly effective. The more people you have on your side the easier this change will be for you and the company. The goal of this book is to provide the learning that leaders will hopefully take back to their enterprises and teach others.

> "The best teachers are those who show you where to look, but don't tell you what to see." — *Alexandra K. Trenfor*

When it comes to teaching, I highly recommend the type of teaching referred to as Socratic Coaching. The goal is to be able to teach complex topics by asking simple questions.

> "If you can't explain it simply, you don't understand it well enough." — *Albert Einstein*

What is Socratic coaching? Socratic Coaching is the art of teaching by asking questions. When asking questions, there are four critical points to the questions:

- The questions must be interesting or intriguing
- They may be leading
- They must be in logical steps
- They must be designed to get the student to see points

> "A Wiseman knows much and says little, a fool knows little and says much." — *Larry McGee*

There are also different types of questions that can be asked to help enable the learner to learn. Those types of questions are:

Questions of Clarification

- What is your main point?
- Can you give me an example?
- What is the source of that idea or information?
- Can you summarize what we discussed?

Questions that Probe Assumptions

- What are you assuming?
- How would you support your assumption?
- Questions that Probe Reasons and Evidence
- What did you observe in the demonstration/experiment?
- What evidence supports your hypothesis?

Questions that Probe Implications and Consequences

- What effect would that have?
- What could you generalize from this observation?
- What does that remind you of?
- What do you predict will happen next?

Before you attempt to use the Socratic Method, you should be intentional about what you are trying to teach. For example, are you trying to teach a specific point, or are you trying to coach the use of a specific process? One should also anticipate how the conversation may go and consider:

- What are some clarifying questions?
- What are some questions that probe assumptions?
- What are some questions that probe Reasons and Evidence?
- What are some questions that probe Implications and Consequences?

> *"Fear = False Evidence (Assumptions) Appears Real"*
> *— Unknown*

The Value of Questions:

- You only get answers to the questions you ask.

- Questions unlock and open doors that otherwise remain closed.

- Questions are the most effective means of connecting with people.

- Questions cultivate humility.

- Questions help you engage others in conversation.

- Questions allow us to build better ideas.

- Questions give us a different perspective.

- Questions challenge mind-sets and get you out of ruts.

When you first try to switch from directly telling people what to do to a Socratic approach, your team may feel frustrated. The same person that was giving them answers yesterday is now only asking questions. They may even want to choke you. The key is to stick with it.

> *"Asking questions creates independence, giving answers creates dependence." — Unknown*

Our goal in teaching using the Socratic method is to help the learner "trip over the truth." If they discover the lesson on their own, you do not have to sell them on the idea; they will sell themselves. There is always power in asking the right questions. Albert Einstein once stated, "If I had an hour to solve a problem, and my life depended on it, I would spend the first 55 minutes determining what question to ask, for once I know the proper question, I can solve the problem in less than five minutes." This profound statement highlights the power of asking the right questions. Afterall, you cannot appreciate the solution if you do not appreciate the problem.

GRACE AND MERCY

As leaders we must be very accepting and understanding. Learning new concepts can be a very frustrating process, and being a leader is not easy. The combination of these two can result in a less than optimal leadership environment. Our team should never 'feel the wrath' from their leader. We will get deeper into leadership development later in this book, but there are two major leadership traits that will guide us to always be the best leader we can be. Those traits are grace and mercy.

Grace = Giving someone something good they do not deserve.

Mercy = Withholding something bad that they do deserve.

You make a living from what you get, you make a life from what you give. For Grace and Mercy to be practiced the leader must have true compassion for their employees. This cannot be faked. Everyone deserves compassion. Phil Robertson of Duck Dynasty stated it very well when he stated, "Our culture has accepted two huge lies. The first is that if you disagree with someone's lifestyle, you must fear or hate them. The second is that to love someone means you agree with everything they believe or do. Both are nonsense. You don't have to compromise convictions to be compassionate."

While there are areas in business where you can "fake it until you make it," leadership is not one of those areas. It must come from the heart. I have had this conversation with many leaders over the years. One conversation stands out to me.

"Most leaders miss it by 18 inches, which is the distance between your head and your heart." — *Unknown*

The conversation centered on whether the leader was recognizing his employees. He was adamant with me that he recognized 100% of his employees every single day. This proclamation amazed me and seemed to be impossible. When probed a bit more, he explained that when his employees swiped their badge at the gate, and it worked, that was him telling them THANK YOU for the work they had done the day before.

This is not the type of recognition to which I am referring. I am referring to personal one-on-one recognition. This recognition may be for a good reason, or it can sometimes be for a not so good reason. In either case, it is personal and is intended to strengthen the person receiving it.

SPIRIT vs. LETTER OF THE LAW

As we are coaching teams and driving change, we must ensure we are not dogmatic in our approach. There will be times when the document, form, board, or process is altered based on the current condition. To help deal with this, I like to refer to what is known as the difference between the letter of the law and the spirit of the law. The letter of the law versus the spirit of the law is an idiomatic antithesis. When one obeys the letter of the law but not the spirit, one is obeying the literal interpretation of the words (the "letter") of the law, but not necessarily the intent of those who wrote the law. Again, we should ensure we are not being dogmatic about the implementation of the change. We could also refer to this as "Freedom within the Framework." The framework in this case is the system that management has given the team to help improve the business. Freedom in this case is not getting bent out of shape when they do not use the same font on their forms as another group.

LEVELS OF UNDERSTANDING

Another important aspect to consider when coaching and teaching is that people are at different levels of understanding when it comes to any given topic. We must be able to discern which level our student is in, so we can adapt our approach. The four levels are depicted in the table below:

Levels	Unconsciously Incompetent	Consciously Incompetent	Consciously Competent	Unconsciously Competent
Phrase	"You do not know what you do not know"	"You know what you do not know"	"You know what you know"	"You do not know what you know"

When someone is anticipating being involved in or participating in a learning journey, they will have a level of anxiety; they are afraid their lack of knowledge will be exposed (Unconsciously-Incompetent). Once they learn there is a gap in their knowledge (Consciously-Incompetent), we have created an opportunity for them to learn. In some cases, we assist in closing the learning gaps, and in other cases, the person is responsible to self-learn. If we have exposed to them a lack of understanding, and they choose to not close the gap, we can assume this person is not interested in learning this topic. Depending on their role in the organization, this may be completely acceptable. Those that are interested in closing their gaps are "learners," and we as leaders should feed that learning as much as possible.

> "If you aren't green and growing, you are ripe and rotting."
> — Ray Kroc

When it comes to learning, our stance for leaders should always be that they either grow or they must go. We cannot allow leaders to get stagnant. By growth, I am not referring to promotion; I am referring to development. Once a person has learned a new skill and becomes moderately successful at it, they gain confidence in what they know (Consciously-Competent). After many years of experience, that knowledge will be so ingrained in what they do, they will operate from a basis of knowledge without even realizing it (Unconsciously-Competent). There are times that being smart can work against you. It is called the Curse of Knowledge, where you become a prisoner of your own experience. At times, these individuals will talk over people's heads. Other times, they may not state things for the fear of stating the obvious. This person may think to himself, "That goes without saying." and then not say that which should be said. In either case, they are robbing those around them from having a learning experience. This final stage of understanding should be constantly assessed. There have been many occasions in facilitation where I considered not mentioning something, only to have someone come to me after a training session to state they were glad I mentioned it. What was obvious to me, was not so obvious to the group. As leaders, we also fall into each of the above categories.

"Leaders Read and Readers Lead" — *Various*

The idea of "learning how to learn" came to me when my great-nephew asked me, "If there was only one thing, you could teach me, what would it be?" First off, I was impressed that a 10yr old would ask me that question. Then, I thought about the question for a few seconds and finally responded with, "I would teach you how to learn on your own."

I now teach that great leaders must "learn how to learn." "Learning How To Learn" is a process of forcing oneself into areas that you do not know much about (Unconsciously Incompetent). We do this by reading, watching, discussing, etc. things that are outside of our area of expertise. By doing this, we uncover things that we did not know before, and now we have a chance to decide if we want to continue the learning journey on that topic. Exposing yourself and/or your team to new concepts and ideas is a great way to learn. The thought is to create self-discovery through your own learning process. You will occasionally find connections between different areas in your learnings that you didn't realize existed. These connections can often lead to new discoveries and inventions.

Some people think sitting in a conference or group discussion is not productive. They are eager to get out there and "get things done." Jumping straight to action can often come off as ready-fire-aim. Learning can be productive if that learning will help us become better in the future and help us align around what needs to be done and why it needs to be done. One of the best things we can do is improve someone's mindset in the right manner. That new mindset will carry on long after we are not with them.

STANDARDIZE OR DIE

By far the hardest part of being Habitually Excellent is sustaining the improvements. The first opportunity we must prove our level of discipline will come when Standardized Work and Workplace Organization is implemented. In this case, discipline = freedom. Discipline to follow a standard will free us to see better ways of doing things. There will be more on the importance of these two areas later. If a company cannot sustain these two areas, I would have serious doubts about their discipline to do some of the other hard actions needed to become Habitually Excellent.

Standardized Work = Work Standards + Standard Working

"Standardized Work without Leader Standard Work [ensuring Standard Working] is a complete waste of time."
— Taiichi Ohno

Most companies have lots of paperwork detailing their work standards. You can tell a lot about a business by checking the dates on the standards, policies, or procedures. If the documents have not been updated recently, you can assume they are not following standard work or improving for that matter. If they argue with you that they are improving and just not updating the files, then you can assume they are giving the businesses knowledge away every time they lose an associate. You may also find that employees have handwritten notes that capture what they "actually" do to make your product. Wise businesses use standard work to capture the learning that occurs daily.

"The secret to our success is in our daily agenda."
— Tag Short

Having standards is one of the basics of the development of good habits. If a leader or a team cannot get this right, then there should be concern, and we cannot expect them to move to the next level of improvement.

I am reminded of a story I heard about a new pastor at a church near where I live. The new pastor was hired by the Church's Hiring Committee as the Executive Pastor. The first Sunday, he gave a sermon better than any they had ever heard. They all made sure to tell him how great the sermon was at the end of the service. The next Sunday, he gave the same sermon, but the Committee members did not realize it since they were still enamored by the new pastor. They sensed something was off, but they could not put their finger on it. On the third Sunday, they realized that the new preacher had given the same sermon for three weeks straight. This angered them to say the least. They were thinking, "Was this the only sermon he knew? Did they make a mistake by hiring this Pastor?" They convened an emergency committee meeting after the service and called the new pastor in for a discussion. They assured him that they really enjoyed his sermon, but he had done the same sermon for three weeks. They were eager to hear a new sermon instead of the same sermon each week. The pastor replied with, "I will give you a new sermon, when I see you put into practice what I am teaching you in the first sermon, and not before."

The same scenario plays out with many companies. I have so much I can show them, but I cannot because they will not put into practice what I have already shown them. This lack of discipline to do what is right has crept into many businesses and is costing them billions in profits. Are you looking for a new sermon before you put into practice what you already know is the right thing to do?

Our goal should be to have processes that become routine. As we all know, the first step to learning a new routine is to try it. As an example of this, I was with a client in Puerto Rico headed to lunch. I had been in Santa Isabel for 2 weeks but had not remembered the route to the restaurant for lunch. It had not become routine. My client contact said I should start driving to lunch each day. By driving I learned the route in 2 days. The point is we must let people drive for them to remember. As leaders is it our job to look for opportunities to let them drive.

The true benefit of Standardized Work is creating those routines that can be done without having to think. If the person doing the job does not have to constantly focus on how to do the job (no routine), then they can focus on how to improve the job. The benefits of having a routine can be demonstrated with the analogy of driving the same route home each day. Have you ever arrived home and not remembered how you got there? The reason this occurs is you have a routine, a mindless routine. You were not focused on how to get home, since it is normal to you. You were probably focused on a problem or something you were planning to do in the future. Since this routine is common, you would have probably noticed if there was something abnormal more readily (i.e., car pulling out in front of you). The shift from seeing normal to abnormal is also called the Oddball Effect (V. Pariyadath & D. Eagleman, 2007). The car pulling out in front of you might not be so abnormal depending on what part of the world you live in. In processes that are not standardized, we do not notice the abnormalities as easily, since most of what we do is abnormal. We know we have standardized the process well if we can run processes that were once reserved for skilled labor with unskilled labor. This hits the bottom line with less labor costs. This also helps us onboard new people faster, which allows faster growth.

> "There are two ways to grow; stronger or fatter. We must be very careful to not get fat." — *Unknown*

During a conversation with a client, I was inquiring about the lack of detail in their work instructions. One of the participants spoke up and stated, "We were told to de-content the work instructions." After further discussion, I realized they had been instructed by an external auditor to de-content their work instructions, so it would be easier to pass an audit. The mindset here was that if you say it, you must do it. However, instead of keeping the details and ensuring those details were followed, the team decided to say less in their documents. My question to the team at that point was, "Is your business to pass audits or make products following a documented standard that can be used to capture your organizational learning?" The result was the company lost years of documented learning to pass an outside audit. WOW!

One of the top struggles in any organization is the sustainment of efforts, which is a byproduct of maintaining order through standardization.

Often, leadership believes that if they tell the organization to do something, it will get accomplished and continue to get accomplished until told to do something differently. However, this is not the case. The adage, "You get what you INSPECT, not what you EXPECT" continues to be proven over and over. So, how does one implement a systematized method of "inspection" that ensures standards are followed and improvements are sustained? Leader Standard Work (LSW) is the best-known method today to ensure that important items are checked and verified at the right frequency. One can consider LSW the Control Plan (as used in product quality) for Leadership.

> "What you allow in your presence is your standard!"
> — *Unknown*

One of the largest failure modes I see in business is the failure to follow the known standard. This is due to a lack of standard working. Remember:

Standardized Work = Work Standards + Standard Working

LSW is focused on the Standard Working piece of Standardized Work. Proper Leader Standard Work documents and defines expected behavior for leaders. It is a list of normal tasks that must be done to sustain the World-Class management system. It typically includes checks (of subordinate's standard work), meetings (daily accountability), continuous improvement projects, and process control plans. The focus is on the work being done. It directs the leader to validate visual controls.

As leaders we must set expectations and then manage the exceptions. We cannot manage all the details. LSW specifies the most important things that need to be checked.

LSW is documented for all levels of leadership and is written for the role, not for the person. This ensures that as people rotate through the different leadership roles, the system continues to operate normally. LSW directs the leader to validate visual controls and specifies the frequency at which each task should be completed (hourly, daily, weekly, etc.). Aside from the technical aspects, LSW also translates the desired habits into clear, specific, and measurable expectations. As with any standard, LSW is expected to be continually improved and built upon as the business system matures. The proper use of LSW will help the business to drive continuous improvement at all levels. The combination of all the LSW activities defines our systemic management structure. The four key elements to LSW are:

- Going to the place where value is being added (Gemba)
- Utilizing visual controls and indicators
- Identifying deviations from standard
- Engaging people in countermeasures to deviations from standard while modeling appropriate behavior through the Socratic method

Following these four elements will better sustain safety, quality, morale, delivery, and cost.

LSW is a powerful tool to send the same message of direction from all levels of the management team. Through LSW we align and link all levels of management toward common goals. It creates a linkage between expected versus actual, which leads to continuous improvement.

> "Leader Standard Work is about discipline, sustainment, and accountability. Expecting discipline, sustainment, and accountability without Leader Standard Work is a fantasy."
> — Mike Rother

Another useful outcome of LSW is its focus on defining behavior:

- Behaviors and actions for leaders to model
- Behaviors and actions that can be checked
- Behaviors and actions that are coachable and teachable

LSW provides a convenient, repeatable, and methodical way to get managers to focus their attention on the process that provides the results, which is opposed to simply watching the results and expecting them to change, or worse, declaring that the results changed without a full understanding of how the results are achieved. LSW is a focus on the X's (process and inputs) that lead to the big Y's (results). The stability of the current process as verified through our checks will serve as a baseline for further business and process improvement. LSW also provides linkage of best practices through leadership transitions - new leaders benefit from predecessors. This ensures we have legacy leadership versus a change in direction during each leadership transition.

The approach to LSW is very simple. It is printed, carried, and used as a hand-written list to remind each leader of their daily and weekly responsibilities. A leader will document daily notes, observations, and requests for action or follow-up, disrupters, and action items. It is not simply a checklist. The most important aspect of the LSW to the leader's boss is the uncovering of items (disrupters) that prevent them from following their LSW. LSW are working documents, so we can constantly update to the changing conditions in the business. Each leader must ensure all subordinate's standard work is followed and completed.

> "When leaders neglect to inspect that which they expect, they have abdicated their roles as leaders in the organization."
> — *Unknown*

LSW will take leaders to visual controls. Leaders must scrutinize these visuals, processes, and data daily. The goal is not to get through the process as quickly as possible. You may have experienced this in restaurants. You can tell when the manager is "checking the box" with their dining area walkthrough versus when the manager is truly observing and engaging in the dining room walkthrough. I proved this point during a diner with a client in Oklahoma City. We were sitting in a popular restaurant in the area. I noticed the GM was walking table to table, but not engaging with the customers. I told my client to watch. When the GM asked how things were going, I said, "Things are going horrible." The GM kept walking and was clearly just checking the box. Do not be a "check the box" leader!

When a deviation from the standard is found during the execution of LSW, the leader must help the team determine what steps to take, when to take those steps, and by whom. Some great examples of visual controls are:

- Operator/Service Provider Standard Work

- Operator/ Service Provider daily maintenance boards

- 5S daily task boards

- 5S in general

- Process control boards/charts, equipment calibration signoffs, etc.

A properly designed visual control should show "Normal" versus "Abnormal." It helps the leader focus on the exceptions. This deviation should be evident to anyone visiting the process. When at the visual control, the leader should:

- Verify visual controls in place and up to date

- Ensure the System is working properly

- Verify execution to standard (or visual controls)

- Ensure "abnormalities" are clearly documented

- Ensure appropriate response to deviations

LSW extends all the way to the top of the organization. Executive Standard Work is an audit of LSW happening at the sites. As with the local leadership, the executive is focused on the health of the business system. It is always conducted on-site (no phone or conference room audits). It is always conducted where the work is performed. Typically, a site visit by an executive would start in the conference room and covers the following items:

- Strategic Initiatives update

- What one will see in the work areas

- What was promised during the last visit (show progress)?

- What one will see at this visit

- Followed by a Focused Plant Visit (not a tour!!!)

During the Focused Plant Visit, all progress from the previous visit is shown. The executive is auditing the system. Any error seen in the system is analyzed to discover more information. The site leader takes notes and does a follow-up. The visit concludes in the conference room, where the executive summarizes the visit in the form of a plus (what went well) and a delta (what should change before the next visit). The site leader will then forecast improvement to be seen at the next visit.

In general, an executive should note the following:

- Does everyone on the team know what the strategic initiatives are?
- Can they explain how they contribute to the strategic initiatives?
- Can each person see, immediately, whether they are winning or losing (real-time metric awareness/players scoreboard)?
- Is there a cadence of accountability?
- How often does your supervisor check with you on tactical initiatives (short-term)?
- How often does your supervisor check with you on the strategic initiatives (long-term)?
- What else do you need to be successful in supporting the strategic initiatives (coaching, training, tools, equipment, instructions, response, etc.)?
- Is there a question you wish I had asked?

Hajime Ohba once said, "When you tell people that it is important to do something, but you show them that it isn't important enough for you to check it, they feel you have lied to them and they feel disrespected. Eventually, they stop doing it, not because they are lazy, but because they know from your actions that it is not important."

One final note on plant visits. Be careful of the three lies that CEO's are told during those visits (this also applies to other visitors from corporate):

1. We are glad you came.

2. We learned a lot.

3. We look forward to your next visit.

If you are an executive, make sure you are adding value during your visits, so your team does not have to lie to you.

WORKPLACE ORGANIZATION

As mentioned before, Workplace Organization is a sign of leadership discipline. If you really want to see how the leadership of a plant is doing, you only need to look at the condition of the plant. A dirty plant is a sign of lazy leadership that has not spent the time on the floor focused on setting the right expectations.

Many people simply refer to the Workplace Organization as 5S. the 5S's are:

1. Sort – Remove what is not needed.

2. Straighten – Organize what is needed.

3. Shine – Clean the area.

4. Standardize – Ensure the above is done regularly.

5. Sustain – Management Audit to ensure sustainment and continuous improvement.

Many companies conduct a 5S workshop, which is a 3S (the first 3's stated above) workshop and call it wraps. This is nothing more than "Spring Cleaning," and will have to be done every year or so. This is a sign that the team does not fully understand the importance, the WHY, of 5S/Workplace Organization.

The main goal of the business is to create a profit that will be used to ensure our livelihood into the future. The simple answer to creating more profit is reduce cost and increase revenue. To create cash faster, we need to flow the product or service (order to cash) faster. To ensure this is done repeatedly, we need standard work. To ensure standard work, we need to have the tools and materials in an orderly fashion. Using this thinking, we can consider Workplace Organization more important than spring cleaning. Workplace Organization serves a few purposes. First, it supports Standardized Work by improving efficiencies and ensuring the proper tools are available and the area is uncluttered. Secondly, it corrects some long-term sources of contamination. The side benefit is the area looks better visually, but that is not the main driver. There is yet another longer-term benefit of practicing Workplace Organization is the discipline that it instills into our teams. When an area is in disorder, we can assume there is a lack of discipline in both the associates and the leadership in that area. When I am given tours of facilities, I always go off the main aisle tour to see the real picture of the workplace organization. One can also be assured one's customers are making the same judgment when they visit your factories.

I have heard countless times where a client has won business from their competitor and the reason given was, "They didn't look like they knew what they were doing, but you look like you know what you are doing." Workplace Organization helps with this perception.

A clean well-organized factory (not just on the main aisle) is a sign of discipline. Although the main purpose of Workplace Organization is to support the people doing the work, it also gives the leadership the ability to visually manage the workplace allowing us to manage by exception and not management by every little detail of the business.

To ensure Workplace Organization is maintained, we must ensure leadership is checking that the standards for 5S are being maintained. As we walk, we are looking for violations to standards. These standards must be clear to all and visually manageable. Visual Management is the element that allows a quick check between what should be happening vs. what is happening. You cannot solve a problem you cannot see. You should be able to figuratively ride through your area on horseback and see how things are progressing each day. When developing visual management, remember this, the only thing worse than no visual indicator is an ambiguous visual indicator. No visual indicator will lead to no action, while an ambiguous indicator may lead to the wrong action, so ensure visual management is telling us what is "really" happening.

5S is a tool that improves visual management, one of the three core cultural enablers (Visual Management, Leadership Engagement, and Problem-Solving Capability). It allows us to see problems (deviations from standard) so that we can engage others in solving problems. It improves Safety, Quality, Cost and Productivity as well as positively impacts morale

- Safety – Removes sources of contamination to reduce slips, trips, and falls. Improved ergonomics through point of use staging. 5S also helps remove the unsafe states that lead to larger safety issues if not addressed.

- Quality – 5S supports standardized work, which reduces variation. Makes contamination, which can foul a process, more visible. Removes distractions and allows us to focus.

- Cost – Over time, there is far greater visibility and control of operating expenses. Less occurrences of missing items.

- Productivity – Eliminates search time and excess motion.

- Morale – Creates ownership and pride. Reduces frustration. Builds teamwork and collaboration.

5S ensures that there is a place for everything and that everything is in its place. 5S is far more than a housekeeping tool, 5S ensures that there is no need for special "clean-ups" for VIP visits and can create a competitive advantage (being a showcase for customers and sales).

As mentioned previously, 5S also has a strong connection with safety. 90-95% of injuries begin with one or more of the following states (causes):

- Frustration
- Rushing

- Fatigue
- Complacency

5S serves to keep our process operators out of the four states. Think about if you were an operator and you do not have what you need to complete a task – What is likely to happen? The operator could get frustrated because they do not have what they need and as they search for it, frustration could continue to build. Operators will have to search for the tool/resource and if they are at a critical step in the process or if it is time sensitive this will cause rushing. Operators work shift work so there is already some fatigue in the equation. Extra steps while searching only adds to the fatigue. Operators that cannot find what they need might use the wrong tool for the job or find a work around. This is complacency. A place for everything and everything in its place will allow our operators to have what they need when they need it where they need it, avoiding entry into the states that increase the opportunity for mistakes, and potentially, injuries.

MAJOR PITFALLS

Every morning in Africa, a gazelle wakes up. It knows it must run faster than the fastest lion or it will be killed. Every morning a lion wakes up. It knows it must outrun the slowest gazelle or it will starve to death. The moral of the story is: It does not matter whether you are a lion or a gazelle—when the sun comes up, you had better be running. There are lions and gazelles in the business world, and we must be the Lion and be able to outrun the Gazelles.

We also cannot rest on our current relationships with our clients/customers to carry us through. Our clients are interested in getting the best value for their money. Even if it means going with our competition, so do not get too comfortable.

In today's highly competitive global marketplace, setting one's sights on world-class is not enough. The approach of the past was characterized by big companies "eating" the smaller ones. However, in today's environment, the faster companies tend to "eat" the slower companies. Bigness doesn't always equal greatness.

> "Think small and add small, and we will get bigger. Think big and add big, and we will get smaller."
> — Herb Kelleher, founder of Southwest Airlines

My many years of experience working in many different industries and traveling the globe as a management consultant have brought to my attention four main areas that separate world-class companies from those companies which are mediocre and/or "mothballed". Those four areas are Unity, Direction, Execution, and Discipline. All the teams that have mastered these four areas are considered successful. The proof is in the results they have achieved in their businesses.

> "It is an immutable law in business that words are words, explanations are explanations, promises are promises, but only performance is reality." — Harold S. Geneen

Those teams which have chosen to pursue mastery in these four areas succeed, whereas those teams which fail to choose mastery of these areas are eventually replaced or will selfishly bleed the company into a condition of non-existence if not replaced. Our job as leaders is to stop the bleeding.

When one enters an environment in which the leadership team is divided rather than unified, one may feel as if he/she has entered the awkward family reunion of a dysfunctional family rather than an effective leadership team. Uncle John is running the maintenance department, Aunt Suzy is running the HR department, and Cousin Larry is doing what Cousin Larry does. Cousin Larry is the plant manager only because his dad pulled some strings for him. No one listens to Larry because he is remembered as the little boy running around in diapers. The team cannot get along, and it does not have a common understanding of the business or of the company's principles, concepts, or practices.

> "On matters of style, swim with the current, but on matters of principle, stand like a rock." — *Thomas Jefferson*

The folks on the team do not have a common understanding because they have never taken the time to sit down and discuss the business as a team. The team members are hoping the figurative wheels do not fall off before it is their turn to retire. Everyone is out to protect themselves and what they have accumulated over the years. They do not meet regularly to set and control direction for the company, and frankly, they would prefer to never meet. However, Grandma (Corporate) makes them sit down once a year at the table, hold hands, and say the blessing.

> "Inches apart on strategy at the top leadership level will put you miles apart on execution at the working level." — *Satya Nadella*

Benjamin Franklin famously stated, "We shall hang together, or we will surely hang separately." It maybe not as severe, but the same thing holds true for leadership teams. Disunity is a fatal flaw and can lead to devastating results. The senior staff of every organization has a fiduciary responsibility to do the best it can for the company. After all, there are many people counting on the leadership team to get it right. For each employee on the payroll, another two to three people are indirectly affected by leadership. It is troubling to see companies performing poorly because the leadership is ineffective due to an inability to unify. Imagine what the associates think in this situation. If there is no unity at the top, there is guaranteed to be disunity at the bottom. This disunity shows up as "turf wars" between maintenance, quality, operations, warehouse, etc. Another way to look at disunity is to compare it to a dysfunctional marriage. It is like sleeping in the same bed but having different dreams.

"No one climbs a mountain to get to the middle. We are going to the top." — *Unknown*

The above story is in no way an indictment of family-owned businesses. I have had the pleasure of working with some multi-generational family-owned businesses that have learned to create and maintain unity across different generations of family members. This is no easy task, and these companies should be commended.

However, on the other hand, I have seen plants shut down or move to another location because the leaders at the current site could not or would not get their act together. As a result of these changes real people's lives were impacted. Real families went from eating steak to beans. Little Jimmy does not get that bike for Christmas. I have a problem with that, and I hope you do as well. The good news is that it does not have to be that way. Unity within the team will ensure we are strong enough to weather the storm of competition. However, do not confuse unity with being nice all the time. That is not my point. Keep in mind that diverse teams will have more disagreements, they will be harder to lead, but better at problem solving. Lack of conflict doesn't lead to harmony; it leads to apathy. Everyone needs to be in total agreement as to purpose and objectives., but a great leader will encourage "constructive contention."

> There were three oxen that always grazed together. A lion had his eyes upon them and wanted to eat them, but he could never get at one of them because they were always together. So, he set them against each other with slanderous talk and managed to get them separated, whereupon they were isolated, and he was able to eat them one after the other.

The oxen in this short story are your team, and the lion in this case is your competition. A weak team is easily destroyed. The top leader must constantly ensure there is unity and address any infighting that may develop over time. One of the major causes of the lack of unity among the team is that the team does not have a sense of direction. The good news is that lack of direction can be corrected.

> "The first rule of any game is to know that you are in one."
> — Cisco System 1984

Another pitfall that keeps organizations from exceeding world class is the lack of direction. Imagine for a moment that there is a black box with wheels sitting in the middle of your office's parking lot. On each side of the box, there is a person pushing on the box. They cannot see each other. If each one of them is pushing with the same force on each side, the box will not move. If one were to ask each person if he or she was pushing, the answer would be, "Yes." However, the box is not moving, and the team's energy is wasted. One of the team members has been told the box must be moved, or else. This is typically the direction given to many top leaders when they are hired to fix a business. Understanding the meaning of "or else", that person pushes harder and eventually gets the box to move. If one were to ask the others again if they are working hard, they would again say, "Yes," and might also add that they are working even harder because they did not want the box to come toward them. Now imagine that the four people got together and agreed to push the box in one direction. The box would move faster and further with less effort. The same scenario is playing out in businesses all over the world. Do you know what direction your black box should be moving? Does your team know?

It is extremely important to have a team that is unified and headed in the correct direction. The success of a company is largely dependent upon the leadership team's ability to unite and lead in a common direction. However, it is not enough to be unified around the direction of the company and what actions need to be taken to effectively move the company in that direction, the team must now begin MOVING. Knowing what to do, but not doing it is lazy leadership. That is unless the team does not know how to do it. In that case, the team should seek out a trusted advisor to help (wink, wink).

> "It doesn't make sense to hire smart people and then tell them what to do; we hire smart people, and they tell us what to do." — *Steve Jobs*

This leads to the next pitfall; the pitfall of failing to execute. In addition to the lack of unity and direction, the team may lack a system for achieving the business need. The team may believe publishing the business goals is enough to empower everyone to meet those goals. This is typically not the case. It will be necessary to narrow the agreed upon focus. We call this the privilege of focus. With a narrowed focus, a unified team has a better chance to execute with excellence. In some cases, the team can get their focus down to one thing. In this case, they have decided to put all their eggs into one basket, so my instruction to them is "You better watch that basket." However, too many teams still take on more than they can implement and do a poor job at accomplishing the goals. These teams have created a vision and strategy, and even plan to advance the strategy, but fail to implement. The plan sits on a shelf in a nicely organized three-ring binder (or two rings if you like Leitz binders). This failure to execute in many cases is the result of over-tasking the team. During the planning meeting, the team will agree there are only a select few initiatives for the upcoming year but continue to pile on more tasks during the year. Sometimes it becomes necessary for leadership to say, "That is a great idea, but we aren't going to do it." How disappointing is it to have a plan that appears to achieve the goals only to have it sitting on a shelf somewhere?

> "If you focus on everything, you won't be good at anything."
> — *Unknown*

I sincerely believe that a great team can do anything, but I equally believe they cannot do everything, and simply because you can do something, does not mean you should do it. There will be times when things fall on your shoulders that should be shaken off and not taken on. There is a parable of a farmer who owned an old mule. The mule fell into the farmer's well. The farmer heard the mule braying (or whatever mules do when they fall into wells). After carefully assessing the situation, the farmer sympathized with the mule but decided that neither the mule nor the well was worth saving. Instead, he called his neighbors together and told them what had happened...and enlisted them to help haul dirt to bury the old mule in the well to put him out of his misery. Initially, as the dirt hit the old mule's back, he became hysterical! But as the farmer and his neighbors continued shoveling, a thought struck the creature. It occurred to the creature that every time a shovel load of dirt landed on his back...HE SHOULD SHAKE IT OFF AND STEP UP! This is exactly what he did, blow after blow. "Shake it off and step up...shake it off and step up... shake it off and step up!" he encouraged himself. No matter how painful the blows, or distressing the situation seemed, the old mule fought panic and just kept right on SHAKING IT OFF AND STEPPING UP! It was not long before the old mule, battered and exhausted, STEPPED TRIUMPHANTLY OVER THE WALL OF THAT WELL! The dirt designed to bury him blessed him all because of the way he handled his adversity. Sometimes we have to turn the things designed to harm us around and let them make us instead of break us. There are many teams today that need to "shake it off and step up" to the challenges set before them rather than succumb to the burial of the urgent yet unimportant initiatives for the business.

The final pitfall to becoming world-class is the lack of discipline required to maintain what has been established. It reminds me of a conversation I had with a Japanese gentleman in Toyota City, Japan. When I asked the Japanese gentleman if he believed Japanese people were smarter than American people, the Japanese gentleman replied with a resounding NO, and continued, "Americans are some of the most innovative people on the planet. However, the Japanese people are more disciplined than Americans. Americans like to create standards/procedures and then not follow them."

I think there is a lot of truth in that statement. As Americans, we like to innovate and find better ways to do things. Some call this lazy, but I choose to call it innovative. As soon as a task is presented, we immediately think of ways to do it better. However, this cannot be acceptable when providing a product or service. The customer expects a certain product or service. This is referred to as 'single market quality.' If the customers fail to receive what they have come to expect, they will not come back. However, in many cases the internal customer (next process, sister-company, or affiliate) may not have a choice. These folks are held hostage by a poor internal supplier.

What if you went to Chick-Fil-A and the sandwich tasted differently each time? Would you keep going back? Franchises are a great example of what standardization can do for a product or service. I have personally eaten at McDonald's in 7 countries, and the quarter pounder with cheese may be called something different, but it tastes the same in each case. Being a franchise may not be the goal of your business but consider the possibility of having to create 500 businesses exactly alike. That may motivate you to standardize extremely well. This deep-rooted desire to continually make the job easier, if not managed properly, will pose a challenge for leaders in their desire to create standardization within the company. This challenge can only be overcome by having the discipline to check the process and solve the problems being uncovered.

"Every big problem was at one time a wee disturbance."
— Scottish proverb

This check cannot be done from behind a desk in an office. The old saying "no news is good news" is not true for those leaders looking to create the discipline required to go beyond world-class. If a leader's goal is simply to make the pain go away, then running a world-class business is not in that leader's future. We can move toward world-class only if we sustain and further improve, in a controlled manner, what we have already implemented. If the expectation is that we will continually improve, then sustainment is not an issue. If one knows they are expected to take that next step toward True North (perfection) soon, going backwards would fail to be an option. If the desire to strive forward is missing, measures may be taken to look good vs. really be good. Eventually, the curtain will fall, and the truth will be revealed. Always ensure you are improving in the right manner and know how you are improving so you can continue to improve in the future. Do not ride the tide. A rising tide raises all ships, but when the tide goes out, we can see those who were swimming naked. Always be aware of when you are riding a rising tide and never swim naked.

INTRODUCTION TO THE SEVEN HABITS

Can you imagine with me for a moment, a boat at sea? The boat has all the horsepower it needs and three times the fuel it needs to get to its destination to cover for any major/minor deviations that may be required. However, the rudder is broken. Although this ship has the fuel and horsepower necessary to get it to the destination, it will spin around in the ocean and eventually run out of fuel and never get to its destination. This is analogous to many teams I encounter these days. These teams have enough people, those people are even energized, but they lack clear direction based on principles.

We must ask ourselves, "How is our rudder? How do we ensure clear direction?" To ensure we have clear direction, we must first ensure that everyone on the team has the same understanding about the organization's definition of "success." Our mindsets are governed by the current paradigms that we use to make decisions each day. These paradigms are developed over the span of our entire lives. We would prefer to run our businesses by habits based on principles versus paradigms. Principles are universally applicable and will ensure that all of us are aligned.

A key element of the principles I will be sharing is Lean. I have used Lean Manufacturing principles to align many teams around developing methods to produce their products. The word lean was first used to describe what was happening at Toyota in the 70's. James Womack, Daniel T. Jones, and Daniel Roos wrote, "The Machine That Changed the World" as a result of their research of Toyota. That book was the first time the word lean was used in that context, and the rest is history.

The first paradigm I would like to address is the paradigm of Lean (aka Continuous Improvement, Kaizen, etc.…). Lean IS NOT "Less Employees Are Needed." Once Lean became the vogue thing to do, people started abusing the power of lean by using it to reduce headcount, so the above paradigm was earned. However, we must now earn the right to change that paradigm. Improvement to remove people is not a goal of mine, and it should NOT be a goal of yours. I use lean as a part of a holistic approach called Operational Excellence. In that context, Lean [Continuous Improvement] is…

A system to identify problems and to solve problems
utilizing everyone on the team.

Now, to truly understand Continuous Improvement, one must understand the definition of some terms:

- Problem = A deviation from the standard
- Standard = A challenging target condition that cannot always be met (so continuous improvement is a part of the Lean thought process). A standard could be defined by the cultural, organizational, or technical work.

The work may reside in the…

- Manufacturing Value Stream (flows from raw material to finished goods)
- Design Value Stream (flows from concept to launch)
- Business Value Stream (flows from order to cash)

Our thinking must be that problems are treasures to be mined; not hidden but exposed for all to see. Once we have alignment around the definition of what Continuous Improvement IS, then we must develop alignment around a common set of habits. When it comes to Continuous Improvement, you don't have to be extreme, but you must be consistent. The steps to improvement are evolutionary, but the results can be revolutionary if you stay the course. Having a common understanding of these habits will allow the team to make better decisions and have better habits going forward. Never underestimate the power of a team that can make decisions effectively. If we want to be a continuously improving, world-class, excellent organization, we need to ensure the continuous, universal application of beliefs (behaviors and thinking). We must also be willing to continually address change, responsiveness, and the organization's ability to improve and adapt to its competitive environment.

> "What doesn't improve dies." — *Unknown*

To accomplish this, we must create some habits that are the constancy of that universal application. There are seven major habits that we must understand to ensure this alignment:

- Acting Long-term
- Valuing the Customer
- Embracing the Total System
- Focusing on the Process
- Obsessing Over Quality

- Capturing Organizational Learning
- Respecting People

"Bad habits are like a comfortable bed; they are easy to get into, but hard to get out of." — Unknown

Most of us are motivated to change when the pain of doing the same thing becomes unbearable. For most of us, pain is a more powerful motivator than opportunity. I would like to recommend that we change our thinking to allow the opportunity to become a more powerful motivator, and hopefully we can avoid some pain. In the next chapters, my goal is to explain the seven habits that will help with this motivation. My goal is that anyone can use this text to improve their organization regardless of status or business complexity.

End of Chapter GROUP Reflection Questions:

1. Are we progressing on the actions from our last discussion?
2. What was the key learning from the current chapter?
3. As a team, what do we do well as it relates to the key learning?
4. As a team, what do we NOT do well as it relates to the key learning?
5. What do we need to Start, Stop, or Continue doing as a team to improve going forward as it relates to the key learning?

CHAPTER 3

HABIT 1:
ACTING LONG-TERM

"If your plan is for one—year plant rice. If your plan is for ten years, plant trees. If your plan is for one hundred years, educate children." — *Confucius*

We often get caught up in the here and now trying to LOOK GOOD instead of focusing on the future where we will eventually BE GOOD. The first habit of the seven habits is Acting Long-term. This is when a team has a long-term focus over a short-term focus. One way to ensure long-term thinking is occurring is to apply the concept of True North.

True North on a globe is at the very top, and any step from that point is south. True North in the sense I am using it here is a considered perfection. Examples of True North in business would be, 100% Productive, Zero Scrap, Zero Warranty, Zero Inventory, 100% Market Share, etc. A True North statement will always be absolute (e.g. Zero or 100%). These are clearly unattainable, so True North is not a destination but rather a compass heading. If we have the discipline to hold ourselves and our teams to this high standard, our focus then becomes more about being good versus simply trying to look good. Below are some examples of looking good (short-term) vs. being good (long-term):

Looking Good	Being Good
Adjusting inventories at month end to make the financials look better or other financial acrobatics	Not Adjusting Inventories, earn the right to decrease overall inventory by improving the process
Cost Cutting to the point where capability is negatively impacted	Cost Savings where the capability is improved
Layoff Talent when the market dips	Keep Talent and Develop them so we are stronger than our competition when the market returns
Pulling in orders from future months to hit a revenue number this month (mortgaging the future) or to hit earned hours by overproducing	Only run what is ordered, pressure on sales to sell unused capacity, use idle time to improve the process and cross train

True North gives us a direction toward being good, however if barriers arise, and we dodge them instead of dealing with them head on, it will take us off the path of True North. This behavior of dodging barriers reinforces the idea of short-term thinking. Those barriers, if not dealt with properly, can force us to make decisions that may make us look good today, but will hurt us in the long run.

As a supplier to Toyota, we could get tours that the public would not get. I am not sure if they still do this or not, but when we used to visit the Toyota plants, they would take to us their top problem areas and ask if we have any ideas on how to fix the problem. The first time this happened to me, I was shocked. I asked my guide, "Why do you keep showing me the problems? I want to see all the good stuff you guys are doing. I am told that you are the best manufacturing site in the world." His response to me was, "My job is to be good, not to look good. You are a fresh set of eyes and may see a solution that we haven't seen, so I am going to leverage that to help me be good." Well, that is a different way of looking at things.

> "Being different scares people. Do not let their fear change you. Be Different, Think Different" — *Unknown*

SHORT TERM THINKING

In the finance world, the phrase "Long-term Greedy" is used to signify that a company is willing to take short-term losses for the long-term gain. This thinking will lead to a company "being good" over the long-term. However, when it comes to frequently reviewed P&L statements and Balance Sheets, businesses struggle with the "Being Good" concept the most. If we want to further foster a long-term vision, we must base management financial decisions on a long-term view even at the expense of short-term financial goals. In today's highly competitive marketplace, we often see businesses making decisions with the quarterly report number for the stock market being the primary focus. Leadership knows what needs to be done, but leaders often choose to go against their better judgment to satisfy the day trader culture of "I want it now." Some examples of this short-term thinking can be seen in the following areas:

- Failure to implement planned maintenance on equipment because "we need to run it." Maintenance should not be seen as a repair function. Maintenance if done correctly should be seen as a reliability function. If the Quality Function's purpose is to help assure quality., Maintenance's purpose is to assure capacity; not simply provide maintenance when failures occur.

- Failure to cross train associates immediately because we need experts at each step of the process to cover up process issues.

- Failure to fill openings ahead of known attrition (e.g. retirements), so we can hit our labor cost numbers.

- Overproducing parts to gain earned hours on overtime even though we know those parts can be made on-time without overtime.

In these types of situations, management's focus is on "making a splash" with a short-term impact that gets the manager noticed and positions him/her for the next step in his/her career path. This same leader may look back at the failure of his successor and state, "Look how bad that area is performing now that I left." Not realizing that the poor performance was due to the decisions he made before leaving. These same leaders judge progress by comparing themselves to competitors or to historical results. Again, the overall focus here becomes looking good versus being good. The result of looking good will typically lead to what I call "window dressing." The place looks great from outside or from a distance, but when you get closer you can see the truth.

I learned a valuable lesson in leadership at one of my corporate jobs. I took great pride in being able to improve an area. There was a 100% chance that the area would improve while I was there. This was due to pure brute force on my part. The issue was that the area would not perform as well when I left. A wise leader who was over the areas in which I was being moved pulled me aside and stated that my performance would be measured differently going forward. My new incentives would be based on how an area ran AFTER I left the area. That changed my perspective significantly. Before this change I was focused on getting quick results. After this change, I shifted to developing systems and people to get long-term results. That is when the concept of "go slow to go fast" really clicked with me.

Typical publicly- traded companies have a quarterly focus and, depending on industry, possibly a two to ten-year plan. Conversely, Toyota has a 100-year focus. They are very patient and long-term focused. It took Toyota 60 years to go from laughingstock to #1. Management at Toyota is concerned with preserving the legacy for stakeholders (employees, stockholders, customers, suppliers). I know you may be mumbling that you do not make cars, and your business is different. I wish I had a dollar for every time I heard a client tell me that. The key is to not focus on what is being made or how it is being made, but to focus on the process of how the "how" and "what" is improved continuously. So how do we change this wrong way of thinking in our businesses?

> "A society grows great when old men plant trees whose shade they know they shall never sit in." — *Unknown*

One day in 1671, Christopher Wren observed three bricklayers on a scaffold, one crouched, one half-standing and one standing tall, working very hard and fast. To the first bricklayer, Christopher Wren asked the question, "What are you doing?" to which the bricklayer replied, "I'm a bricklayer. I'm working hard laying bricks to feed my family." The second bricklayer responded, "I'm a builder. I'm building a wall." But the third bricklayer, the most productive of the three and the future leader of the group, when asked the question, "What are you doing?" replied with a gleam in his eye, "I'm a cathedral builder. I'm building a great cathedral to The Almighty." The third bricklayer had a clear understanding of the purpose of his work which in turn improved his work.

There is an old saying that states, "The best time to plant a tree was 20yrs ago, but the next best time is now." The problem with some businesses these days is those needing to plant those trees aren't willing to do so. If the leaders are nearing retirement, they know they won't see the value of the expense/work, so why bother. They may even be negatively impacted by the expense/work since the return on the investment won't materialize until much later.

As leaders, we must have a philosophical sense of purpose that takes priority over short-term decision making. We must understand our place in the history of the company and work to bring the company to the next level. This cannot be done if every leader tosses out what the previous leader was doing and starts a new direction. Consider running your business as a relay race. The race is going to take the business from where it is today toward True North. When the next leader assumes your current position, you are essentially passing the baton. That leader should continue going in the same direction. Could you imagine running a relay race where, when the baton is passed, the next runner goes off the track in a direction that will not take them to the finish line?

This focus on True North should create a constant state of healthy dissatisfaction with the current condition. This is also referred to as a constancy of purpose. We are never finished improving until one of two things happen: one, we achieve True North (highly unlikely), or two, we hand off the baton to the next generation (more likely), which means that the next generation is never done until True North is achieved, or the baton is passed. It is always important to have that next generation ready to take over the business. We must have a strong bench from which to pull future leaders. Afterall, if your business cannot run without you, you do not have a business, you have a job.

Setting goals can be very tricky for a team. If there is no guidance on what goals to set, a general rule of thumb to set challenging goals is to double the good, and half the bad. However, a full understanding of True North can also help us set better goals and targets for our team. The traditional approach to setting a target is to arbitrarily set an incremental target (think inch-stone vs. milestone) from where we are today. If you start with True North and ask what is keeping us from having that today, and if you compromise slowly, you will develop goals that are 20% - 30% higher in improvement.

LONG TERM FOCUS

Leaders sometimes ask me the question, "Where do I and my team need to spend our time to ensure a long-term focus?" The answer is best explained using the graphic below:

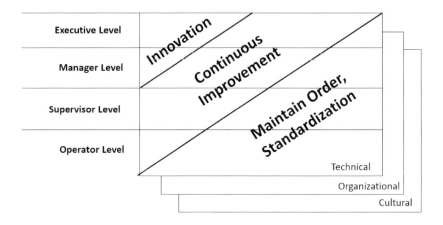

The diagonal lines signify the time spent between each section. The horizontal levels show the shifting center of attention as the level within the organization rises. You will also notice the layers that align with the elements of change discussed in a previous chapter. In total, the entire organization should spend half of its time focused on maintaining order and standardization (make today good) across all elements. Making today good is simply following the standards that we have put in place to ensure we provide a quality and consistent product or service to our customer. This may sound simple, but it is not easily sustained. Many companies spend their time dealing with the backlash of not maintaining order and standardization in technical, organization, and culture. This time spent reacting to backlash is very distracting.

Another 30% should be focused on continuous improvement (make tomorrow better). This also applies to all elements. If everyone in the business was thinking about how they could make tomorrow better and implementing those thoughts, we would be in a very different place. Imagine if many improvement ideas are being conceived and implemented daily. The key is for leadership to create the thinking that triggers ideas. These idea triggers (Lean Thinking, Theory of Constraints, Variation Reduction, etc.) open our eyes to what "could be."

> "One of the features of the Japanese workers is that they use their brains as well as their hands. Our workers provide 1.5M suggestions per year and 95% of them are put to practical use. There is an almost tangible concern for improvement in the air at Toyota." — *Eiji Toyoda.*

To continuously improve, we must solve problems. As we look for problems in our process, there are what we call opened-ended problems and closed-ended problems.

Open-ended problems are problems where we have not shown that we can ever create the desired outcome. These types of problems are reserved for innovative approaches and typically cost more money, due to heavy Research & Development costs. This would be a good spot to clarify the difference between Research and Development. The words are often combined to show similar meaning. However, they are very different. If you ask your team if the idea being considered will work, and more than half of them say yes, then you are Developing the idea. If you ask your team if the idea being considered will work and more than half of them, say no, then you are Researching. Researching is more about coming up with breakthroughs into areas of the unknown, while Development is simply incrementing things that we already know. To be good at research, you must be confident with nonsensical things. Most breakthroughs were thought of as crazy ideas until they were not. When breakthrough is first conceived, they think you are crazy, then they fight you, and then you change the world. Most companies do not have the patience or tolerance to allow the team to get through all the bad ideas to land on the great idea. Sometimes, you must be willing to kiss a lot of frogs to find a prince.

Imagine the first time someone came up with the idea of jumping into a stranger's car for a trip across town or staying in a stranger's house with or without them being there or sending a stranger money over the internet to purchase a product that may or may not be delivered. Well, Uber, Airbnb, and eBay, respectively, did just that and have generated 10's of Billions of dollars of value for their users. Sometimes the best ideas are the ones that seem to be bad ideas in the beginning.

As mentioned before, innovation is often dealing with an open-ended problem. A method that can be used on open-ended problems is called TRIZ. TRIZ is the Russian acronym for the "Theory of Inventive Problem Solving." According to TRIZ, universal principles (40 principles to be exact) of creativity form the basis of innovation. TRIZ identifies and codifies these principles and uses them to make innovation more predictable. The underlying thought is that whatever problem you are facing, somebody, somewhere, has already solved it (or one very like it). Patent databases are a great source of inspiration when using this approach.

A great innovation/paradigm shift question to ask your team is, "What is seen as impossible to do today in our business/industry that would change the game if we could figure out how to do it?" To understand the impossible, one must venture past the possible. However, this is only beneficial if you actually get to work figuring out how to do said thing. Don't fall for the fallacy that since it has never been done it can never be done. Some leaders manage from a posture of fearful safety when what they need is thoughtful courage to try what hasn't been tried before. To operate in this manner, you must be very comfortable with having confidence in nonsense.

One of many examples of finding solutions outside of one's industry came to me during my work as a consultant for a client in Honduras. I was touring a furniture factory in Tennessee. The factory had just won Industry Week's "Plant of the Year" award, and as the tour progressed, I could see why. The team there had done an outstanding job on flow and the team members were very polite and welcoming. As we were touring, I noticed a machine that was adhering two boards together, and the operator could handle the part immediately. This interested me, since I had been working to solve a problem at a wooden toy factory with parts taking too long to cure after gluing. At the toy factory, we had balanced most of the processes to cycle fast (seconds per part), but this one area still had a 20-minute cure time. We would have to queue up 20 minutes' worth of parts and put them in a press for 20 minutes. The accumulation of parts in this area always bothered me, but I did not have a solution. That was the case for a long time until I saw what I saw at this furniture factory. I immediately asked the tour guide to show me the machine. I then had him explain to me how it worked. It was basically an RF gluing process. The glue is applied to the parts, the parts are combined, and for lack of a better term, microwaved. The heat from the microwaving caused the polymers in the glue to fuse almost instantly. Fast forward a year, and that process was replacing the 20-minute cure press at the toy factory.

Another aspect of TRIZ is the focus on system contradictions and how to overcome those contradictions. Creative problem solving with TRIZ involves finding a solution and adapting it to your problem. An example of this can be seen in every large hotel chain. The problem was the shower curtain used with tubs would rub against you while you are taking a shower. If you have ever experienced this, you know that it is a very unpleasant feeling. The first thought may be to make the tub larger. However, that would contradict with keeping the floor plan smaller in the bath area. To solve the contradiction, the team developed a curved rod to allow the curtain to be farther from the person while maintaining the same tub footprint.

There are different levels of invention to consider when working with TRIZ. Those levels are below:

Level #1 is simple improvement of a technical system. They require knowledge available within an industry relevant to that system.

Level #2 inventions include the resolution of a technical contradiction. They require knowledge from different areas within an industry relevant to the system.

Level #3 is an invention containing a resolution of a physical contradiction. It requires knowledge from other industries. Levels #2 & #3 solve contradictions, and therefore are innovative by definition.

Level #4 is to develop a new technology. It is developed by using breakthrough solutions that require knowledge from different fields of science. This fourth level also improves upon a technical system, but without solving an existing technical problem. Instead, it improves the function by replacing the original technology with a new technology. For example, a mechanical system is replaced with a chemical system to perform the function.

Level #5 involves the discovery of new phenomena. A new phenomenon is discovered that allows pushing the existing technology to a higher level.

There are also some TRIZ Basic Principles that help guide one to break the psychological inertia created by old thinking. Those principles are:

The ideal end-result - Thinking out of the box is a good principle to achieve an ideal end result. TRIZ encourages people not to be satisfied too quickly with the solutions to a problem, but to be always open to even better ideas. This is very similar to the concept of True North.

Less is more - There is not always a need to invest a lot of money to arrive at the best idea. Innovation can be realized with existing materials and sometimes the solution is close at hand. This is very similar to the concept of "Creativity Before Capital" and "Master Manually before Automating."

Solutions already exist - TRIZ helps people define problems in terms of frequently used and general principles, which enables searching for solutions outside their primary field of expertise.

Search for fundamental contradictions - Innovating equals problem solving, which mostly exists of contradictions. When these contradictions are defined, the solution is often imminent.

Lines of evolution - Systems do not evolve randomly. There are fixed patterns that make the evolution of technology predictable,

TRIZ is a great approach to the open-ended problems that one will face in the business. The closed-ended problems are problems where we can achieve the desired result most of the time or at least 5% of the time. There are two different types of closed-ended problems: acute (special cause) and chronic (common cause). The approaches to deal with these problems are basic problem solving, and variation reduction, respectively. Operators are best suited for basic problems solving, since they are closest to the process when the special cause occurs, while the variation reduction is typically led by engineering due to the statistical nature.

Now back to where the organization should be spending its time. Finally, 20% of the time should be allocated to innovation (make the future brighter). If we are following standards and improving our work daily, we should be building a large amount of new learning. This new learning should lead to innovation. It is top leadership's duty to recognize this tipping point and take advantage of it. We must look at innovation differently since it often is the opposite of standardization. It is trying new things that have not been tried before. Other avenues of innovation can come from industry trends, new technology, improved capability, or looking at the product and process from a modularity standpoint, etc. The great power in innovation is when significant innovation occurs, everyone else in the industry is set back to zero. This happened with the Swiss in the watch industry. Toyota did this in the automotive industry. Apple did this in the phone industry. The list can go on and on, but the point is you want to be the first to innovate in your industry.

While continuous improvement typically implements low-cost to no-cost solutions, innovation starts requiring more resources to accomplish the goals. Resources may be in the form of research to develop the innovation, money for new capital investment, and/or a high-level team to implement the innovation. An operator or supervisor typically does not have the time and in many cases the clout to get those things done, so we leave innovation to the Managers and Executives. However, there are exceptions to this rule. While top leadership is most accountable for imagining the future, I firmly believe that innovation should be distributed accountability and designed into every single role in the modern organization. The number one rule is always "Do the right thing." If having a process operator lead an innovative initiative is the right thing, then do it.

Now that we have discussed the organizational-level time divisions, let us look at how this applies to each role within the business. At the Operator level, most of the time is to be spent maintaining order and following standards. A smaller percentage of the operators' time is spent on continuously improving the work that they do. Their improvement is mainly on task level items. This will require that the operator be trained in basic problem-solving methodology to improve their chances of success. This continuous improvement is sponsored, coached, and supported by the Supervisor level.

The Supervisor level spends part of their time maintaining order (via Leader Standard Work) and ensuring standardization, whereas a larger part of their time (compared to that of the operator) is spent on continuous improvement. The supervisor's focus on continuous improvement is focused on the process level. The process typically consists of multiple tasks. They are responsible for improving the performance of the processes for which they are responsible. Managers should ensure there are proper metrics in place to monitor this improvement. The metrics should be assigned to those that have "line of sight" to improve the things that drive the metric. It is demotivating to give someone a metric over which they have zero control. Typical improvement metrics are related to safety, quality, delivery, and cost. The importance of the metrics is in that order. We will discuss the reason for that order in a later habit.

As we reach the Manager level, we see that most of management's time is spent on making tomorrow better rather than making today good. While they do have Leader Standard Work, it is not as structured as the Supervisor's. Management's focus on continuous improvement is targeted at the system and/or value stream (the flow of value to the customer) level. The key is for the manager to check the system health and if the system is being followed.

Regardless of the intention of the system, if no one is using it, it is worthless. I have seen many occasions where management has implemented very nice well-intentioned systems only to have them ignored. In my opinion, the bigger issue is when management does not correct the fact that they are not being used and therefore condones the behavior.

The amount of time an Executive spends on standards is primarily devoted to creating policy for the entire enterprise and performing their Leader Standard Work, which typically includes focused site visits, and monitoring the implementation of the corporate strategy through policy deployment and management. This level manages the setting and controlling of direction for the entire business. We also see an increase in the time an Executive spends on innovation. They are the Chief Innovation Officers. In their book, "Jumping the S-Curve", Paul Nunes and Tim Breene cover the concept of the s-curve whereas businesses start, grow, level-out and decline.

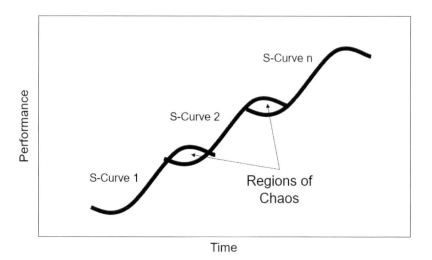

In the book, they discuss the importance of finding the next s-curve in your business rather than allowing the business to diminish into obscurity. This is easier said than done. If you are looking for and taking advantage of new businesses or new ways of doing your current business, for a while, you are having to manage both ways of doing business, the old way, and the new way. This is not easy to do for some of the best managed companies, to the point where some of them create special groups outside of themselves to manage this tension. For those that decide to keep the current and emerging business together, the test is how they respond in the area where one curve is starting, and the other curve is ending. This is called the 'Region of Chaos'. Some companies do what is easy and go back to doing business as usual, but the great companies fight through this chaos and overcome the organizational memory to create the new way of doing business. The key is to be on the lookout for the emerging future and ask your team, "Are we prepared to take advantage of what could happen?" Be careful, to not fight over every detail. There is an old saying that states, "One should pick his battles." A question to ask yourself is, "Am I willing to die on this hill?" Our goal should be to win the least number of battles that will win the war. We don't have to win every battle.

As stated before, the top executive should spend a large portion of their innovation time finding the next s-curve for the company. This may mean a shift from chasing current market to creating a totally new market. I have had VP's tell me that they must focus 80% of their time on running the business. My initial thought is, they must not have the right team under them if that is happening. If the top leaders are too focused on running the business, they will neglect to improve and innovate. I often see that leaders are working one level down (referring to the graphic shown in the Organizational Time Management discussion above) from where they should be working. This will keep the company from being able to reach its full potential.

A few examples of this happening are:

- IBM – They were convinced that there was no need for Personal Computers. They were late to the PC game.

- Xerox – They were focused on copiers and did not see value in their R&D. They had developed the mouse and what would eventually become Windows® and iOS® operating systems. While they innovated these ideas, they did not profit from them.

- Sears – They were the first big catalog company. They were the Amazon of their time. However, they failed to adjust their business model and now they do not exist.

- Kodak – Developed the first digital camera but did not see the value in the idea.

- Swiss Watchmakers – The Swiss did not make the shift to quartz (even though they invented it) and the Japanese now lead the market in quartz movement watches.

I can go on and on, but the idea is, as leaders we must keep one foot in today (run and improve the current business) and one foot in tomorrow (innovation).

A McDonald's innovation that stood out to me was the fact that they cooked both sides of the burger at the same time using these clamshell type griddles. I did not appreciate it at the time (I was only 16) but looking back there were several innovative systems being used. For example, each cooking area had a different tone buzzer. Regardless of where you were in the kitchen, when you heard a buzzer you knew which way to turn and start walking. This level of thinking went into everything you did at McDonald's. All the way from onboarding to exit interview. I am certain this forward thinking helped catapult them to success.

Many companies think they do not need to be on the lookout for their next S-Curve. However, they should at least be looking to ensure they are not on the downside of the current S-Curve. In his book, "How the Mighty Fall," Jim Collins describes the five stages of decline that a business will see. These stages are listed below:

Stage 1: hubris born of success (Rising)

Stage 2: undisciplined pursuit of more (Rising)

Stage 3: denial of risk and peril (the Peak- enjoy it while you can)

Stage 4: grasping for salvation (Falling)

Stage 5: capitulation to irrelevance or death (Crash)

Stages 1 and 2 can be misleading since the business is still showing improved performance. Leadership should always be conscious of all stages and ensure their businesses are not at risk. We must be in tuned enough to notice the issues during the rise and find that next jump off point to keep the business alive. That is the job of the Top Leadership Team.

A good example of finding the next curve can be seen in CarMax. Their original business was Circuit City, but they pivoted to cars, and the rest is history. With what has been happening to big box retailers lately, I would say that they made a smart move with their capital and talent.

In the organizational time management figure above, I showed where our time should be spent on an organizational level, when we move to where time should be spent on an individual level, we use the Eisenhower Model. This model was popularized by Stephen Covey in his book "The Seven Habits of Highly Effective People."

The model is shown below. It is arranged in quadrants to which I will refer later in this chapter.

	URGENT	NOT URGENT
I M P O R T A N T	**Quadrant I: Job Description Related** • Crises • Pressing Problems • Deadline-driven projects • Daily, routine tasks **Addresses Today** *People who stay in this quadrant get to keep their job*	**Quadrant II: Goal Related** • Prevention/solving of problems • Planning • Continuous Improvement • Personal Growth & Developing others • Reflection **Addresses Tomorrow** *People who stay in this quadrant get promoted*
N O T I M P O R T A N T	**Quadrant III: Other Duties Related** • Interruptions • Some phone calls • Some mail • Some reports • Some meetings • Proximate, pressing matters • Non-specific items • Traditional, Inherited tasks *People who stay in this quadrant get very, very busy*	**Quadrant IV: Wasteful Behavior** • Trivia • Busy work • Some mail • Some phone calls • Time wasters • Pleasant activities • Fun stuff • Idle time *People who stay in this quadrant get fired*

In a 1954 speech to the Second Assembly of the World Council of Churches, former U.S. President Dwight D. Eisenhower, who was quoting Dr J. Roscoe Miller, president of Northwestern University, said: "I have two kinds of problems: the urgent and the important. The urgent are not important, and the important are never urgent." This "Eisenhower Principle" is said to be how he organized his workload and priorities.

Eisenhower recognized that great time management means being effective as well as efficient. In other words, we must spend our time on things that are important and not just the ones that are urgent.

To do this, and to minimize the stress of having too many tight deadlines, we need to understand this distinction:

- Important activities have an outcome that leads to us achieving our goals, whether these are professional or personal.

- Urgent activities demand immediate attention and are usually associated with achieving someone else's goals. They are often the ones we concentrate on and they demand attention because the consequences of not dealing with them are immediate.

When I engage with a group, they are already busy, so I have them use this model to determine where they spend most of their time. They are often caught up in the tyranny of the urgent. The goal is to remove items from their plate that are not adding value to the business. We always find items to remove.

> "Being busy is a form of laziness – lazy thinking and indiscriminate action" — *Tim Ferriss*

Depending on your role, the goal would be to have the proper balance between Q1 (urgent and important) and Q2 (not urgent and important) activities. We should work very hard to not have any Q3 (urgent and not important) or Q4 (not urgent and not important) activities. Q1 and Q2 align with Organizational Time Management discussed above. Any time spent in Q3 and Q4 is taking away time that should be spent on important tasks. In some cases, you will have individuals spending all their time in Q3 and Q4. These people are majoring in the minors and/or giving the trivial many activities too much of their time. If you consider that their important work is not getting done as a result, you will begin to see the negative impact on the business. Either you are over staffed (giving them too much idle time), under deliver to the customer, or over work others as a result. This is not fair to the business, customers, or employees, respectively. The leader should help the person determine what actions need to be taken to shift one's time to the important tasks for the business. If the individual cannot make the transition, the leader should follow a progressive discipline process.

Some examples of each quadrant are shown in the graphic above. A good exercise for teams is to have each person track their time in 15min increments for an entire week and categorize each 15 min segment into the quadrant that represents how the time was spent. I mainly do this as a learning opportunity, not to point fingers. My goal is to enlighten the individual as to how things that are not important creep into their schedules, or how they have simply accepted things as important that are not important.

When we know which activities are important and which are urgent, we can overcome the natural tendency to focus on unimportant-urgent activities, so that we can clear enough time to do what is essential for our success. This is the way we move from "firefighting" into a position where we can grow our businesses and our careers. You will find there are those that love "firefighting," so you will need to find another outlet for their skill sets or risk losing them.

LEVEL PLUS ONE

A clear indicator that a group lacks long-term focus can be seen when the people of that group work below their level (see graphic below). We recommend leaders work at their Level Plus One.

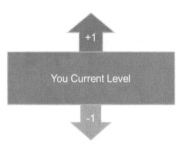

When one acts in a Level Plus One manner, they are learning what it takes to move to the next level. They are also allowing their boss to work in a Level Plus One manner. While it is important to understand the work being done at the next level down, one should not work at that level. This prevents that lower level from being upwardly mobile. It also keeps that level from doing their work, since it is being done for them. While they should not do the work at the next level down, the leader should be able to coach the work being done at that level. Leaders must be focused ON the business not IN the business.

> "If you are willing to do more than you are paid to do, eventually you will be paid to do more than you do."
> — *Unknown*

I was working with a client in an electro-polishing operation and noticed that the plant manager was the busiest person there. While I was primarily there for a technical issue, I always give my advice on anything I see that should be addressed. In this case, I had the plant manager stop what he was doing and look around. I showed him that one guy had been smoking outside for the last half an hour (not break time), one lady had been reading the paper all morning, and I was not sure what the guy on the fork truck was doing, but I know I had not seen anything on his forks all day. The point I was making with the plant manager is he was working a level down, and due to this fact, he could not manage his team. They were perfectly content to sit there and draw a check while he did all the work. Unfortunately, he never recovered from that style of leadership and was placed in a position with the company that suited him better. He was much happier, and so were we.

STANDARDIZATION

One of the first steps for any organization starting their improvement journey is to standardize what is being done today. This standardization must be done by the people doing the work. These are the people that know what is happening. It cannot be delegated to someone else in an office somewhere away from where the work is being done. Those in the office think they know what is happening, but all too often they are wrong. Only the people doing the work can write the standards and improve upon them later. It is our jobs as leaders to give them the support to document the standards and a process to improve them on an ongoing basis.

I often must remind engineers that they have only built or designed one of any given product, while the operator has built hundreds or thousands of that same product. The engineers understand the theoretical outcome, but the operator sees the real outcome that includes the common and special cause variation that is present in all processes. Therefore, the operator knows more about what is happening. I wish engineers had that same deep understanding of a product that comes from building it repeatedly, but that isn't always practical. However, I do recommend engineers build the first 5 – 10 units of a new product design. This forces them to see the errors in their design and the variation in the process, this makes them better engineers in the long run.

Once we have standardized, we can then consider further improvements. Standardization gives us a stable platform from which to do all other improvements. If we try to improve from an unstable base, we will not have lasting improvements. We must have an "All Deviations from Standard are Evil" approach. The concept here is "stabilize before improving." Stabilizing is so important that I have had to instruct my clients to add temporary labor, temporary inventory, and/or temporary capacity to become stable. On the surface, adding these goes against True North. However, it allows us stability at which point we will slowly reduce them to the correct levels, which is typically well below the level at which we originally started.

Standards are owned by the team. They do not have to be perfect in the beginning; never let perfect be the enemy of good. The key is that there are standards created, trained to, and audited. The team can then improve upon what they have. It is expected that the standards be revised frequently to reflect the latest standard. If there are no updates to the standard in months or years, we can assume there is no improvement taking place. This lack of improvement is a problem with leadership in the area and should be addressed with the leaders directly. Typically, I find that either improvement is not expected, or it is happening and not being documented (this is a violation of the Capturing Organizational Learning habit that will be discussed later in this book). Both are dangerous to the longevity of the business.

Having standards also ensures we are allowing the people to do the right thing by providing the proper method, materials and machines or tools to do their job. Then and only then can we expect the right safety, quantity, and quality from them. Leadership expecting the process operator to do their part without the leaders doing their part first is unfair and disrespectful. I believe most people want to do what is right for the company that feeds their families. However, we often force smart people to do dumb things when we neglect to provide what they need to do the job right.

Once standards are created, we must train the team members on how to do the work by following the standard. Regardless of the work to which we are training, we must have a robust training process. Training Within Industry (TWI) is the method adopted by the Toyota team after World War II and is an excellent method to training. All training at Toyota is conducted using a derivation of this process.

Once we have created the standard and provided the items to achieve the standard, then we can ask, "Are the team members following the Work Standards?" The job of all leaders in the business is to ensure the standards are being followed. As mentioned previously, leadership also has standardized work to ensure the proper checks are conducted during each shift to ensure standards are being followed. Depending on the level of leadership up to 90% of a leader's work should be standardized. This concept (Leader Standard Work) was covered in detail in the previous chapter.

Individual Leadership Reflection:

True North

Leader Thinking

Never satisfied.

It will have a bullseye on it until it is perfect.

Every "solution" is a temporary countermeasure until something better is found.

Dodging barriers leads me away from my True North ideal.

Target conditions are a compromise from True North (vs incremental improvement from current condition).

Leader Behaviors

I use True North as a compass heading and make sure that everyone's actions align with it.

I earn the right to achieve the target by addressing barriers; not dodging them.

When coaching, I press for what else can be done to improve further.

Leader Reflection

Do I think and act this way? If not, what must I adjust?

With what situations have I become satisfied rather than holding a True North mindset?

Spending sufficient time in making tomorrow better (Q2)

Leader Thinking

I get the majority (80%) of my long-term results from my Q2 (Not Urgent, but Important) activities.

I own the development of the team. I must stay cutting edge (develop myself) to succeed here.

Daily reflection is one of the most valuable things I can do.

Leader Behaviors

I schedule Q2 activities daily, making it my top priority (provide time).

I ensure that my leaders (n-1) spend sufficient time in Q2 (provide people to ensure the proper span of support).

I do, and I encourage my leaders to work a level plus one.

I reflect while I am at a high energy point in my day.

Leader Reflection

Do I think and act this way? If not, what must I adjust?

How does my Q1/Q2 ratio fit with my current level (organizational time management)?

End of Chapter GROUP Reflection Questions:

1. Are we progressing on the actions from our last discussion?

2. What was the key learning from the current chapter?

3. As a team, what do we do well as it relates to the key learning?

4. As a team, what do we NOT do well as it relates to the key learning?

5. What do we need to Start, Stop, or Continue doing as a team to improve going forward as it relates to the key learning?

CHAPTER 4

HABIT 2:

VALUING THE CUSTOMER

"I would rather lose money than trust." — *Robert Bosch*

I was with a client discussing the reasons why they were having issues with one of their customers, and after he explained to me how they were handling the customer, I told him that I knew what the problem was. They were treating their customers like mushrooms. He looked at me strangely and asked how. I further explained by stating that they were keeping the customer in the dark and feeding them crap. This got a laugh out of him, but he acknowledged there was some truth in the statement, and he would personally work to improve the situation.

Sadly, this mistreatment of customers is not uncommon. Some businesses think the customer cannot handle the truth, so they say things to appease them. It is not the customer that is the problem, it is them, the supplier, trying to save face. Eventually, the truth comes out and the customer loses a little faith with each occurrence. If this cycle continues the customer may simply look for a new supplier.

"You can shear a sheep many times, but you can only skin it once." — *Unknown*

I have also seen where customer quality groups will make up a root cause to a problem just to get the customer off their back. In one instance, I had a zero-mileage customer return, and I tracked down what had happened, and implemented what I thought to be a brilliant countermeasure. When I submitted the Root Cause Corrective Action to the customer quality group, they told me I could not use that root cause, because they had used it before. They had told the customer that the problem was permanently solved. This was the same quality professional that explained his role to me as being my diaper. When asked to clarify the statement, he stated, "I am here to catch all of your SH%@!" You cannot make this stuff up. I would much rather have had a quality professional that was aimed at helping me solve problems and reduce variation versus simply seeing themselves as a police force of quality.

If asked, most people understand the importance of the final customer, and there are things that you would never do to the final customer. However, we do those things to ourselves (internally) all the time. Imagine extending our understanding of "customer" to include the notion that the next process IS the customer, and we treat that next process with the same importance as we treat our external/end customer.

Every step in our process has a customer-supplier relationship. In this relationship, we must strive to not make defects in our current process, not accept defects from the supplying process and not send defects to the next process. No matter what your job or role, the process that receives the work you produce is your customer, and we must give our customers what they need, when they need it, and how they need it. The word need is very intentional here. Notice I did not say what they want, when they want it, and how they want it. They may want every option you have, available all the time, and sitting beside their line (at your cost). To understand what they really need will require us to ask them what they need, when they need it, and how they need it. We must never guess! There are two quick methods we can use to ensure we are not guessing. One method is what is called the Voice of the Customer (VoC) and the other is called Focus Groups. Voice of the Customer will be discussed in more detail in a later chapter and focus groups are simply getting a group of your customers together and discussing their needs. Both VoC and Focus Groups are good tools to understand the needs of the customer from their point of view.

There is another more analytical method for gathering customer input which is called Quality Function Deployment. This method can be used to get the most detail from the customer. This method is best used when developing a new product and you want to ensure you are getting all the fine details required to ensure the new product meets the customer expectations. The output from this method feeds into the engineering properties development and later into technical solutions to meet those properties.

One of the concepts within the habit of Valuing the Customer is called Upstream Management. By practicing Upstream Management, we ensure we do not AMPlify (Accept, Make, Pass) defects. Quality cannot be inspected only at the end of the process just prior to delivery to the final customer. We must ensure that quality is passed from step to step in each process. This is referred to as "built-in" quality. If you are building in quality all along the process, the final inspection is simply a formality and should never reveal a failure.

W. Edwards Deming explained the difference in quality between the US and Japan by using toast as an analogy. He stated that American toast would be burnt during the toasting process, scraped at the end, and shipped to the customer. We refer to this as "inspected-in" quality and it can be very costly. Some companies are very proud of the fact that they have 100% (I have seen some up to 400%) inspection at the end of the process. Obviously, this is not the ideal way to produce products. I am not suggesting you go out and stop all inspections. That would be crazy. One must earn the right to not have to inspect by correcting the process(es) upstream. In the case of our Japanese counterparts, the toast would be burnt once, they would work to understand the problem, the toaster would be adjusted, and future un-burnt toast would be sent to the customer.

If we allow defects to exit a process, we are not being respectful to the next process, which we now know as our customer. If this failure is not addressed, it will also set the stage for the downstream process to allow defects to be created and passed on to its customer. At this point, the quality death spiral will ensue. As a management team, we must stop and fix quality the first time.

> "If you don't have time to do it right the first time, how will you find time to do it the second time?" — *Unknown*

You will be tested daily on whether you truly believe quality is first. How you respond will determine the ultimate quality of your product or service. We do not have time to keep solving the same problems over and over. There is one thing on this planet of which we cannot create more, and that is time, so we must be very protective of how we spend our time.

SOMETIMES YOU HAVE TO KICK A GOOSE

There are times when we must do something that will not benefit us directly. We do it simply to protect the next process (or person in the case of this story). My youngest son and I were riding our motorcycles in the outskirts of our town one afternoon. I was in the lead as I am most times. As we were rounding a bend in the road, I saw a goose coming out of the grass on the side of the road. I recognized that that goose would miss me if I swerved to the left. However, my mind shifted to the fact that if I dodged it, it would most definitely hit my son. With that thought in my mind, I swerved closer to the goose and give it a swift kick to send it back into the grass. After kicking the goose, I looked back to see the goose spinning on the side of the road. Assured my son would make it pass the goose with no issues, I motored ahead to the next stop sign. At the stop sign, my son signaled for me to stop. He said, after the goose stopped spinning, it looked back toward me like, "I can't believe you just kicked me." We laughed, and I told my son,

"Sometimes you have to kick a goose." I am not sure if he got the full meaning of the phrase, but I always get a laugh when I think about it.

LINE BACK

As we focus on the customer, we will eventually conclude that there is also a customer-supplier relationship between the support groups, including management, and the value-added flow. Value-added flow is the part of the business where the value for which the customer is paying us is being added to the product or service. Line Back is the concept of everyone and every group in the company understanding that the company does not exist for each group's benefit. The company exists to add value to the customer, and the people directly adding value to the product or service comes first. The other groups are necessary and value-aiding at best. In some extreme cases, the support groups may be inhibiting flow. Value-aiding is in support of the value-adding activities (e.g. supplying materials, maintenance of machines, payroll, calibration, etc.) Therefore, the support groups must determine what must be done to support the value-added flow and remove inhibitors to flow (aka Enemies to Flow, which we will dive into later) from the value-added flow. Once the support groups have determined how they can provide support and remove waste, then the support groups must do it as efficiently as possible, even if it means taking the waste into their groups where they then work to reduce or eliminate the waste. Too many times I have seen functional groups focusing on functional excellence while moving their function's work to the value-added flow in the name of efficiency. I have also witnessed support functions removing resources to improve their costs. However, they were not being effective in the eyes of the customer (value added flow) before removing the resources, and now they do not have the resources to become effective. This is often seen in maintenance, material handling, quality, and human resource groups. The practice of effectiveness before efficiency means that we are meeting the needs of our customers prior to removing resources in any given area. How do you know if you are meeting the needs of your customer? Ask them!

For example, below are the 5R's as they relate to Planning and Materials:

Right Part

Right Quality

Right Quantity

Right Price

Right Place

If the planning and materials group lived by these 5R's, they would be modeling the lineback concept. However, if they are not satisfying these 5R's, but are hitting their internal function targets, they would be violating the lineback concept.

Another example would be for the Quality Function. What if quality was focused not on policing quality but helping improve process quality, which will lead to product quality. In addition to improving the quality of the product and process, this would also improve the working relationship between the value added flow and the quality group. Some companies have already made this transition, but there are many more that have not.

The one question every support function should ask themselves is "If my customer (internal or external) could get the services we offer from anyone (inside or outside of the company), would they still choose my group?" Support groups should not want their customer to only be using them simply because they must use them due to being in the same company. I have been in the situation where I was forced to use a sister company for services and goods that I could have easily gotten cheaper and with higher quality from somewhere else. This never made sense to me.

While working at Bosch, we would always say each function should be so good at what they do that they could be consultants in their field. This came true many years later when I and others separately embarked on the adventure of starting our first companies. We WERE consultants in our fields to the point where we could consult other companies. We used the skills we learned to help make Bosch successful and then started business consulting firms. We were having fun and saving tons of cash for Bosch. Those were good times, but the best is yet to come. Some people reminisce about the good old days. I would like to think that today is the good ole days, so have fun!

ANTICIPATE NEEDS

In the voice of the customer and focus groups, we allowed the customer or potential customers to tell us what they needed from their perspective. There is another method referred to as Market-In that will enable you to be tuned-in to your customer well enough to understand and even anticipate their needs in relation to what they need, when they need it, and how they need it. Thinking back to earlier in this chapter, the customer in this case is both the next process and our external customer. Market-In is a way to ensure we anticipate our customer's unstated needs and desires. It is quite possible that the customer has needs that are not even known by them, but we can anticipate those needs and create delighted customers.

> "If I had asked people what they wanted, they would have said: Faster Horses." — *Henry Ford*

As an example of this, Toyota came to the US to film customers using cars. At that time, they did not have cars in the US (or at least not a lot), but they wanted to learn how Americans used cars. They knew that cars were used differently in each culture. Toyota filmed numerous interactions between people and vehicles. These examples were then studied by Toyota. A famous example was filmed in the parking lot of a large US grocery store chain. The team of Japanese observers filmed a mother leaving the store. She had a screaming child in one arm, and a bag of groceries in the other arm. When she reached the car, she fumbled for her keys, found the round one (Remember having two keys; one round and one square?) and unlocked the trunk. She then looked around (not sure why) and with her knee pushed the trunk to the open position. Standing there, she had a decision to make. She had to put down one of the items in her arms. She decided to sit the child down first. At this point the child started screaming even louder. We can only imagine what was going through the child's mind at that point. She then gently sat down the groceries, collected the child, and moved to the side of the car. At that point, she unlocked the door, placed the child in the car, got in the car herself, found the square key, started the car, and she was on her way. Upon analysis of the video, Toyota was able to make the following changes to their car design that are now industry standards across all cars.

1. The opening of the trunk was lowered by extending the sheet metal to the lid and making the opening flush with the bumper, so customers would not have to lift the groceries so high to get them in the trunk. They had noticed how she struggled and was on her toes.

2. Key Fobs were introduced to open the doors and trunks without anyone having to insert the key.

3. Kick Plates on the trunks were installed to ensure the trunk opened on its own once the latch was released.

If Toyota had asked the lady what she needed in a car (focus group approach), she most likely would not have considered the items outlined above.

Toyota did not only look at the end customer, they also looked internally to their processes. You can see evidence in how the roofs of cars are designed today compared to in the early days. The stamping and assembly of the roof was very problematic as it was done as one large piece. They redesigned the roof to what you see today, which is three separate pieces; left, right, and top. Those valleys on either side of the roof are where those three pieces are connected. This improved the manufacturability of the car. Look at older model cars, and you will not see those valleys.

Market-in is a very valuable process. Steve Jobs famously stated that he did not like focus groups, because people did not know what they wanted. In some respects, he was right. You need someone who has a good grasp of what technology is being developed and how to link that technology to what customers are struggling with. The customer may not even know they are struggling, since they have been struggling for so long. If Apple would have solely relied on focus groups, we may have simply gotten a better version of the flip phone.

Another example is Laundry Detergent companies were focusing on whites being whiter and colors being brighter. However, when they conducted market-in studies they noticed people did not compare the whites or colors, they smelled the clothes. The learning was that the consumer cared more about smell. This learning significantly shifted their marketing strategy to focus on smells.

Watching our customers use our products or services (or a similar product/service) will lead us to discover many improvements our customers do not even know they might want or need. When observation and implementation is done properly, your customer will say things like, "Wow! They have thought of everything!"

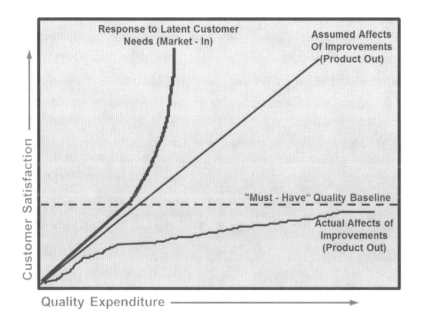

The figure above is called the Kano Model. I often use the Kano Model to explain the impact of quality on the customer. The old thinking was that by focusing on product quality (Product Out), we would exceed customer expectations. However, as we have learned over time, the customer expectations are continually changing. Therefore, the actual effects of improvements create an asymptotic line that never reaches the "must have " quality baseline.

> **"One must be able to scratch an itch that the customer doesn't even have yet." — Unknown**

As an example, consider the transition in quality of the automobile. In the beginning, you would buy a car and get a tool kit to repair the car. The same can be said for motorcycles. Today, we expect our cars to last for 100's of thousands of miles, with very little maintenance. There are even some aspects of our cars that are maintenance free. When is the last time you put water in your battery? That used to be an owner maintenance item.

Our expectations have changed over the years, yet we are still dissatisfied. The aim of Market-In is to surpass the customer's expected quality baseline. Imagine if the makers of the Video Cassette Recorder (VCR) only focused on making the VCR better. This would be a Product Out focus, and they would have the best VCR on the market that no one wants.

> **"If you wait for the customer to tell you what needs to be done, then it is too late." — Unknown**

There is an old saying in the business world that states, "The early bird gets the worm, but the second mouse gets the cheese." I share this statement as a cautionary note to not get too far ahead of the market or technology. There are many instances where the first company to market failed and the second one succeeded. The first mouse in this case got the rod across the back of their neck, while the second mouse came and got the cheese with no concern for danger. A case of this happening was with a Silicon Valley company called General Magic. This company was way ahead of its time and was led by a leader that most people would not remember. While the company failed, the ideas that came out of that company were the building blocks for the iPhone, which is now the #1 revenue generator for Apple. There is a great documentary about this titled, "General Magic." I highly recommend you watch it. Another example of the second mouse getting the cheese is Myspace (1st mouse) and Facebook (2nd mouse). Facebook set back and while Myspace made mistakes and leveraged that learning into Facebook. The result is there are many more people on Facebook, and some people have never heard of Myspace.

Another quick story concerning Facebook that I think can serve as a caution to businesspeople is related to letting someone else understand your business better than you do. This happened to the Winklevoss brothers. They had the original idea of what they called the Harvard Connection. They didn't understand coding, so they had this unknown fellow Harvard student do some the programming for them. This unknown student as Mark Zuckerberg, and he later founded Facebook and the Harvard Connection never really took off. My advice is to only outsource things that are stable and widely known, but never outsource what is considered to be (or will become) your competitive advantage.

WHAT IS YOUR PICKLE?

Bob Farrell, the founder of Farrell's Ice Cream Parlor, was a master at customer service. He understood the importance of wowing the customer. He is best known for his mantra of "Give them the Pickle." The idea of giving them the pickle originated from a letter Bob had received from an irate customer. The letter is below:

Dear Mr. Farrell,

I have been coming to your restaurant for over three years. I always order a #2 hamburger and a chocolate shake. I always ask for an extra pickle and I always get one. Mind you, this has been going on once or twice a week for three years.

I came into your restaurant the other day and I ordered my usual #2 hamburger and a chocolate shake. I asked the young waitress for an extra pickle. I believe she was new because I had not seen her before. She said, "Sir, I will sell you a side of pickles for $1.25." I told her, "No, I just want one extra slice of pickle. I always ask for it and they always give it to me. Go ask your manager."

She went away and came back after speaking to the manager. The waitress looked me in the eye and said, "I'll sell you a pickle for a nickel." Mr. Farrell, I told her what to do with her pickle, hamburger, and milkshake. I am not coming back to your restaurant if that is the way you are going to run it.

As the owner of the business, Bob took this personally and resolved to give this person, and anyone else for that matter, the pickle. This later led to him becoming a motivational speaker where he would tell his story and ask the audience to determine what was their pickle. "The Pickle" is simply something that you do that goes above and beyond what the customer would expect. A perfect example given was a father and son duo that collected garbage, but they would start lawn mowers for people as well. As they were collecting garbage and would see someone in their yard struggling to start the lawnmower, they would do it for them. Starting lawnmowers was their pickle and it led to them getting more customers in the garbage collection business. What is your pickle?

IT IS MY PLEASURE

When you read the title to this section, I would be willing to bet you are thinking of a very popular fast-food restaurant that was founded in the South, Chick-fil-A. Every time you say, "Thank You" your order taker will say "My Pleasure." Sometimes I will demonstrate this to my kids by saying "thank you" more than once. The most I have gotten to is five "My Pleasures" before my wife made me pull around. The use of this phrase was very important to S. Truett Cathy. He did not think saying, "No Problem" or "You are

Welcome" conveyed the proper sentiment to his customers. He wanted his customers to know without a doubt that he and his team thought serving them was a pleasure. He had gotten the idea from staying at some five-star hotels. If you have ever stayed at a five-star hotel, you have seen the pinnacle of customer service.

On a personal note, one thing that stood out to me during one of my visits to a five-star hotel was when I asked where the restrooms were. The person did not simply point down the hall and say, "Go down there and take a right, it will be on your left." The person stopped what they were doing and escorted me to the restroom. To this day, I use the phase, "Don't Point, Escort" when it comes to showing someone where something is or showing someone how to do something.

As the story goes, Truett suggested the use of the phrase "It is my pleasure" long before it was widely adopted by his franchise owners. This was due to his laid-back management style when it came to the franchise owners. He was not seen as a dictator, but more of a collaborator. However, he eventually had enough and made it very clear that this phrase would be used, and he expected to be greeted with the phrase during any visit. The managers of the restaurants did not simply go back and make their teams say "It is my pleasure" to satisfy Truett. They sensed the urgency in Truett's mandate and owned it with their teams. One of my pet peeves is a leader that will go back to their team and make them do something by telling them that "the boss" said it had to be done. This undermines the leader that says it, and they become a mouthpiece for the boss. We do not need these kinds of leaders in our business. We need leaders like the Chick-Fil-A leaders that took ownership of the request and made it happen at their sites.

Simply giving the customer "the pickle" or saying "it is my pleasure" is not enough. The genuine care for the customer must be internal to the customer facing team members. The process of ensuring you have the correct people facing the customer begins with the hiring process. I cannot speak for Farrell's, but Chick-Fil-A has managed to hire some of the nicest teenagers I have ever met. I contrast this with some of the other fast-food restaurants and there is no comparison. At some of the other restaurants, I get the feeling that the person taking my order would rather I not be there.

Valuing the Customer is about knowing who your customer is, what they say they need, what you think will wow them, and making sure they realize you and your team care.

Individual Leadership Reflection:

Line Back – "Serve the value providers"

Leader Thinking

I am here to support the value-added flow. The value-added flow is not here to support me.

Leader Behaviors

I remove inhibitors to flow from the value-added flow even if it means putting it upon myself (and other support).

Leader Reflection

What inhibitors to flow currently exist in my value-added flow and what can I do to remove them?

As I manage the relationship with my supervisor, how does she utilize my outputs?

As I manage the relationship with my direct reports, how do they utilize my outputs?

End of Chapter **GROUP** Reflection Questions:

1. Are we progressing on the actions from our last discussion?

2. What was the key learning from the current chapter?

3. As a team, what do we do well as it relates to the key learning?

4. As a team, what do we NOT do well as it relates to the key learning?

5. What do we need to Start, Stop, or Continue doing as a team to improve going forward as it relates to the key learning?

CHAPTER 5

HABIT 3:

EMBRACING THE TOTAL SYSTEM

"If you want to go fast, go alone. If you want to go far, go together." – *African Proverb*

Earlier in this book I discussed a boat at sea with no rudder. The same issue occurs in business where the teams are not aligned to the total system and do not understand that everything impacts everything else. Everything exists in the context of something else. In this chapter we will cover the habit of Embracing the Total System. This habit is where we continually examine each part of the organization to determine how each function interacts with and affects an event, situation, or problem. We strive to ensure that changes in one part of the organization do not negatively affect other parts of the organization. This idea is opposed to functional thinking. Functional thinking divides and isolates. This creates waste, conflict, and inefficiency. In business, there are no isolated, autonomous systems; every system affects every other system.

"...dividing the cow in half does not give you two smaller cows. You may end up with a lot of hamburger meat, but the essential nature of "cow" — a living system capable, among other things,

of turning grass into milk — then would be lost. This is what we mean when we say a system functions as a "whole". Its behavior depends on its entire structure and not just on adding up the behavior of its different pieces." — Kauffman, 1980

Below is a comparison of Functional View vs. a Systems View:

Functional View:	Systems View:
View things in a vacuum	Things understood in context
Value stimulations, highs/lows crises	Value harmony, stability, balance
Manage events and things independently	Manage relationships and fit
Separate people and isolate for control	Bring people together into teams
Function cause and effect only	Appreciate multiple factors
Individual performance valued at the expense of the system	System performance outweighs individual performance
Drive with fear, become risk averse	Create an environment for change

"How am I supposed to win, if I am always worrying about [how you are going to respond to my] wrecking?" — *Dale Earnhardt*

There is a saying that states, "I would rather stay with the devil I know than to take a chance on a devil I don't know." This statement is driven by the fear to change or the desire to settle for less than you deserve. Fear can equal Forget Everything and Run, or Face Everything and Rise; you decide. Fear can hamper everything we are trying to accomplish, and no one is protected from fear. However, we can choose how to respond when fear creeps into our lives. Fear can get in your head and tell you things like, "You aren't good enough, or you will never meet your goals, or you aren't as smart as others." The truth is, "fear is a liar." You are good enough, you will reach your goals if you put in the work, and you are as smart as the others; maybe not in the same subjects, but you are as smart at the things that are in your sphere of concern.

When Mikhail Gorbachev took over as what would be the last leader of the former Soviet Union, he was giving a speech to the masses. In his speech he was admonishing the behaviors of his predecessors when in fact he was on their staff. A voice from the back of the crowd yelled out, "Why didn't you do anything to stop them from doing what they were doing?" In a very stern voice, Gorbachev asked, "Who said that?" He waited for what seemed like minutes, but no one responded. He continued with, "And now you know why I didn't speak up." The same fear that existed in this example also exists to some degree within companies. Our job as leaders is to ensure that fear is eliminated.

SYSTEMS THINKING

Systems Thinking, also referred to as Living Systems in some circles, is a body of knowledge aimed at educating us on the importance of healthy systems and the benefits understanding systems can bring to any business or society. Systems are very powerful and if managed correctly can bring about great efficiencies.

Consider the small system of a man riding a bike. According to a study that measured the efficiency of locomotion for various species on the planet, the Condor was the World's most efficient animal. The measurement used was the amount of energy used to cover one kilometer. Humans were unimpressive when compared to other animals. However, when you create a system where the man is riding a bicycle and compare that to a condor, the man wins by far. Some may say this is not a system at all, but it is the man simply using a tool to make him more efficient. However, riding a bike is more than just using a tool. There is a constant feedback loop that keeps the bike in balance and moving in the correct direction. There is harmony between the man and the bike. Without balance, the bike would fall over. Without direction, the bike and the man would end up somewhere the man did not plan on being. The same harmony should be targeted in the larger system that governs our businesses. The larger system has many more "balance and direction" points than the man on the bike, so much care must be given to the health of the business system. In my opinion, this is the main job of the top leaders.

The system within an organization should behave much like that of a natural system. The key understanding must be that the outcomes from a natural system are a product of the relationships, not the individual parts of the system. In a natural system, satisfactory results come from parts of the system being harmonized in patterns of relationship. The conclusion is that harmonized relationships create satisfying results.

The concept of "Systems Thinking" originated in 1956, when the Systems Dynamic Group (SDG) was created by Professor Jay W. Forrester at the Sloan School of Management at MIT. The team utilized computer simulations and different graphs and diagrams to illustrate and predict system behavior. The significance of Systems Thinking in the framework of running a business is large. Systems Thinking is in direct contradiction to the Mechanistic Thinking that has propagated in the world of business across the globe. Very few companies have resisted the pull to be mechanistic in their management of the business. The companies that have fallen into the mechanistic approach have taken a reductionist view of the business by breaking it into the individual parts and thinking they can improve the entire system if they master the individual parts. This could not be farther from the truth when dealing with natural-living systems. As mentioned before, the interactions between the parts are more important than the parts themselves.

INTERDEPENDENCE

An organization is much more like an orchestra than a bowling league. In a bowling league you simply add up the individual scores to get the team's score. In an orchestra the entire group is playing from the same sheet of music and making minor adjustments as the music is being played. If you were to isolate (or have the instrument players put in earplugs) each person in the orchestra and have them play from the same sheet of music, it would not sound the same as it does when the entire orchestra is together harmonizing and making those small synchronizing adjustments. The role of a leader in this case, is the conductor. The conductor cannot necessarily play all the instruments, but the conductor can and does help manage the harmony. This is analogous to the leader in a business. The leader must manage the harmony.

While the interdependencies of an orchestra and organization are similar, an organization is much more complex that an orchestra. An organization must be run with an understanding of the many interdependencies, and as stated previously, the organization's leaders must be the ultimate conductors. An example of a violation of Embracing the Total System is incentivizing different parts of the business with contradictory goals. For example, we measure the producers of the product on the amount they produce, or we measure the services offered on the value of the services offered. We also measure the quality department on the quality of the products or services being delivered. In the above scenario the producers want to ship everything, and the quality department does not want to ship anything. What if we incentivize sales and the Sales Group sells many products that are on the edge of the company's product portfolio, ensuring that our delivered costs are too high to make a profit? Or, what if we incentivize purchasing on purchased material variance, ensuring that the materials come from low-cost countries at the expense of lead time, quality, and responsiveness? Can you see how this can cause a conflict? Have you ever seen this in your organization?

> "There's nothing so useless as doing efficiently that which should not be done at all." — *Peter Drucker*

Having the entire team focused in the right direction can help the team work smarter and not harder. The graphic below demonstrates the effects of having a misaligned team as compared to one that is unified. In the first condition (Working Hard, Misaligned), many forces pull on the organization. The net effect is that the organization cannot move upward. Upward (in this case) is toward True North. Regardless of all the work being done, there is no movement. The second condition (Working Harder, Misaligned), we have the organization putting more effort toward moving toward True North but failing to remove the other forces acting upon the organization. This is typically due to a strong leader being placed in the area and that leader is forcing the change requested from the top leadership. The net effect is a slight move toward True North, but that movement cannot be sustained. In the third condition (Working Smart, Aligned), we have removed the things that are distracting (left to right) and directionally incorrect (those items pulling us away from True North). The net effect is the team has much more upward momentum without having to add more effort.

Another symptom of not having the team Embrace the Total System is "Interpersonal Conflict." The graphic below is called the GRPI (grip-ē) model. The model came from research conducted by Harvard while I was at Bosch. It is now called VGRPI, since I added the "Values/Vision Aligned and Internalized" after the model was initially created to show the importance of the WHY. The most engaged people in your organization work for you, not because of WHAT you do. They work for you because of WHY you do it. Make sure you have explained the WHY to them. The values and vision of the company should explain the WHY; no vision can lead to no decisions.

Another way to reduce interpersonal conflict is by using Mutual Learning instead of Unilateral Control. We will discuss the topic of Mutual Learning in more detail later in this book. You will notice that "Interpersonal Issues" is at the bottom of the inverted pyramid. My experience has shown me that "Interpersonal Issues" are rarely the cause of organizational dysfunction. If interpersonal issues do exist, you can expect to have what are called muted conversations, meaning people simply do not talk to each other or speak their mind. This social silence can drive the team apart. There will be virtually no candor among the team. This is very scary from a leadership standpoint. Remember, no news is NOT good news. However, the true cause of this is not the people on the team. It is more often a result of failing to have the items shown higher up in the pyramid correct and/or poor leadership of the team. It is a lack of alignment. I teach that we should work from the top down. The values/vision of the company must be aligned to and internalized (The Why). The goals (The What) for the team must be shared (not competing) and aligned to meet the needs of the business, universally understood roles and responsibilities (The Who), and processes and procedures (The How) which are defined and followed. If these things happened, the interpersonal issues will be at best non-existent or at worst manageable. The problem is when we try to fix the bottom of the pyramid without addressing the top.

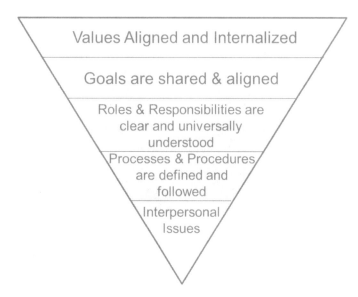

The above model combined with a resource matrix (which will be covered later in this book) can clearly demonstrate what projects are going to be completed to allow us to meet our goal and who (roles and responsibility) will be driving each project.

ABILENE PARADOX

Alignment is great if it is directionally correct. There are times when the team aligns around the wrong goal or direction. In the Abilene paradox, a group of people collectively decide on a course of action that is counter to the preferences of many or all the individuals in the group. It is the opposite of groupthink. It involves a common breakdown of group communication in which each member mistakenly believes that their own preferences are counter to the group's and, therefore, does not raise their objections to the course of action. A common phrase relating to the Abilene paradox is a desire to not "rock the boat". This differs from groupthink in that the Abilene paradox is characterized by an inability to manage agreement. In essence everyone agrees, but not for what is being planned. This sounds crazy, but it happens.

The term Abilene Paradox was first introduced by management expert Jerry B. Harvey in his 1974 article "The Abilene Paradox: The Management of Agreement".

The name of the phenomenon comes from a comedic anecdote that Harvey uses in the article to elucidate the paradox:

On a hot afternoon visiting in Coleman, Texas, the family is comfortably playing dominoes on a porch, until the father-in-law suggests that they take a [50-mile] trip to Abilene for dinner. The wife says, "Sounds like a great idea." The husband, despite having reservations because the drive is long and hot, thinks that his preferences must be out-of-step with the group and says, "Sounds good to me. I just hope your mother wants to go." The mother-in-law then says, "Of course I want to go. I haven't been to Abilene in a long time."

The drive is hot, dusty, and long. When they arrive at the cafeteria, the food is as bad as the drive. They arrive back home four hours later, exhausted.

One of them dishonestly says, "It was a great trip, wasn't it?" The mother-in-law says that she would rather have stayed home but went along since the other three were so enthusiastic. The husband says, "I wasn't delighted to be doing what we were doing. I only went to satisfy the rest of you." The wife says, "I just went along to keep you happy. I would have had to be crazy to want to go out in the heat like that." The father-in-law then says that he only suggested it because he thought the others might be bored.

The group sits back, perplexed that they together decided to take a trip which none of them wanted. They each would have preferred to sit comfortably but did not admit to it when they still had time to enjoy the afternoon.

A video has been produced showing this skit and is a good watch for leadership teams. This paradox happens a lot in business, and as leaders we must be on the lookout to prevent it. One way is to always have an outside set of eyes looking at the business and the plans being created for the future.

STRATEGIC ALIGNMENT

Earlier in this book, we mentioned that one of the jobs for leadership is to provide hope to their teams. However, hope alone will not get us where we want to go as an enterprise.

> "Hope Is Not a Strategy." — *Unknown*

Another goal when planning the direction of the team should be to always avoid the Columbus School of Management. Columbus's School of Manage can be summed up as follows:

> *When he left, he had no idea where he was going. When he got there, he did not know where he was. When he returned, he did not know where he had been. He did it all on borrowed capital.*

We need a strategy that works, so when developing our strategy, we must remember that strategy is all about the three C's

Choice: You have limited resources
- By focus we can build strength together.
- You do not want to be a jack of all trades and a master of none.

Clarity: Keep It Simple
- Enables sharing and understanding
- The more complex your business, the simpler your strategy should be.

Consistency: Long term and committed
- There must be a sense of direction
- Welch's strategy- If it cannot be #1 or #2, fix it, sell it or close it.

WHAT IS STRATEGY?

This seemingly simple question is quite complex, and many different definitions exist. I believe that strategy is defined as "how we internally respond to outside factors that are currently impacting our business or could impact our business in the future." Some examples of those factors are:

- Competitors
- Customers
- Law, Economy
- Pandemics
- Suppliers

Jim Rohn stated, "It is the set of the sails, not the direction of the wind that determines which way we will go." In business, the outside world is the wind, and our strategy is how we set the sails. When we respond to the outside world, we do so from inside the business with our internal processes; therefore, strategy is an internal response to external factors. Regardless of our strategy, it is only effective in terms of our ability to change our processes quickly enough to respond to the external. Consider what happened to the US automotive industry in the early 1970's. There was an external factor (oil embargo) that created a shift in the US consumer sentiment (vehicles with improved fuel economy). The Big Three (Ford, GM, and Chrysler) were not responsive enough to the change and subsequently lost considerable market share. Those three companies never recovered from the market share impact of those days. At the time of this publication, these companies, now called the Detroit Three rather than the Big Three, continue to struggle to make a profit on their smaller models.

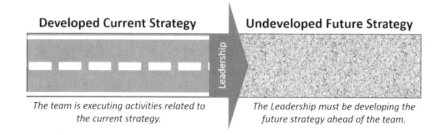

Developed Current Strategy	Undeveloped Future Strategy
The team is executing activities related to the current strategy.	The Leadership must be developing the future strategy ahead of the team.

As the leader you must have a strategy that is always out front. Do not let your team out pace your ability to create the strategy. The leadership team must be very diligent about staying ahead of the team executing the current strategy. If the team runs out of strategy, it is analogous to a car running full speed on a paved road and suddenly hitting gravel. I literally had this happen to me on a motorcycle once, at night. Not Fun!!

CONTINUOUSLY IMPROVE

If the Big Three would have known that a shift in the market was coming, they would have certainly prepared. However, one does not always know what is around the next corner, so a good approach is to continuously improve the following:

Stability – Reliability – Flexibility – Speed

We have already covered the importance of Stability and how we must stabilize before improving. We must also constantly be improving the reliability of the team, our equipment, and our products. Our flexibility comes from being able to efficiently change resources from doing one activity to doing another activity. Our speed is reflected in our ability to respond to customers and to changing conditions in the marketplace, thereby turning over resources faster, e.g. – inventory (flow creation). Some examples of speed, reliability, and flexibility are outlined below:

Speed:

- Inventory Turns (faster is better) = Material Portion of CoGS / Inventory (Raw Materials, Work in Process, and Finished Goods)

- Order Lead Time (shorter is better) = the time between when you pay for the materials to the time you get paid for the finished goods produced with those materials, or the time from when the customer places an order until you get paid for that order; whichever is greater.

- Sales per Employee (higher is better)

Reliability:

- Assets that perform when needed

- People who are present and perform when needed.

- Information which always remains current and accurate

Flexibility:

- Assets that can change from one product to another.

- People who are multi-skilled and cross trained

Constantly improving speed, reliability, and flexibility will allow us to be better prepared to respond to any changes in external forces in the marketplace. Another thing to keep in mind is the fact that more isn't always better, but better is always better, and sometimes better means less. For example, one should never hide problems by adding more unneeded Inventory, more Capacity or more Labor and call it increasing flexibility. The improvement in flexibility must be real and is to be accomplished before we NEED it. Improvement and change is hard enough, and we all know it is exponentially more difficult to improve and change during a crisis.

Creating a strategy for the company cannot be completed in a vacuum. Many have pointed to Toyota as a model for strategic planning. Indeed, Toyota has skillfully created and deployed their strategy over the years, so it would be wise to look at their methods, which is what I did.

Their Strategic Improvement Planning comes from a process called Hoshin Kanri, which means "shiny metal" or "compass." Some U.S. companies use the term "policy deployment." Hoshin Kanri is more like strategy management. Hoshin Kanri could be translated as "setting and controlling direction." It is a planning method that captures strategic goals and actions and combines them with the means to make those goals achievable. At the request of many of our clients, I have moved away from the Japanese phrase, Hoshin Kanri, to the phrase Strategic Alignment.

WHAT IS STRATEGIC ALIGNMENT?

Strategic Alignment is a systematic and disciplined process to align, communicate, and execute business strategy. I recommend you create, or at least revisit, your strategic plan yearly. The risk of planning too far out is that you shift from strategic planning to strategic guessing. There is a time when to speculate about the future, but your strategic plan is not that time. We will cover speculation in the section on Scenarios Planning. The risk of planning too short is you do not challenge the leadership to make significant shifts in the way they do business. We always want to be just outside of what the team thinks is possible. This stretches the team's thinking and leads to breakthroughs. It is like rock climbing. When you are first learning how to rock climb, the instructor will tell you to reach just past where you can see to keep climbing the rock. The same is true when creating your strategic plan. Don't take the easy route. Strategic Alignment focuses on those vital few breakthrough objectives which give us a competitive advantage. This is opposed to the trivial many in which lots of companies get caught up. Focusing on the trivial many is like trying to boil the ocean. The Strategic Alignment process ensures the entire organization is working on the right things. We use a simple one-page document (A3) to manage efforts and we create meaningful metrics with accountability for reaching targets.

As part of the process, we must consider our metrics. The metrics we use to motivate the team are critical, since some metrics divide and isolate rather than build unity. People with the targets will probably meet those targets - even if they must destroy the enterprise to do it. It is key to have counter balancing targets to ensure this doesn't happen in your organization.

When two elephants (management) fight, the grass (employees) loses. — *Japanese proverb*

Some traditional functional tactics that drive the "tug of war" mentality is below:

- Purchasing: Lower piece price (can lead to lower quality and longer lead times)
- Logistics: Lower inventory (can lead to running out of parts)
- Design: More functionality (can add cost and complexity to manufacturing)
- Accounting: Lower cost (can overburden the resources, can cut into the capability of the business)
- Operations: Increased output or maximizing earned hours (can lead to excess finished goods inventory)
- Quality: Lower delivered PPM defects (can lead to over processing, aka Gold Plating the product)
- Sales: Revenue (can lead to selling negative margin products)

"Running a business should not be like playing tug of war. As leaders, we must ensure the total enterprise is pulling in the same direction." — *Unknown*

None of these metrics are inherently bad. However, when functions are assigned competing metrics, it exacerbates the tug-of-war mentality. It is crucial to align key measures. One of the newer trends is to have a balanced scorecard, which has the teams focused on too many trivial metrics. At one of our clients, we transitioned from 42 competing metrics to aligning the entire team to eight tiers of shared measures. Typical Tier 1 Metrics include items like:

- Customer Satisfaction Index
- Cost of Quality
- New Product Development Cost
- RONA – Return On Net Assets
- EBITDA – Earnings Before Interest Tax Depreciation and Amortization

The tiers below this level must have some linkage back to this level. However, many functions that have metrics in the 5th or 6th tiers may have to subjugate their work "to the greater good of the entire business."

TRUE NORTH

We discussed True North in detail in Chapter 1. When working with teams on defining perfection, we walk them through a process of defining True North for their organization. This process helps the team visualize what perfection looks like as it relates to them. As a reminder, when doing this, we must ensure the team does not see True North as a destination but rather a compass heading. Once everyone is clear on True North, we can then compare our decisions to our compass heading. If the decision will move us closer to True North, we call that decision "directionally correct." If the decision will move us away from True North, we call that decision "directionally incorrect," and we should reconsider the decision.

When you are navigating you must follow where the compass is pointing. If you navigate with your sight, and you see briars, you will go around them. If you use the compass, you will have to face the briars and go through them. True North is our compass, the briars are the barriers that must be dealt with; not ignored.

Another exercise that proves beneficial involves discussing those practices that make us look good rather than be good. Be careful not to confuse nice "window dressing" as being good. One of the most common items that appear on the LOOK GOOD list relates to managing inventories. There is typically a habit of lowering inventories at the end of a period (month, quarter, and/or year) to make the financial reporting LOOK good. The inventory numbers are much higher if checked during the period. Because the inventory was not measured correctly at the beginning of the inventory game, the process must then rely on incorrect, unreliable numbers at the end of a period and the beginning of the next.

If you were to ask everyone in your company the following questions, what would be their replies?

- How do you know if you had a "good day" today?

- How does what you are doing contribute to the long-term success of the company?

- What should you STOP DOING because there are other activities that will yield more bottom-line results?

The response to these questions will let you know how well your company's strategy is being deployed.

The expectation is that every company starts out with an annual strategic plan. As the company matures in its strategic planning process, these expectations can extend into longer range planning sessions. The three types of planning sessions I use are:

- Annual Strategic Planning

- Long Range Planning

- Scenarios Planning

PROCESS TO CREATE ALIGNMENT

This may seem like a daunting task at first but creating alignment within any enterprise is possible if you apply the right process. It also goes without saying that a team is highly encouraged to use a facilitator that is not part of the team that will be affected by or required to implement the plan. It is very hard for a leader or anyone else on the team to balance their role as a member of the team at the same time as being a facilitator of the team.

"Failing to plan means planning to fail." — Unknown

In this section, I will detail a process through which we can create, align, and deploy our strategy. Our focus early in the strategic process is to identify gaps in our business that need to be addressed in the coming year. While there are many processes that can be used to uncover gaps in the business, I will focus on the following processes:

- Previous Year's Performance
- SWOT Analysis
- Voice of the Customer
- Market-In
- Kill the Company
- Pre-mortem

PREVIOUS YEAR'S PERFORMANCE

In this step we simply want to reflect on the previous year's performance to our plan (process) and the metrics (results of the plan). The goal is for the team to have a candid discussion using the following questions:

How would we as a team judge our targets and strategic activities?

O = Met Target

Δ = < 15% Off Target

X = > 15% Off Target)

Where did we do well?

Do we know why we did well?

Do we need strategic focus in those areas?

Where did we fall short?

What were the causes? (Note: focus on those things which we can control)

What were our strategic efforts in those areas?

Were they completed on time?

Did they get the expected result? If not, what was our recovery plan?

Did we identify the right projects? Did we identify enough projects?

Did we provide the needed resources? Did we remove the barriers to success?

The outcome of this discussion should be in the form of gaps we will consider later in the strategic planning process.

SWOT ANALYSIS

Strengths-Weaknesses-Opportunity-Threats (SWOT) Analysis is a process by which the team considers many internal and external aspects of the business. Strengths and weaknesses are internal to the company; opportunities and threats are external to the company. Below are examples and thought triggering phrases to help better understand the SWOT tool:

Strengths (internal) – what do we do well?

- Results from brilliant processes rather than hero effort
- Culturally embedded vs. personality dependent
- Possesses organizational advantages
- What we do better than all competitors
- Unique or low-cost resources
- Embodies strength in the market
- Unique Selling Propositions (USP's)

Weaknesses (internal) – where do we need to improve inside of the business?

- High-Cost Structure
- Lack of Technology / Innovation

- Poor results from poorly developed people
- Poor results from broken processes
- Good results from broken processes through hero efforts and workarounds
- Things we should avoid
- Seen as weaknesses in the market
- Hidden Factories (things we do not know we do that cost us money)
- Factors that lose us sales

Opportunities (external) – where can we grow?

- Developing Disruptive Technologies
- Where we could employ market-in
- New markets in which to expand
- Existing markets in which to penetrate
- Hidden Bank Accounts (Things that we do that should make us money, but don't today.)
- Changes in government policy related to your industry
- Changes in social patterns, population profiles, lifestyle changes, etc.

Threats (external) – where are we vulnerable?

- Market / Economy / Commodity volatility
- Supplier Stability (Quality, Deliver, and/or Cost)
- Shifting Consumer Sentiment
- Disruptive Technology from Competitor or Newcomer
- Economic issues
- Regulatory issues
- Social issues

When conducting a SWOT analysis, the team should brainstorm all the possible items that apply to the SWOT, consolidate them as much as possible (affinity), and clarify the consolidated list for later use in a gap analysis.

VOICE OF THE CUSTOMER

Voice of the Customer (VoC) is the process of intentionally soliciting the "voice" of one's customers. These customers may be internal, external, or end customers. The goal is to not assume we are doing a good job for the customer; we must be intentional about ensuring we are doing a good job for the customer. Below are some simple questions to be asked when face-to-face with customers:

- What are we doing that we should CONTINUE doing?
- What should we STOP doing?
- What should we START doing?

MARKET-IN

We discussed this concept in the chapter on Valuing the Customer, but I will do a quick recap here as it fits with the process of developing a strategic plan. This concept is also referred to as Ethnographic Study. However, I think Market-In sounds more appealing. Market-In is an additional VoC approach where one observes our customer using our product/output. This approach is very different from focus groups. Focus groups only capture customers' wants and needs based on their perceptions given their current situation. Watching the customer use our product/output allows us to discover latent wants and needs. With this knowledge, we can then provide products and/or services that have customers saying, "They have thought of everything."

KILL THE COMPANY

Mark Cuban said that he often likes to strengthen his businesses by asking himself this question: "If I was going to kick my own #$@, what would I do?". Then he goes and makes sure that cannot be done by his competitors.

I first have the client brainstorm what it would take to kill (or seriously injure) the biggest competitor within two years. This seems to go easily for the team and sets up this next exercise.

What if you (our clients) were able to compete with your own company? Your goal is to take all your customers and put yourself out of business. Having worked for your company for many years, you know the inner workings of the company. What would you do? The team brainstorms what it would take to destroy their own company within a year and then creates countermeasures to those items.

PRE-MORTEM

The key here is to envision failure now and develop counter measures to reduce the risk of such failure. Think of it as a Failure Modes Effects Analysis (FMEA) for your strategic plan. Fast forward to the end of the planning cycle and assume the plan failed. Why did it fail? What can we do now to prevent those failures?

Once the leadership team has created a list of all the gaps using the processes mentioned above (in addition to any other processes or data), it is time to determine which gaps the team will focus on in the coming year.

DETERMINE VITAL FEW

The Greek poet Archilochus wrote, "The fox knows many things, but the hedgehog knows one big thing." When it comes to our strategy, we must think like the hedgehog. This is where we must make some tough choices. Sometimes success is not determined by what we choose to do, but by what we choose NOT to do. This means we may say NO to some very good ideas; and that should be acceptable to the team. The resulting vital few gaps will be what drive the plan and alignment going forward.

The process of determining the vital few for the coming planning cycle must include every function's leader and maybe even their direct reports. The goal is to gain consensus on the plan. If this process is done in a vacuum, you will not have support for the plan and there will be competing initiatives throughout the year.

> "The essence of strategy is choosing what not to do."
> – Michael Porter

With all the gaps identified in the previous brainstorming sessions, the next step would be to group the common gaps into common groups. This is called an affinity exercise and the result is an affinity diagram. This reduces the number of gaps to families of initiatives that will be considered in the next step of the process.

The next step would be to determine those vital few initiatives for the coming year. One method I like to use in narrowing the initiatives is the Mathematical Consensus Model. When you have a large group of people trying to prioritize items, you have them each put a one next to the one they think is the most needed, then a two, three, etc. You rarely need to go higher than five. Then you flip the numbers. Those with five get one, four get two, etc. This is so that items that did not get a lot of votes will have the right number on them. Those with no votes get pulled out. With the ones that remain, you then add them all up and sort them from highest to lowest. At this point, the team agrees to work on the top items, or has further discussion as to why they would not focus on the top items. When the team has reached consensus, then they are ready to create their response to closing the gaps in the vital few initiatives. There are several ways to address these gaps. Below are the most common approaches are used:

Projects (A3):

- Used when the actions needed to achieve the target condition are not understood.
- Cross-functional participation with a sponsor and team leader.
- Timeframe is typically mid-term (6 months) to long-term (9 months).

Rapid Improvement Events (RIE's – can also utilize an A3):

- Scoped to ensure that 80% of the actions needed to achieve the target conditions are completed within a one-week timeframe using a cross-functional team.

- Many actions will not be understood prior to the event.

- There is about one month of pre-work and an expectation that the remaining 20% of the remaining action items are accomplished within one month following the event.

- Follows the staffing rule of thumb of 1/3 (from the process), 1/3 (touching the process), 1/3 (outside eyes – resources from other parts of the business).

- 30-60-90-180 Day follow-ups are scheduled to ensure the results are sustained.

Just Do Its (JDI):

- Used when the actions are understood.

- Resources are assigned with potential need for reference resources on an ad hoc basis.

- Typically, a limited timeframe.

- Functional Excellence:

    - Like JDI, but for a specific function (e.g. – HR) to carry out.

    - These actions typically fall into the purview of that function.

- The timeframe on these can vary greatly.

Just Stop Its (JSI)

- These are unimportant things that we are doing that we simply need to stop doing.

ADDRESS WORKLOAD

In many cases, when the team first begins their strategic planning process, they must address the team's current workload. This workload is not part of any strategic plan, but it keeps the team members very busy. There is a process referred to as the 5D process (aka Clearing the Plate) which facilitates the removal of items from the teams' responsibilities.

There are five known ways to reduce the number of initiatives to improve focus and the likelihood of success:

1. Delete - Simply stop doing it.

2. Delay – Set a later date to do it.

3. Delegate - We will do it, but with different people than we had originally intended. The item may provide a development opportunity for someone lower in the organization. This also supports the Level-Plus-One approach to development discussed in a previous chapter.

4. Dedicate - Remove people from daily activities to focus solely on an initiative to get it completed faster.

5. De-content - Still conduct the initiative but limit the scope.

Areas to which we can apply the 5D's are:

- Initiatives / projects / tasks

- Meetings

- Reports

The key here is to ensure we are not overwhelming the team with all the "Feed the Beast" type activities, projects, meetings, and reports. The beast in this case is typically corporate or a customer whom we have failed to delight.

"Feed the Beast" refers to activities aimed at supplying data and/or reports to other groups in the business. I have seen this activity distract leaders from the real focus of business, which is flowing value to the customer.

Once we have assigned owners and leaders to address our vital few gaps, we should conduct a resource roll-up as a final check to ensure we have not underutilized or overburdened an individual or a department. Below is an example of a resource roll-up:

	Project #1	Project #2	Project #3	RIE #1	RIE #2	RIE #3	JDI #1	JDI #2	JDI #3	Totals
Associate # 1	1	2	1	1	2	1	1	1		10
Associate # 2				2						2
Associate # 3			1	2	1	1	1			6
Associate # 4		1	1							2
Associate # 5				1	1	2				4
Associate # 6			1		1		2			4
Associate # 7				1	1	1		2		5
Team Totals >	1	3	6	5	6	5	4	3	0	

1 = Team Member or Sponsor
2 = Leader
= Underutilized
= Over Burdened

Now that we have identified countermeasures to our gaps and assigned the resources, we need to deploy those countermeasures throughout the organization. With mature organizations, we do this at the gap phase, and solicit countermeasure proposals from the process level teams, conducting a roll-up of impact, and determining if the countermeasures will fully close the gaps and/or meet the business's needs. This process is called "Catchball." This up/down communication may occur several times before the plan is finalized. During this process, the leader must ensure we are doing Catchball not Dodgeball with initiatives. There are those that are adept at dodging work. I had a boss at a past company tell me that his main goal in meetings is to leave without any actions. We all learn from our leaders. Some you learn what to do, and others what NOT to do. While the task dodger boss was bad, he was not the worst. The worst boss I ever had was what I would call an Industrial Psychopath. He would literally sabotage his own team. It was the strangest thing I had ever seen, and that was the worst 8 months of my professional career.

"You can't play Catchball without a ball" — *Unknown*

Once all the plans are created, we create a "Glass Wall." Glass Wall signifies our efforts to make the business plan and results transparent to the entire organization. The glass wall is where we will keep score. Some people call this a Mission Control Board or a Strategic Improvement Board. The glass wall is a place in the organization in which all the metrics are displayed along with the initiatives (Projects, RIE's, FE's, and JDI's) aimed at closing the gaps.

An example of a simple glass wall is shown below.

At this point, we have set a clear direction for the organization, and everyone should know how we keep score.

The worst thing that can happen is to find ourselves on a road to hell that has been paved with good intentions. To prevent this, we must have a group that is focused on controlling direction. This is much different than simply reviewing the business performance which can sometimes be solely focused on being good today. This is a focus on our intent to be better tomorrow. By controlling direction, we understand there may be some adjustments needed throughout the year. Some projects may not get the intended results, so adjustments will need to be made to the plan. We refer to this group as the Enterprise Steering Committee. Some also call this the Operational Excellence Steering Committee, Lean Steering Committee, or simply the Senior Leadership Team. This team is composed of high-ranking people within the business who have the power to remove barriers and add resources as needed. The members of this team will also serve as sponsors (coaches and mentors) to the teams implementing the improvements. Our goal as mentors is to help the mentee "stretch" to a new level of knowledge and/or performance. One way to do this is to set high standards with assurance (e.g. "I know this is more than you have ever done, but I have faith that you can do it, and I will be here to help you not fail.") To stretch themselves they must have faith that they can do it. The role of the mentor is to help build that faith. Zig Ziglar once stated, "The reality of faith is that faith must come before reality." The role of the sponsor is to provide resources (time to work on initiatives, people, funding, etc.,) remove barriers, coach, teach and facilitate the improvement process. I also highly recommend an outside observer to check on the progress of the Strategic Plan execution. This prevents directionally incorrect thinking and allows for course corrections along the way. There is a formal process for conducting these reviews, which is called Check/Reflect/Adjust (CRA).

CHECK / REFLECT / ADJUST (CRA)

There must be some level of accountability to get any plan executed. This accountability typically comes from the top leadership, as it should, but there is also value in having an outside set of eyes check the plan. We must be focused on whether the plan is achieving the desired results (lagging measure). This process of checking is called Check / Reflect / Adjust. Through this process I partner with the client and provide an outside set of eyes on the improvement plan for the year. I help determine if the intended results were achieved following the correct process and why we did achieve or failed in achieving the desired results. We also determine what must be done differently to recover and ensure we achieve the targets going forward. These Check / Reflect / Adjust sessions are the key to keeping the team on track since they tend to fall into the whirlwind during the month or quarter. This process is a must-have to ensure we are controlling direction.

A proper CRA session begins well before the actual meeting. The pre-work involved will look at the following:

1. A Review of the Strategic Plan

   a. What were the key gaps?

   b. What were the key countermeasures?

   c. What was the original execution schedule?

2. A Review of the last CRA Reflection

   a. What did the plus-delta tell us last time? What adjustments do you need to make?

   b. What problems did we encounter last time?

   c. What did the team agree to execute / adjust last time?

3. Ensure business measures (initial, current, and targets) and Strategy A3 metrics are updated.

4. Schedule staff for CRA session.

5. Ensure report-out is scheduled with executives that aren't in the CRA to review the findings.

6. Ensure each initiative leader is ready to report-out with their updated A3's.

7. Ensure department leaders are prepared to speak to their Control Boards and Improvement Projects.

During the CRA session, the group will look at what was promised from the last CRA session to ensure it was accomplished. Then, the group will CHECK how things are going according to the Strategic Plan. They will REFLECT on what they see and make suggestions for ADJUSTMENTS. Adjustments could be due to lack of execution, lack of resources, barriers, or changing markets / economics. The key is to check and adjust as needed. Don't stick to a plan that isn't getting results or taking you closure to your Ideal Target Condition.

LONG RANGE PLANNING

"I skate to where the puck is going to be, not to where the puck has been." — *Wayne Gretzky*

Long range planning is not the same as Annual Strategic Planning. The deliverable for an Annual Strategic Plan is a plan that will take us through the next year. The deliverable from a Long-Range Plan is a set of choices that uniquely positions the business in its industry to create sustainable advantage and superior value relative to the competition. In his book, "Playing to Win," A.G. Lafley laid out 5 tenets of a long-range plan.

Those tenets are:

- A winning aspiration – The purpose of your enterprise, a constant state of FOMO (Fear Of Missing Out).
- Where to Play – A playing field where you can achieve that aspiration.
- How to Win – The way you will win on the chosen playing field.
- Play to our strengths - Core capabilities and competencies. The set and configuration of capabilities required to win in the chosen way.
- Management systems - manage what matters. The systems and measures that enable the capabilities and support the choices.

The leadership team must know the answers to these questions, and ensure the annual strategic plans support this long-term direction.

SCENARIOS PLANNING

If you do not know where you are going, any road will get you there. — *Lewis Carroll*

The 14th of March in 2008 was a very bad day for Jim Cramer. Jim Cramer had a spectacular career in finance and is now the host of Mad Money, a popular TV program. Just three days prior, Jim had instructed his listeners to hold on to stock in Bear Stearns; however, on this day the shares dropped by 92%. Jim is a smart guy, so how did this happen? Despite his intelligence, Jim attempted to predict the future, which is impossible. While this prediction proved disastrous for Jim and his listeners that had stock in Bear Stearns, the problem with predicting the future is much more widespread. Many businesses attempt to do this very thing in their strategic planning processes by trying to set up a strategy while assuming there is only one potential future and ignoring the probability of many alternate futures. The only thing we know for sure is that the future will be different from the present in some capacity. Considering the impossibility to predict the actual future, we must, nevertheless, plan for multiple future scenarios. How can a business improve their ability to better predict the future? I propose using Scenarios Planning as this method.

WHAT IS SCENARIOS PLANNING?

Scenarios Planning is a method of organizational planning that prepares for three different time periods / ranges into the future. Sometimes called Scenarios Thinking or Scenario Analysis, Scenarios Planning is a strategic planning method that organizations use to make flexible long-term plans. Previously, we detailed the annual improvement planning process, also referred to as Strategic Alignment. Businesses also try to keep an eye out for near term trends in the market and conduct Long Range Planning, which covers the next 2 to 5 years. The focus of Scenarios Planning is to focus on the "Up to 10 Years" timeframe.

Scenarios Planning is a complex method to make bold predictions for the next decade. The goal is not to predict the future, but to explore what the landscapes could look like when considering multiple futures.

The military uses Scenarios Planning for strategic and tactical planning: training for "likely events." This way, if a situation does occur, they can simply "implement protocol #6", just as they have been trained to do. We, of course, want to be able to do the same thing in our businesses. For example, what would a petrochemical company do if 98% of their revenues were usurped by a major technology change, such as electric cars? Or, what would a snack cake company do if there was a complete shift to a gluten free product? Is there a plan? Not just a desire, but a plan? Scenarios Planning creates the conversation that gets things moving. This is what keeps us from simply creating an annual improvement plan year-after-year without considering the long-term implications of external forces.

EXECUTING THE PLAN

"Not every opportunity is an obligation." — *Clayton King*

The idea of spending the time to select the vital few gaps for our strategic focus is to help the team to not fall into the trap of intentionally focusing on too much at one time (leaning too far over one's skis). However, I have repeatedly seen clients create a plan with vital few items and then let other items creep in throughout the year. This is a struggle for many companies, and it must be dealt with during each plan review; check/reflect/adjust cycle. We cannot continue to wait until the end of the planning cycle and ask, "What happened?" We should know what happened long before then.

In his book "The Four Disciplines of Execution" Sean Covey describes a survey of the Fortune 500 companies. The survey asked, "What is the number one gap within your organization?" The overwhelming majority stated that EXECUTION of their strategic plan was the number one gap. When we dive deeper into the reasons for this gap, we find that results are driven by two factors— those we cannot control (economy, competition, and market) and those we can control (strategy and execution).

In the case of strategy (what we can control), there are two facets:

1. Stroke of Pen Strategy (most companies do not struggle here)

    - Capital Investments

    - Expansion of Staff

    - Acquisitions

    - Change in Policy or Programs

2. Behavior Change (most companies do struggle here)

    - Improved Customer Experience

    - Process Adoption

    - Higher Quality of Service

    - Faster Responsiveness

    - Operational Efficiencies

When we consider that most companies struggle with executing Behavior Change, we conclude that this is the area in which we must focus our efforts. However, looking more closely at occurrences within any given business, we see there are two forces constantly competing against each other.

Our Day Job (The Whirlwind or Quadrant 1 from the Eisenhower quadrants)

- Required to keep the doors open; maintain operations

- Be good today

- Urgent

- It acts on us

Goals/Improvement (New Activities, Quadrant II from the Eisenhower Quadrants)

- Moves the organization forward

- Helps us be better tomorrow

- Important

- We act on it

When our day job (the whirlwind) and our goals/improvement (new activities) are competing for our time and attention, which one typically wins? The whirlwind wins, of course. The challenge for any leadership team is to execute the strategy during a 100mph whirlwind. To do this, we must narrow our focus on what Sean calls, the Wildly Important Goals, not on the whirlwind. While we can narrow our focus on wildly important goals, we cannot narrow our focus on something that acts on us, the whirlwind!

Below is another statistic from Sean's book where he surveyed Fortune 100 companies.

NUMBER OF GOALS In Addition to the Whirlwind	2 - 3	4 - 11	12 - 20
GOALS ACHIEVED With Excellence	2 - 3	1 - 2	0

The data supports the conclusion that fewer goals will generate a better chance of success for the business. The easiest way to paralyze an organization is to over-goal the business and let the whirlwind take over completely.

There will always be more good ideas for the organization than there are resources to execute those ideas with excellence. One must remember that simply because you can do something, does not mean you should do it. There are two focus traps that we must be aware of: turning everything in the whirlwind and saying YES to every good idea. Most companies believe they can do anything, which is probably true, but they cannot do everything. Thinking you can do everything in the middle of a whirlwind is "playing not to lose" rather than "playing to win."

"We are the most focused company that I know of or have read of or have any knowledge of. We say no to good ideas every day. We say no to great ideas to keep the number of things we focus on very small in number so that we can put enormous energy behind the ones we do choose. The table each of you are sitting at today, you could probably put every product on it that Apple makes, yet Apple's revenue last year was $40 billion."
— *Tim Cook, Apple CEO (the company now has a market capitalization of $1.4T)*

When Steve Jobs returned to rejuvenate Apple in 1997, he said NO to many things that were asked of him and the business. The company had fallen into both focus traps mentioned above. His first order of business, after ousting the CEO at the time, was to reduce the complexity of the organization. He consolidated departments, reduced the product line by 70%, and reduced the research development to a handful of projects. When he was finished, all Apple products could be placed on a single, small table. The strategy at the time was to develop desktops (personal and business) and laptops (personal and business). The whirlwind was around these products. In this case, Jobs was able to reduce the whirlwind by reducing complexity, so they could narrow their focus on the strategic path. Their strategic focus was in research, where they were focusing on what would later become the iPod, the precursor to the iPhone, and the iPad. The iPhone now comprises greater than 70% of Apple's sales, and the iPad makes up >12% of Apple's sales. In the design department, simplicity became the mantra, and in the supply base, the number of supply partners was reduced from one hundred to twenty-four key partners. The results speak for themselves.

"The difference between successful people and very successful people is that very successful people say no to almost everything."
— *Warren Buffet, Berkshire–Hathaway CEO*

My experience shows the following to be the key gaps when execution is not where we want it to be:

- Too many initiatives for the resources available
- Did not take enough OFF the plate
- Said YES to too many good ideas
- Lack of time to work on the strategic items
- Allowed the whirlwind to win

If we find ourselves in the execution gap, we must ask ourselves the following questions:

> What is keeping you from being fully successful with strategic initiatives as planned?
>
> What should we do differently?

Having too many metrics can also increase the effects of the whirlwind. We must decide what metrics we will use to run the business. I recommend that we use the following classification:

- Critical goals (Tier 1): Required to keep the business running and to keep our jobs (not meeting these will get us fired)
- Necessary goals (Tier 2): Related to achieving the strategic improvement plan (not meeting these will hurt our future)
- Maintain goals (Tier 3): Everything else that we need to simply keep in the static state. Trying to improve these, in addition to the critical and necessary goals, will lead to a focus trap.
- Trivial goals (Tier 4): Typical for large organizations and related to a functional VP's project. These goals are often not aligned with the critical or necessary goals. (not meeting these will get us yelled at)

The lower tiered goals should have a link up to the tiers above to ensure goal alignment. When measuring the necessary and critical goals, we must have different levels of metrics. Those metrics should fall into two groups: leading (process) or lagging (results). Leading measures are measures that, if met, will lead us to the goal (lagging measure). Leading measures are things over which we have control. Lagging measures are result measures that tell us if we have met the goal because of improving the leading measures. An example of these two measures being applied to everyday life is the situation where one wants to lose weight, the goal of weight is the lagging measure. Meeting the goal requires one to focus on the leading measures (caloric intake and exercise). This is referred to as energy balance. When there is excess energy (more calories in than out), one can expect to gain weight. Where there is a deficit in energy (more calories out than in), one can expect to lose weight. Weighing oneself each week and expecting a reduction without a plan to reduce calories and/or increase exercise would simply be a fantasy.

At this point in the strategic planning process, I am assuming we have answered the question, "Which thing(s) (no more than three, and awesome if you can get it to one) would transform the business if we focused all of our resources on it(them)?"

Now, we need to ensure we have daily accountability for focusing on the leading measures (process focused) that will help us ensure the lagging measures (results/goal focused) are met. Systems that allow us to assess the leading measures are below:

- Leader Standard Work
- Managing Daily Improvement (MDI) Boards
- Problem Solving
- Tiered Meetings
- Performance Evaluations

These systems, if monitored and followed correctly will ensure the proper execution of the plan and highlight any issues with the execution of the plan. Strategic Planning should be the setting and controlling of direction. We set the direction for the business by completing and communicating the plan. Now it is time to control that direction. Consider these systems the front-line indicators of the effectiveness of the plan. Leadership's job is to ensure these systems are working properly. They will also learn if there are other initiatives creeping in if they manage these closely.

BUDGETS

Earlier in this chapter we discussed the importance of metrics and how some metrics can drive the wrong behavior. Another long-standing item used in the business can have the same effect. That is the use of Budgets. IMO, the poorest performance measures any manager could be judged by is variance to budget. Why?

Budgets are collections of guesses. Some simple statistical analysis shows that a budget is not worth (as a performance measure, anyway) the paper on which it is written. The budget should only be used as an estimate/forecast or to detect a special cause problem(s) in spending. As with any forecasting, you must be willing to be wrong all the time. The problem is that we use budgets to drive decisions even when the budgets are wrong. What happens if demand for your product increases or decreases? What if there is a new opportunity that was not present when the budget was created? Budgets are static and do not adjust to changes in your business conditions. For all these reasons, performance to budget is the worst possible performance measure you could ever select.

I have literally had managers tell me they do not have the thousands of dollars in their budget to pay me to save them hundreds of thousands of dollars by fixing their business. As is customary with my business, I was willing to guarantee them the savings, and they still would not do it. This only happens with the managers of businesses. If I tell the owner (or someone that thinks and acts like an owner) that I can save them at least 2x for what they pay me, they ask how much they can pay me, since they know they will get $10 back for every $1 they give me. It is a no-brainer to the owner.

When it comes to measuring the success of the business, the KISS (Keep It Simple and Standardized) principle works best. Profit = Revenue

- Expenses. It is that easy. How much $$ came in and how much $$ went out. This is the bottom-line performance measure for any company. No matter what the mission of your business, there is always a bottom line. Even if your goal is to "Save the Turtles from Straws", you will not be in business long if you spend more than you bring in! Profit focus has absolutely nothing to do with greed, or at least it does not have to. Profit in a business ensures the livelihood of those employed by that business. Profit allows us to develop products and markets for those products. I like to refer to this as profit with a purpose.

In the past, the manufacturer dictated the price and the amount of profit they would make on their products, as described in the equation below:

Price = Cost + Profit

This was an easy approach for the manufacturer, since they could simply build the product for whatever cost, add the profit margin they wanted, and simply pass it on to the customer. In this case the manufacturers controlled all three variables (Cost, Price, and Profit). They were basically printing money, and you can imagine the behavior that drove. They did not have to concern themselves with Cost because Price and (more importantly) Profit were under their control.

This was especially a problem in the early years of the automotive industry. The prices were high and the quality low. That was until the competition from Asia entered the market with a cheaper to buy, cheaper to operate (fuel economy), and higher quality automobile. The first response of the Big 3 automakers (GM, Ford, and Chrysler, now simply known as the Detroit 3) was to attempt to have the government put tariffs on the imports to the point where they could not compete on price. However, the government did not get involved and allowed the imports with normal tariffs. This forced the US automakers to improve quality and price. At the end of the day the consumer won, and the US automotive market was forever changed.

"What you think the customer will pay is in your head, what the customer will actually pay is in your wallet." — *Unknown*

Another downside to cost plus pricing is the fact that the market, in some cases, may be willing to pay more for the product. In this case, the business has left money on the table. In today's global economy, price is dictated by the market and is no longer controlled by the manufacturers. The market will determine what price it can bear. The market is also willing to pay more for increased value, so do not underestimate the market. For example, coach and first-class land at the same time, but those people in first class (minus the upgraded ones) are willing to pay more to be treated differently. When the market sets the price, the manufacturer controls only one variable (Cost) and their ability to earn a profit is directly proportional to their ability to control Cost.

Profit = Market Price – Cost

In this new environment, everyone is trying to control costs. So, we must understand where the costs are in the business. A common breakdown by category is below:

Cost = Labor + Material + Overhead

If we dive into part of Overhead in the above equation, we can break down costs by function.

Cost = Sum (Engineering, Procurement, Quality Assurance, Accounting, Manufacturing, Logistics, Maintenance, et al.)

From this level of understanding, poor decisions are often made. For example, it is easy to look at labor and assume the quantity of labor is fixed. With that assumption, the only variable is the labor rate. This leads to offshoring to reduce costs instead of making the current labor more efficient and using less of it. Another pitfall is optimizing functions. When costs are broken down and understood by function, improvement efforts tend to be functionally focused. As discussed earlier in this chapter, when a function is optimized independently of the system of which it is a part of, the system almost always suffers. For example, the most efficient way to do logistics is to move large quantities of material infrequently. However, this rarely adequately meets the needs of manufacturing who now must wade through piles of material on the shop floor or worse use the wrong material, since more than what is needed is always present in the area. Thus, giving the process operators more options from which to choose, and leading to the wrong choice.

I had an example of this happen to one of my clients. They were struggling with a product not mixing well. The operator would load bags of ingredients into a mixer, then turn the mixer on for the specified time. However, the mix would not be homogeneous at the end of the mix cycle. The operators noticed that this started happening when they got to the older material that was a little dryer and had clumped. It was drier than usual and clumped, since it had been sitting there for a long time; longer than it used to sit. As a work around, they started breaking the bags up manually before loading them. This added considerable time to loading of the mixer, but it solved the problem. The issue is the reason for this happening was not addressed. The real issue was the purchasing group had gotten a price reduction for ordering extra supply. The extra supply had to sit in the warehouse longer and would harden in the bags. They showed a cost savings on the raw material but did not include the added cost of labor and the lost capacity due to longer mixer loading and cycle time. The stated savings is visible on the P&L, but the added cost is hidden. The visible savings created a hidden factory. If you take the time to analyze your business, you will find lots of examples of "silo" optimization that is driving your total cost in the wrong direction.

"The bitterness of poor quality [and sub optimized processing] remains long after the sweetness of low prices is forgotten" — *Unknown*

That was a lot to cover on one habit, but I believe having complete alignment and being focused on the total system, is that important.

Individual Leadership Reflection:

Breaking silos / Cross-functional collaboration

Leader Thinking

When each function tries to optimize their piece, the system / outcome suffers (functional sub-optimization).

$1 + 1 > 2$ (Synergy)

Leader Behavior

I increase my engagement (and influence) in cross-functional activities.

I do not self-constrain and self-limit my influence when engaging with other functions.

I engage key stakeholders from other functions to find the optimal system solution.

Leader Reflection

Do I think and act this way? If not, what must I adjust?

What more can I do to fully understand all functions' contributions to the value stream and my role in it?

Organization alignment (values, goals, roles, process, interpersonal)

Leader Thinking

I must align my team to the why, the what, the who and the how, in that order.

Interpersonal conflict between individuals and departments is a sign of organizational dysfunction / misalignment.

Leader Behavior

I seek feedback on my team's performance and fit (what we should stop doing, start doing, and continue doing).

I provide feedback to other teams on their performance and fit.

When conflict arises, I use the VGRPI model as a diagnostic tool to align / realign where needed.

Leader Reflection

Do I think and act this way? If not, what must I adjust?

What are the interpersonal conflicts that I should address with functional alignment?

Strategic Planning

Leadership Thinking

I believe Strategic Planning is a key to organizational alignment.

I believe having too many initiatives will ensure we will not execute well on any of them.

The workload must be balanced among my group.

I value Long Range Planning and Scenarios Planning as being as important as annual planning.

I ensure the execution of the plan is monitored closely to allow for quick course corrections as needed.

Leadership Behaviors

I see to it that Strategic Planning is an integral part of the business cycle.

I am disciplined to only allow the vital few initiatives into the plan, and initiative-creep is not allowed.

I ensure the workload is balanced.

I see to it that Long Range Planning and Scenarios Planning is part of the business cycle.

I personally ensure that Check/Reflect/Adjust is being conducted.

Leadership Reflection

Do I think and act this way? If not, what must I adjust?

Do I check the health of the plan and the execution of the plan through the planning cycle?

Do I spend more time checking on the daily tasks than I do the strategic plan?

End of Chapter GROUP Reflection Questions:

1. Are we progressing on the actions from our last discussion?

2. What was the key learning from the current chapter?

3. As a team, what do we do well as it relates to the key learning?

4. As a team, what do we NOT do well as it relates to the key learning?

5. What do we need to Start, Stop, or Continue doing as a team to improve going forward as it relates to the key learning?

CHAPTER 6

HABIT 4:

FOCUSING ON THE PROCESS

"If you can't describe what you are doing as a process, you don't know what you are doing." — *W. Edwards Deming*

In Western culture, the separation of means (how things are done) from ends (the result) has often been accompanied by a belief that the end, or result, is permanent and the means are ever changing. Therefore, to most, the ends seem more concrete, tangible and more valuable than means. This leads some leaders to a willingness to resolve moral cognitive dissonance over a clash between worthy ends and despicable means by turning a blind eye to the means and condoning acts that in themselves, apart from the goal, would never be tolerated. In other words, "the end justifies the means." Have you ever heard that? Have you ever said that? The result of this way of thinking is that managers seldom address moral issues if the goal is being met. The endgame in the most egregious cases, is a spot on the local or national news, or sometimes the case does not have to be that egregious if it is a slow news day.

For a business to succeed, there must be a shift from Managing by Results, for the reasons given above, to Managing by Means. One must see that means are simply results in the making. Focusing on the outcome is no way to improve the process. Trying to do so is considered managing by fear and causes good people to make bad decisions. Those managing by results are solely focused on the bottom-line, and considers any means, regardless of how destructive, justified by the end. Our target must be to get rich ends from simple means. I believe process yields results, and if we focus our efforts on creating a process that is brilliant, we can get brilliant results. Too often, companies develop broken processes that must be run by brilliant people, and this is one of the main issues at the heart of our talent gap. There simply are not enough brilliant process minded people out there.

I find myself quoting Deming on many occasions. People outside of the manufacturing sector will tell me that you cannot put what they do into a process. Well, see chapter quote. There is always a process, and only the intellectually lazy will not take the time to find it. In this chapter we will cover the habit of Focusing on the Process. Focusing on the Process helps us understand that both the process and the result that is achieved (paying attention to what is done and how it is done) are important. The result will not change unless we change the process. While being results focused can get us short-term gains, having a process-orientation yields results in a more sustainable manner. If you do not know what you did to get a result, how will you get it again? When clients are celebrating an extraordinary day, I always ask, "What did we do differently today?" Sometimes they know, but often, they cannot tell me what was different. This "not knowing" is a lack of process focus.

If you put me in a tennis match with the best tennis player and have them focus on the scoreboard (the result) while I focus on the ball (the process), I will win every time even though I do not play tennis. Many managers focus purely on the results regardless of the process that one must follow to gain the result which is the same as focusing on the scoreboard and not the ball. Have you ever heard someone say, "Just get it done, I don't care how you do it"? Have you ever made that statement to your team? If you have, this may be an indication that you lack a process focus. If we focus on the process that yields results, we are more likely to be able to improve those results over time rather than just taking whatever we are getting while still failing to understand why. There is an adage that states, "The person who knows how to do a task will always have a job, but the person who knows why the task is being done will always be the boss." As a leader, you must understand the WHY.

PEOPLE WORK ON THE PROCESS > PROCESS YIELDS RESULTS > IGNORING PROCESS REDUCES CHANCE FOR RESULTS > IGNORING RESULTS RISKS MISSING NEW IDEAS!!!

You would think that developing a process would be easy once one understands the need for a process. However, in the past I have found that we often define processes up to a point, and then for some reason (either lack of understanding or patience) we stop defining the process. Therefore, we have incomplete processes within business. However, the product must get shipped or the service must be delivered, so we put the process into action and let the people responsible for running the process deal with it. This leaves a "fog" in the process where the process has not been clearly defined. The people who get us through this fog are the operators of the process. Consider this, we are asking operators to put their livelihoods at stake while they are bridging the gap in the process, all the while those operators understand that if they make a mistake, they may face punishment or even termination. At the very least, they will have their own "ribbons of shame" to bear. However, they do it for us day in and day out without issue in most cases. Most often each operator bridges the gap differently which creates a larger problem. This non-standard processing will give us inconsistent results. Those inconsistent results are passed on to the customer. It is short-sighted to believe the customer cannot see the difference.

When there is not a clear standard to run the process, and we leave how to run the process up to the operator, we find ourselves in the position of having processes that only a select few can execute. The excuse given by management in these cases is this process/product is partially science and partially art. This is a clear sign that the process/product is not fully understood, and management's countermeasure is to put in skilled operators when management should be focused on demystifying the process. This is another example of management debt. These skilled operators cover up the fact that we do not understand the process in the name of "art," This is referred to as tampering. These skilled operators are considered highly valuable to the company. Through no fault of their own, these operators' actions keep a broken process running, by tampering. The effects of tampering were first taught by the late W. Edwards Deming in his Funnel Experiment. The results of tampering always increase process/product variation. The only way to deal with this tampering is to create the standard, remove the skilled operator, and have an unskilled operator run the process. The reason for removing this skilled operator as a test of the standard is that, in some cases, the skilled operator is the head-tamperer and will tamper without even realizing they are tampering.

"Never attribute to malice that which is adequately explained by ignorance" — *Derivation of Hanlan's Razor*

When the unskilled operator faces an issue, he or she will not know how to tamper, so he/she is forced to stop and call for help. The process can then be corrected, the standard updated, and the process continued until the unskilled operator can run the machine as well as the skilled operator. In this scenario, the accountability is placed (as it should be) on the leadership and engineering teams to fix the process.

A true story that I use to demonstrate holding the right people accountable is the Maynard story. Jimmy (pseudonym) was from Kentucky, but he was living in Detroit and working for one of the Detroit 3 when Toyota was deciding to build a plant in Georgetown KY. Now, if you are from Kentucky and living in Detroit, you have one goal in life; get back to Kentucky. Jimmy's mom knew he was looking to come back to KY, and she wanted him back there as well. She had seen in the local paper that Toyota was hiring for positions at the new plant. She called Jimmy and asked if he saw the same thing in the paper in Detroit. Jimmy looked and did not see anything in the paper.

There was a reason he did not see an ad for hiring in Detroit. Toyota was not looking for people with automotive experience from the Detroit area. It would be easier for them to teach new people the skills needed instead of having to unteach the old skills and then teach new skills. Kentucky had lots of people with the farmer's mindset. Toyota had lots of luck working with farmers in Toyota City, Japan. If you have ever been a farmer or known a farmer, you know that they are some of the most hard-working people you will meet, and they get things done regardless of the issue. If a plow breaks in the middle of the field, they fix it. If they cannot fix it, they find someone who can and pay back the favor later. They know the true meaning of the phrase, "You better cut hay while the sun is shining." Jimmy did apply for a job and managed to get hired.

Toyota sent a large group of them to Toyota City to train on the assembly line there. They were so intentional that they paired the team members together from the very beginning. Jimmy was paired with a guy named Maynard (pseudonym). Jimmy noticed that Maynard was holding the armrest tight; white knuckled tight. Jimmy asked, "Is this your first time on a plane?" Maynard responded, "This is my first time out of the county." Jimmy could tell that Maynard would not be the smartest guy he would meet on this trip, but he was looking forward to sharing this adventure with him.

When they arrived in Japan, Jimmy and Maynard were also roommates. This pairing was also maintained at the plant. Jimmy would run a station and the next day Maynard would run the same station. Jimmy noticed that while everyone else on the line had one trainer that would stay with the trainee for a couple hours in the morning and then leave them for the rest of the day, Maynard had two trainers for the entire day. This told Jimmy that Maynard must be struggling with the processes. Now knowing this, Jimmy would work with Maynard at night in the room to help give him some pointers on the station that he would be operating the next day. This seemed to be working, so it became their routine.

Then, one day, Jimmy was on a station that ran horrible. The process was a stamping process. The trainer had told Jimmy that if the part slipped out of position during the stamping process, the stamping die would crack. However, the parts did not want to stay in position. Also, the oven from which the part came was turned 180 degrees from the line and was blowing hot air on him the entire day. It was extremely hard for Jimmy to keep up with the line that day. He would later state that it was the worst day of his career, and if every day had been like that he would have gladly gone back to Detroit. Well, that night in the room, he did not waste much time working with Maynard. He knew that there was nothing he could do to make Maynard successful due to the nature of the poor process.

The next day, as expected, within 3 cycles of the line, Jimmy heard a huge crash. He looked back to Maynard's station and there it was a crashed press with a cracked die, and Maynard standing there with a dumb look on his face. Jimmy was thinking, "Well, he gets to go home." Jimmy had seen this kind of thing happen in his past career and it never ended well for the operator. As Jimmy watched, since the line was now completely stopped, he saw men running out to the line. The longer the line was down the more people came (this was an escalation policy in action). They would point at the line and point at Maynard.

Eventually, an older gentleman showed up at the line. This man was very important. Jimmy could tell he was important by how low the other men bowed to him. This is a sign of respect in Japanese culture. The other men began talking to the older man, pointing at the machine, and pointing at Maynard. After a while, the man began walking toward Maynard. At this point, Jimmy was thinking, "Yep. This is it. A free ticket back to Kentucky."

So, what happened next totally blew Jimmy's mind. Jimmy was correct in his assessment of the old man. He was the top leader for the site. The man approached Maynard and in broken English stated, "I apologize for allowing a process to be made that allowed you to fail. My engineers will work all night to correct it and you will run it tomorrow with no problem." At this point, Jimmy is standing there with his jaw to the floor. The plant was shut down for the remainder of the day, and the engineers went to work on improving the process that they had poorly designed and haphazardly implemented.

As promised, the next day when Jimmy and Maynard arrived at the plant. The process was different, and it was clear that the engineers had not been home. They had worked through the night to correct the problem. The fixture was improved, the die was repaired and hardened to prevent cracks, and the oven was moved to only be 90 degrees from the station with a heat shield added. All the things that Jimmy was working with, and hating it, were corrected. Jimmy had been covering up a problem, and it took Maynard to uncover it. Now that the problem had been exposed and corrected, Maynard ran that station that day with no issues. By holding the right people accountable, the process was improved for all future operators. Maynard is still with the company, and they found a unique job to take advantage of his skill set. He now works in process development. When they develop a process, they ensure he can run it. If he cannot run it with no issues, they correct it and try again.

Early when I referred to holding the right people accountable, this is the level of accountability to which I am referring. Could you imagine the plant manager or functional leader apologizing for and ensuring the correction of any failure in the process that causes the process operator to either fail completely or fail to deliver as promised. There has been a lot of improvement in this area in business over the years, but we still have a long way to go.

A TOYOTA VIEW

"We get brilliant results from average people managing brilliant processes. We observe that our competitors often get mediocre results from brilliant people managing broken processes."

Typically, when a process is not running to standard, the operator does not report this issue, or they did report the issue at one time, and no one helped. At this point, the operator simply figures out another way of getting to the end result. I am reminded of a story told concerning Abraham Lincoln. He could not remember the military command for instructing his troops to cross a fenced area, so he simply dismissed the troops and stated they would regroup on the other side. When we do not have our processes defined and stabilized, we are doing the same thing to our operators. In effect, we are closing our eyes and letting them figure it out for us. The issue is each one of the operators will "cross the fenced-in area" in a different manner. As mentioned before, I call this tampering. We may end up on the other side, but in many different conditions.

Operators are not the only ones that tamper with processes. The idea of tampering can also be extended to the leadership. Leaders tamper when they pull profits from a future period into the current period, drop inventories at the end of a period, play games with the P&L or Balance Sheet, or any number of games or financial acrobatics that are intended to make the business look better than it really is.

If we want to combat tampering, we must standardize our tasks. Standardized tasks are the foundation for continuous improvement and employee empowerment. To ensure we are process centered; our focus must be on sustaining improvements. The world tends toward disorder unless a countermeasure is put in place. This is called entropy and is a natural progression if not halted. Standardized Work is that countermeasure that prevents regression of improvements over time.

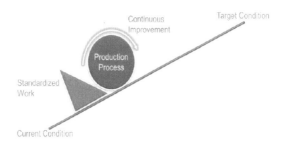

The graphic above shows how standardized work serves to sustain our continuous improvements toward our target condition. As mentioned before, to truly have Standardized Work we must have two things in place:

- Work Standards (What we say will are going to do)
- Standard Working (Doing what we said we were going to do)

In all cases, we will see evidence of Work Standards inside businesses. These work standards are the results of engineers pouring their knowledge into a document to ensure the process is at least partially defined. However, what we do not often encounter in business is Standard Working. Standard Working means we are checking that the work standards are being followed. A well-developed work standard is useless if it is not being followed.

STANDARDIZED WORK

Standardized Work is intended to allow us to use stable, repeatable methods everywhere. Standardized Work is the foundation for flow and pull in a process. The Work Standards are designed to capture the accumulated learning about a process by standardizing today's best practices.

> "Most companies don't need millions of dollars' worth of technology; they need $5 worth of brains." — *Edward Deming*

However, we must allow creativity (by the way, there is no creativity in buying solutions. In fact, money suffocates creativity. Think Low Cost or No Cost) to improve the standard, and then incorporate that standard into the new work standard, so that when a person leaves the process, we can hand off the learning to the next person.

During a trip to Toyota City, I visited the Takaoka plant that builds, among other products, the RAV4. I had the pleasure of having Hayashida-san, a former Toyota executive, with me. His time with Toyota was spent both as a factory manager and in Toyota's headquarters as the Director of Production Engineering. Some notable accomplishments of Mr. Hayashida:

1. He pioneered the use of robotics in welding at Toyota (working directly with Taiichi Ohno).

2. He designed a factory that was used as the basis for future plants built at Toyota.

3. He became the plant manager of the very plant he designed. Exactly why he humorously declares he was always the person to blame no matter what the problem; as he both ran and designed the facility.

As we were walking through the facility, it was amazing to see Hayashida-san in action; quickly pointing out errors in standard work and waste on the assembly line. You could tell he had spent many years in "Ohno circles." One example that stood out to me was when we were on a catwalk. He stopped, pointed at a workstation, and said, "That operator is not able to work to standard." Notice the phraseology of his statement. He could have said, "That operator is not working to standard." However, he was intentional in making it the process's problem, not the operator's problem. I looked, but I could not easily tell what the issue was, so I asked him to be more specific. He then proceeded to show me that the operator was having to overreach the station to get a tool during each cycle. He said they would have never designed a station where that was the norm. When the assembly line is built to make abnormalities visual, the problems become much easier to see. However, Mr. Hayashida-san had not run a factory in decades, and he did not run the facility in which we were standing. How could he be so attuned to these details within another factory? We do not see this level of expertise with most executives. So I asked him, "When you were plant manager, how much of your time was spent at the Gemba?" His response astonished me. "Unfortunately, due to many meetings and other items of focus, I could only spend 80% of my time at the Gemba." Really? He is apologizing for 80%?!!! Most plant leaders spend far less than 50% of their time and fewer still apologize for only spending 80% of their time on the floor! This is the level of commitment it takes to ensure standard work is followed.

STABILIZE BEFORE IMPROVING

While a lot of companies try to jump straight into the improvement cycle, we stress the importance of stabilizing first, which I call "Stabilize Before Improving." Stabilize Before Improving is a constant process by which we standardize what we do, THEN improve to make it better, safer, and easier. In this case, standardization IS improvement. Through this stabilization process, we will create work standards. Work standards are the safest, healthiest, best, and easiest way to complete a task. As we mentioned above, following these work standards requires self-discipline. Standardized Work is designed to create the needed discipline, and it is the leadership's duty to ensure standard working.

Standardized Work, it takes much longer to reach the target condition. The graphic below shows the result of improvement efforts where there is no standardization.

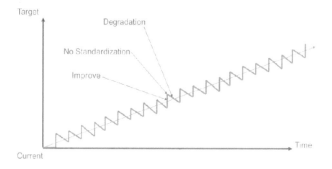

With Standardized Work, incremental improvements build upon each other, and the target condition can be achieved quickly. The graphic below shows the impact of using standardization to sustain the gains of each improvement. If done correctly, we can get a higher performance with less improvement activities.

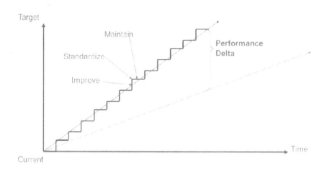

Standardized Work enables flow. Flowing value to the customer can be hampered if we do not have the habit of Focusing on the Process to create processes that support the value-added flow.

The goal of any business (profit or non-profit) is to have the resources available to support the mission. One of these resources is always money. Money affords the enterprising businessmen and women the luxury of doing all the other cool things businesspeople like to do. The best way to get cash is to provide exceptional value to customers. Value is defined as:

Any activity that changes fit, form, or function (or progresses the order) in accordance with the customer's expectations.

This definition implies the customer is willing to pay us for those products and/or services that add value to them personally or to their business(es). In world-class companies the percentage of time spent adding value to the product is 5%. In businesses where no concentrated efforts are made to improve flow, the percentage of value-added activities is approximately 0.1%. It is important to note that this time is as it relates to the information and materials. It is also important to create production flows where the material becomes the information once the schedule is started. Scheduling more than one part of the process will lead to mismatches in flow. The answer to this mismatch is not to "schedule harder." We must look at the process and determine why we schedule the way we do and fix that first.

As it relates to value-added time, the timer starts the minute you order raw materials (in the case of manufacturing) or when the customer schedules (in the case of services), and the timer stops once you are paid. I use order material as the start time for manufacturing since some companies store lots of product in stock. Therefore, using the customer order as the start time gives them a false sense of true lead-time. The % is based on the amount of time you are adding value to the product (or conducting the value part of the service) divided by the total time (customer asking to you being paid). If you are a make to stock company, I am not simply referring to when you are shipping from stock. The 0.1% is referring to the complete order to cash value stream which includes raw material to finished good manufacturing. Order to cash also includes the concept to launch. Concept to Launch is a value stream when you are an engineer to order business. In the case of value-add only being 0.1%, the bad news is there is only 0.1% value added. The good news is there is a 99.9% opportunity to improve the business's flow and thus reduce the total cost of our product or service. This in turn will allow us to grow our market share. As we increase this percentage, we will see our lead times go down significantly.

The importance of lead time was studied by George Stalk, Jr and Thomas Hout and documented in their book, "Competing Against Time." After studying many products, across many industries, manufacturing types (Craft in Europe, Mass in US, and Lean in Japan) and many countries, they concluded that, regardless of the type of manufacturing, if you reduce your order lead time by ¾, you will double productivity and reduce overall cost by 20%. With this understanding, I always work to reduce lead time, and in 99% of the cases, the lead time is being driven by inventory (information and materials).

One method I use to explain the impact of inventory on lead-time is below:

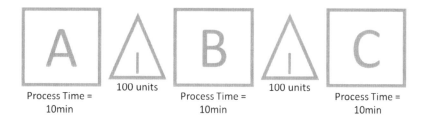

The first pieces of information we need are how long we work each day and how many parts does the customer want each day. With this data, we calculate what is known as TAKT time (the selling speed of the product) in the lean world. For this example, let us say we work for 480 minutes (remove breaks and scheduled down time) and the customer wants 48 parts per day. This would give us a TAKT time of 10 minutes / part (480 minutes / 48 parts).

Using the graphic above, you will notice that we have balanced our line to meet the customer demand. I would never balance a line directly to TAKT, but I will in this example to keep the math simple. Also, when showing this live, I may show one station slower than the others to make the point about bottlenecks.

The first question I ask the group is, "How long does it take a part to pass through the system described in the model?" In most cases there is a consensus that a part will take 30 minutes to pass through the system. However, they are not considering the impact on the lead-time due to inventory. Now that we know the time-value of a part (10 minutes), we can put a time-value to the inventory. Assuming we follow FIFO (first in first out), a new part introduced at process A will be in the system for 2030 minutes before it exits process C. There is only 30 minutes of actual processing taking place during this time. Inventory makes up 98.5% of the total lead-time in this example. I am always given many reasons for the existence of inventory in any given system. I always agree and then ask how we can solve the problems and reduce the inventory.

Another large driver to lead-time is the order backlog. While order backlog isn't physical inventory in the system, it is inventory in the form of information and must be considered when determining the total lead-time in the system. If the backlog is growing, one should look at the performance of the system to determine if additional capacity (processing speed) should be added to burn down the backlog. This additional capacity may be short-term or long-term depending on the market conditions.

The best way to combat inventory is by implementing pull systems, but one must do this wisely. If you simply remove the inventories without knowing why the inventory is there, you may cause other problems. The typical reason for inventory is to cover up problems. Problems like equipment reliability, lack of trained operators, quality issues, change over times too long, imbalanced cycle times, etc...

Using the same example above, I usually show the group the impact of connecting processes when they are unreliable. Let us imagine each of the processes (A-C) has an uptime of 90%. The system performance with the inventories in place will be close to 90% since the machines will not all go down at the same time and the inventories will buffer that downtime impact. However, when you link them, when one goes down, they all go down. Where you once had a 90% system uptime, you now have a 73% (.9x.9x.9) system uptime. This will force you to improve the uptime of all the processes, or you could improve them before coupling if you know there is going to be an issue.

The negative impact of coupling processes is what drives us to want to have simple machines with very high uptime. As you add more complex automation to your processes, you risk impacting flow in a negative manner. My experience has shown me that the more technologically advanced a process the lower the reliability.

Using the chart below taken from Mike Rother's book "Creating Continuous Flow", I always try to target Level 3 automation:

An Important Concept:
AUTOMATIC EJECT OF FINISHED PART

		Load Machine	Cycle Machine	Unload Machine	Transfer Part	
	1	👷	👷	👷	👷	Note: One-Touch Automation
Levels of Automation	**2**	👷	Auto	👷	👷	
	3	👷	Auto	Auto	👷	
			The Great Divide			
	4	Auto	Auto	Auto	👷	
	5	Auto	Auto	Auto	Auto	

Level 3: • Makes one-piece flow more natural
• Helps separate operator from the machine

The "Great Divide" is where costs start increasing and reliability starts decreasing due to auto loading and auto transferring.

Flow and lead time are synonymous. With the understanding that lead-time reduction will improve our productivity and cost, our primary objective should become to improve flow which will allow us to flow value as fast as possible to the customer. This enables us to convert demand more quickly into cash. Below are the five typical flow patterns you will see in a business:

Build to Order	Order Raw Material	Customer Order	Manufacture / Deliver Service		Distribute	Cash
Build to Stock	Order Raw Material	Manufacture / Deliver Service		Customer Order	Distribute	Cash
Engineer to Order	Customer Order	Engineer	Order Raw Material	Mfr/ Srv	Distribute	Cash
Pre-Pay	Customer Order	Cash	Order Raw Material	Manufacture / Deliver Service		Distribute
Product Innovation /Commercialization	Problem	Engineer Solution	Order Raw Material	Manufacture / Deliver Service		Distribute

There has been no effort to ensure these flows are scaled properly. The above diagram is simply demonstrating the steps in the flow pattern. When referring to flow, regardless of the pattern, I am referring to the complete time in all steps.

The noteworthy step in the Product Innovation/ Commercialization is the Problem step. This step is referring to the finding and solving of problems via new products or services. The start of this value stream is the active search for problems that need to be solved. The problem being solved may be to improve a current product's functionality, make a current product more affordable, or a completely new product where no such product currently exists. In any case, once a problem is solved, the company should ask can the solution be sold, or was there a product developed that should be commercialized.

It goes without saying that if you can manage to get it, Pre-Pay is the best option, since it basically gives you infinite cash flow (aka Negative Cash Conversion). In the other scenarios, you have cash tied up in engineering time, raw materials, and/or finished goods. These tied up cash issues have caused lots of companies to go out of business even though they had strong demand for their product.

A shorter lead-time should translate into a competitive advantage. You must know the value you provide and charge for it. If a customer wants a quick ship outside of your normal lead-time, then it must be of some value to them. Your job is to figure that value and get paid for it. Remember, poor planning on their part should not equal an emergency on your part without you getting paid.

I was in the General Manager's office at one of my clients. and an urgent call came in from a customer. This was the nuclear industry and plant downtime cost them $2000/min. We had improved the client's lead-time from 18 weeks to 2 weeks. However, we had not fully leveraged this improvement other than the reduction in cash tied up in inventory. The team had been struggling with how to further leverage the lead-time reduction, so the call was timely. While the new lead-time was 2 weeks, we knew we could get to 1 day if we pulled out all the stops. At the other end of the urgent call was a frantic purchaser from a nuclear plant. He wanted to know how soon we could get a replacement part for them, and how much it would cost. Having been part of the team focused on the lead-time improvements, the General Manager knew we could get it there in a day, but we had not agreed on the price premium at that point. The normal cost for this part was $8000, so I was eager to hear what number he gave. He looked at me, and told the purchaser, we can get it there tomorrow, but it will cost $80,000. The purchaser said, "Sold!" The General Manager slammed down the phone and said, "Damn! I should have asked for more." At that point, we knew the value for quick shipping of their product was not going to be a single- or double-digit percentage adder, but a multiplier (10x) of their current price.

There are eight types of flow within a business:

1. The flow of cash
2. The flow of raw material
3. The flow of work-in-process
4. The flow of finished goods
5. The flow of operators
6. The flow of machines
7. The flow of information
8. The flow of engineering

All these flows are important and must be improved. When our focus is to improve flow, we must find what is inhibiting flow in all the areas above. In other words, we must be on the lookout for the three enemies of flow: Waste, Variation, and Overburden.

WASTE

When performing a task or service, we must ensure we are doing it in the least-waste-way. Wastes are those activities that do not add value (what the customer is willing to pay for). Those wasteful activities can be classified using the following acrostic (DOWNTIME):

Defects	Making a defective product or having to redo a service.
Over Production	Producing more of an output than can be used by the next process or customer immediately. The worst form of waste since it creates or amplifies the other forms of waste.
Waiting	Waiting for materials, information, people and/or other assets (such as equipment) to be productive.
Not Utilizing Creativity	Failing to tap into the team's creativity to improve their processes.

Transportation (excess)	Moving of parts, information, and products.
Inventory	Excess material which is consuming cash, and floor space (direct result of overproduction)
Motion	Stepping away from the value-added work to obtain or search for materials, tools, or information or to work the next process.
Excess Processing	Giving the customer something for which they are not willing to pay extra (e.g., non-painted will do, but we paint it anyway.) All testing and rework (hidden factories) are considered excess processing.

The above definitions are as the waste relates to a manufacturing process. We have also extended these wastes to leadership. Below are the leadership wastes:

Defects

Checking (due to not trusting), fixing after the fact, too many surprises, switching objectives or measures.

Overproduction

Requesting more than what is required to get essential work completed (Data, Reports, Measures, Capital, Plans, People, etc.)

Waiting

Starting meetings late, delaying essential decisions or communications, avoiding critical issues or barriers to change.

Not Utilizing Creativity

Not listening to ideas, not including people on initiatives in their area, soliciting ideas without acting on them, treating people like a "pair of hands" the old management style thought that managers should think, and employees should do. That has never been a good way to improve. Knowing cannot just be the boss and doing cannot just be for the associates. Bosses need to do and associates need to know.

Transportation

Personal travel, transport of documents and/or personnel to complete plans, decisions, or reviews.

Inventory

Holding onto reports, people, data, and facilities that are no longer needed.

Motion

Not clear on direction, objections, measures, or clear meeting points.

Excess Processing

Not being clear about expectations, "Just In Case" (JIC) work, reactive or arbitrary changes in the process, multiple levels of approval

The discussion around waste can be extended to all parts of the enterprise. The key is that we are taking the time in each part of the enterprise to look for the wastes.

VARIATION

Variation drives many issues within the value stream. Variation in how the work is done by each member of the team and can appear as internal quality and efficiency issues. This variation in doing the same job differently is driven by failing to have standardized work. Variation in work content between process operators will result in unbalanced lines. Variation in the schedule can cause days in which there is over demand on the system and other days when there is not enough demand on the system. Variation in features and functions can drive internal and external customer complaints.

Variation in product design to satisfy customer's demands for unique products, can drive lots of inefficiencies in the manufacturing process if not managed correctly. The challenge for the business is to create a modular product architecture. A modular product architecture is a strategic means to deliver external variety (to the customer) and internal commonality (to the manufacturing organization). This approach is best taken when designing new products but can often be done on existing products as long as management is willing to invest in the changes (technical, organization, and cultural) needed to meet the requirements of modularity.

There is also process variation. Common Cause vs. Special Cause variation is an idea that is used broadly in the Statistical Process Control (SPC) world. It is used to show the variation hidden within a process. It also informs the approach we should take to improve the process. We can also apply this thinking to the way we manage. Management trying to demand root cause from operations on a common cause issue is not fair. Common cause issues are a part of the system, which is owned by management, not operations. The process used for common cause should be to focus on reducing the variation. Management should only expect root cause on special cause issues since there is an assignable cause for special cause issues. This allows the manager to manage by exception vs. managing every deviation. This requires managers to be able to tell the difference, which is simply understanding the variation in the system and setting limits (Green, Yellow, Red), where Green means we met the target, Yellow means we didn't meet the target within the common cause limits, Red means we didn't meet the target outside of the common cause limits. There is some math involved in setting these limits that all engineers should know. I can spend all day writing about this topic, and it would be well deserved.

OVERBURDEN

Overburden occurs when we operate our processes and/or teams beyond a reasonable capacity and/or capability. When we overburden our processes, the processes develop reliability issues and often become bottlenecks to the overall flow of the product or service. When we do this to the team, we damage morale and experience high turnover and absenteeism rates.

As we see these enemies to flow within our businesses, we must be able to provide effective countermeasures to reduce and eventually eliminate them. The recommended countermeasures for each are listed below:

Enemy to Flow	Countermeasure
Waste	Lean Tools
Variation	Statistical Tools (Six Sigma) and Modularity
Overburden	Theory of Constraints

Note: Theory of Constraints should also inform on what areas we should focus our improvement. Focusing improvement on a non-constraint area will NOT improve the flow for the overall value stream. Any time saved on a non-bottleneck is a mirage.

Individual Leadership Reflection:

Focusing on the Process

Leader Thinking

If I can create robust (brilliant) processes, all employees can be successful.

The key to stability is standardization.

The waste, variation, and overburden exist. I must learn to see it better.

Leader Behavior

I am constantly focused on improving processes by placing accountabilities on the x's that yield our y's.

I engage people by starting with the standard.

Leader Reflection

Do I think and act this way? If not, what must I adjust?

How much time do I spend in Gemba, focused on the process?

End of Chapter GROUP Reflection Questions:

1. Are we progressing on the actions from our last discussion?

2. What was the key learning from the current chapter?

3. As a team, what do we do well as it relates to the key learning?

4. As a team, what do we NOT do well as it relates to the key learning?

5. What do we need to Start, Stop, or Continue doing as a team to improve going forward as it relates to the key learning?

CHAPTER 7

HABIT 5:

OBSESSING OVER QUALITY

"The continual lowering of your quality standards (product and process) is the equivalent of boiling a frog." — *Unknown*

I have always taken the Napoleon Law approach to quality. In the US we have a justice system that states that one is innocent until proven guilty. In Napoleon Law, one is guilty until proven innocent. While Napoleon Law is a terrible approach to people, I think it is a great approach to quality. I always suspect that the product is bad until proven innocent, and our quality system is the judge and jury. After Safety, Quality is the most important aspect of any business, and one should never lower their quality standards to extend their reach. There are two sides to quality: the culture side and the science side. Many companies have mastered the science of quality, but most companies lack the culture of quality. How leaders engage and ask questions around quality will drive the culture side of quality. Most leaders spend their time asking questions around delivery (over quality) and then wonder why they have internal scrap and warranty issues with their product. The same leaders may encourage shortcuts to simply get an order out. This sends a horrible message to the team.

"By taking shortcuts, you only make a defect faster."
— *Unknown*

In the 1950's and 1960 's, W. Edwards Deming helped fuel the quality revolution in Japan. That same revolution eventually made its way to the US. However, it was twenty years later before most US manufacturers took notice of this way of thinking. The old mindset was to build sub-quality products which customers had to buy since there were no other options.

"We cannot solve our problems with the same thinking we had when we created them." — *Albert Einstein*

The message being taught by Deming at the time was promoting an Obsession for Quality. The main premise: quality should drive all our decisions, and all other parts of the business are subservient to quality. We must have the mindset to get the job right rather than just getting the job done. This new mindset was hard for US manufacturers to embrace in the beginning since it meant fewer products would be sold due to higher quality standards (meaning products would last longer). The immediate impact to the business would be a net loss in sales. The manufacturers failed to realize the long-term cost benefits of having quality processes and products which, in turn, drive the overall cost down, thus allowing for a larger market for their products.

As crazy as it may sound (with all the talk about Toyota), I am a huge fan of KIA Motors. My relationship with KIA started in the 90's. I bought a KIA Sophia while I was in college. I bought the loss-leader off the lot in Anderson, SC. A loss-leader is the cheap car that is put in the sales paper to get people to come to the lot, so they can sell them a more expensive car. That trick didn't work on me. I needed a cheap car to get me out and back to school each day, since I did not stay on campus. The salesman that sold me the car, tried his best to get me to buy another car that had more options. However, I was content with having a car that did not have a radio, power windows, or air conditioning, since it made the car cheap. The cost of the car was great, but the thing that impressed me the most was how KIA responded when there was a problem. They offered a 100K mile warranty and corrected any issues I had. They also gave me a loaner car (better than mine) each time, so that was not too bad. I have owned several KIA's over the years because of this level of service. They are now one of the top ranked quality cars in the world. With all the returns from their 100K mile warranty they were able to improve the quality of their cars, and it shows. But wait, there is more.

My latest KIA was an Optima. I can now afford those options that I once could not afford. Another example of how KIA thinks was when I was driving my KIA Optima up from Chattanooga TN to Knoxville, TN and the engine started making this awful knocking noise. I almost made it to a truck stop but ended up in the entryway. My first call was to my dealer to ask if I had the extended warranty, since my car had 104K miles on it. He assured me I did have the extended warranty. My next call was to AAA to have my car towed to the dealer. The next day, my dealer called me and stated that KIA knew there was an issue with that model engine, so they extended the warranty to 120K miles. This meant I would be getting a new engine at no cost to me. Boom! What company would extend their warranty to ensure they capture all the failures? KIA does, and they use that failure data they find during their failure analysis to make their cars even more reliable. As a result, they now offer a 200K mile warranty. Some companies would rather put their heads in the sand and pretend they do not have quality issues instead of seeing those failures as treasures. This is most likely due to them seeing the same failure repeatedly, and they have simply given up.

THE CULTURE OF QUALITY

Deming's revolution fueled what I am calling the science of quality. There has been much focus on the science of quality (FMEA, Control Plan, MSA, etc.). If one does not have these tools and they implement them, they will see an improvement. However, few companies have truly embraced the culture of quality. To build that culture of quality, we must do the following:

- Stop to fix problems.

- See Something, Say Something

- Believe that quality for the customer drives value.

- Don't Make, Pass, Accept a Defect!

- Build into the equipment the capability to detect problems and stop automatically whenever a problem occurs.

- Leaders must be present at the value-added processes and looking for problems.

- Don't simply write standards; ensure they are followed.

- Develop a visual system to alert leaders that a machine or process needs assistance.

- Build into the organization support systems to quickly solve problems and implement countermeasures.

- Build into the culture the philosophy of stopping or slowing down to get quality right the first time to enhance productivity in the long run.

Developing a culture of quality has eluded many leaders. To truly have a culture of quality, we must have systems that help expose and solve problems. Problem exposure means we are not covering up problems with excessive inventory, labor and /or capacity. This is paying, since inventory, labor, and capacity cost money, to hide problems. That sounds crazy, but I see it happening all the time. Problem response is leadership reacting when problems do occur and ensuring root cause and corrective action is taken. Problem solving at the Lowest Level is when we support and coach the operators who do the improvement work. I think Theodore Rubin said it best, "The problem is not that there are problems. The problem is expecting otherwise and thinking that having problems is a problem."

GET AMP'D

We briefly touched on this earlier in the book, but I think it deserves more explanation. The culture of quality is not something that can happen overnight. It will take serious leadership presence and example-setting to create a culture which supports all aspects of quality. There is a concept called AMP, which explains how defects are to be viewed in a customer / supplier relationship. The concept is demonstrated below:

- One should never **A**ccept a defect from their supplier (the previous process).
- One should never **M**ake a defect in their process.
- One should never **P**ass a defect to their customer (the next process).

With this understanding we can make the statement of Do not Accept, Make, or Pass a defect. If the entire organization understands this concept and the leadership ensures it is being enforced, the quality levels of the product and process will improve. However, if we continue to pass defects from station to station and expect the end-of-line inspection or test to catch it, we will have a higher production cost and poor quality which will eventually slip through to our final customers. This not passing of defects also applies to support departments and leadership.

ESTABLISHED PRIORITIES (S$_4$Q$_2$DC)

As we move toward this new mindset, our dedication to the mindset will be tested. There will be constant pressure to make decisions related to quality, cost, safety, and delivery. Sometimes there will be intense internal conflict when determining which one of the four areas takes priority. We don't have unlimited resources, so we must determine where to best spend our time, talent, and treasures. Dealing with this intense internal conflict will require the following prioritization. Safety is always first. Safety can and should be seen in four different ways. Personal Safety, Process Safety, Psychological Safety, and Product Safety.

Personal Safety is measured by how safe people are. This is typically the only safety that is focused on by companies. Process Safety is measured by how safe the process/environment is around where people work. I added Process Safety to my teachings after the incident that occurred in 2005 in Texas City Texas, where 15 people were killed due to process safety that had gone undealt with by management. This site had been recognized for an outstanding safety (focused on personal safety) record just prior to this incident. Another much overlooked component of safety is Psychological Safety which is measured by how people feel psychologically after a full day of work in the current process/environment. The idea of psychological safety is not considered often but can have huge consequences on a company's morale and output. Product Safety is when your product can involve a safety aspect (e.g. Food Safety, Airplane, Anti-lock brakes, etc.). A few of my clients deal with food, pharmaceuticals, and transportation, so their products could pose a significant safety issue.

For example, one of my clients produces airplanes for the agricultural industry. As you may know, the airplane industry is very heavily regulated. Afterall, most of the regulations for the aircraft industry are written in the blood of those that came before us. My client's planes are used to spray crops, drop seeds, or other fertilizers on crops and forest, so the performance and quality of the plane become very important. The leadership there is hyper conscious of product safety. In any case, safety is paramount regardless of the product or service for all the reasons mentioned above.

Quality of the Product and Process is second, Delivery is third, and Cost is fourth. Cost and Delivery can be debated, but Safety is always first since there is no improvement worth personal injury. If, at the end of the workday, we cannot send people home the same or better than when they arrived, we have no business working with people. Quality is always second since Quality drives both Cost and Delivery. Cost is the result of doing Safety, Quality and Delivery well. We are not just referring to products when discussing quality. We are referring to the quality of the Product, People (a reflection of our recruiting, screening, hiring, onboarding, training, and retention processes; not the people themselves) and Processes.

Process quality is what we can do to reduce waste and variation in the process of making the product. A good process will yield a good product.

Something important to remember here is quality is determined by the customer not the supplier. I had a client arguing with their customer about how a part was performing in the customer's process. The customer was telling my client that the part was not fitting correctly. My client told them that the part was to print, so the problem was on the customer's side. Fortunately, level heads prevailed, and we discovered there was a property that was critical to performance at the customer that was not considered on the print. I refer to this as a performance specification vs. dimensional/property specifications. You can meet all the dimensions/properties, but if that part/product does not perform at the customer, YOU have a problem. Had we not gotten over this issue, I am sure the customer would have taken their business elsewhere.

The graphic below summarizes the priorities:

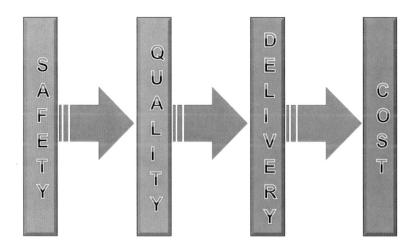

As a leader, you must earn the right to work right.

There are thousands of examples I could share where these priorities were out of order, but I will share one where it seemed like they were doing the right thing on the surface. Their automation team was charged with installing robots to auto load an oven. I inquired about the reasoning behind the installation. I was told it was to reduce headcount, so I put that in the Cost bucket. Robots are not bad. When used to support the operator or address a safety concern, they are perfect. The impact of installing these robots was going to be 4 weeks of downtime on a line that was already in a backlog situation with their customers. Knowing that the client was struggling with Quality and Delivery, I challenged the team to reconsider installing robots until we stabilized the process. The leadership team had not earned the right to focus on Cost in an area where Quality and Delivery were not being met. Now, if the robots were going to improve Quality and Delivery (in that order), then we would not have had an issue. Also, Safety was never an issue at this client, they had earned the right to move past Safety.

CUSTOMER FOCUS

We cannot have a discussion around quality without discussing the customer. As discussed above, there are still high-level leaders in manufacturing who believe that if a product is built to print/specifications, then that product is good regardless of what the customer says. This might have worked in the old days when there were not as many choices for products. However, in today's highly competitive landscape, what the customer thinks and feels does matter. I have had some very heated discussions with executives about product quality. Some stand firm in their belief that if the part is to print, the customer must accept the part. The people who believe this have a stand that is purely a contractual one. I propose that having customers who WANT to do business with us is preferable to having customers who MUST do business with us. As mentioned before, we should constantly be asking ourselves, "If our customer could do business with anyone else, would they still choose us?" As mentioned in Embracing the Total System, this thought also applies to internal support departments supplying products and services to other departments. Do not mistreat your suppliers simply because they are part of the same company! On the other hand, don't get mistreated by your suppliers. Your money doesn't break after you give it to them, so their parts shouldn't break after they give them to you.

A few years back, I had a few days home and was looking forward to getting some of my "honey-do" list completed, when I got a call from a client to go visit their Springhill LA. plant. It was a Tuesday and they wanted me there the next day. From the sound of the caller's voice, I could tell the request was urgent. I am always up for a challenge, the harder the better for me, but I wanted them to know that an airline ticket with such a short notice would be expensive. It turned out the caller was the plant manager, and he told me the cost of the ticket did not matter. The problem they were experiencing was costing them $15K per day. I was on a plane to Springhill LA early the next morning. I landed in Shreveport LA later that morning and drove 1 hour East to the manufacturing site. The town was very small, and I remember thinking, "Why would they put a plant out here?" I later learned that it was due to the CEO's wife having grown up there. It was a gift to the community.

Once at the site, I spent the morning "talking to the parts (a skill I had learned as a master problem solver)," speaking with operators of the problem process, creating a mini process flow diagram, and putting together my response to the leadership team that was scheduled that afternoon. The defect being seen was tubes splitting inside the coil during the expansion process. There were lots of tubes per coil so the opportunity for a split was high. If one tube split, the entire coil was scrapped. I had gotten wind that members of the leadership team had already concluded that the problem was a supplier issue. No surprise there, since I get that a lot. The sooner people can blame a supplier, "art," or mother nature, the sooner they do not have to work on the problem; someone else gets to work on it.

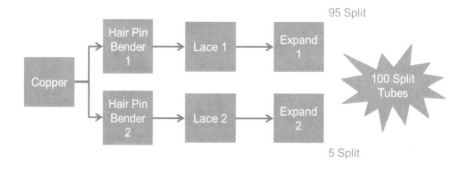

In the spirit of speaking with data, I was armed with the above data when I went into the meeting with the leadership team. I started the meeting with, "I can say without a doubt, your problem is not the supplier." At that point, the Quality Manager became indignant. He stated, "You have only been here a few hours and you are telling us that we don't know what is going on. We know it is the supplier and they will be here next week to either fix this issue or we will get a new supplier." My immediate response was, "Well Robert, we have a bigger problem than I thought." As he sat there with a quizzical look on his face, I continued, "We have what I call smart copper." He asked, "What is smart copper?" I drew the above diagram on the board and stated that based on the data in this diagram, for copper to be the problem, the bad copper would have to know to go to the top flow and the good copper would have to know to go to the bottom flow. After I responded to him with those facts, he stated, "Well, if you put it that way."

Now that we could not blame the problem on our supplier, we worked to find the root cause. It turned out to be the setup of the rollers in the straightening process just prior to the hairpin bender operation in the top flow. The problem was corrected. Had we replaced the supplier, we would have had the same issue with the new supplier and the headache and financial cost of changing suppliers. There were lots of opportunities at this site, and I spent the next couple of years helping them with their technical issues. I never got the chance (not that I did not try) to work on organizational or cultural issues. The leadership was not open to change. That unwillingness to focus on that non-technical change coupled with the fact that population in the areas was declining led to the plant being closed. As a result, some good people lost their jobs. This still bothers me. I was asked to come back and develop all areas technical, organizational, and cultural at the new location. The leadership team at this new site was awesome. They worked hard to make the plant better, and now that site is now a model for manufacturing in the division.

UPSTREAM MANAGEMENT

Another way we can improve our ability to develop and sustain quality is by going upstream to manage processes. Managing upstream requires one to address errors and defects before those errors and defects get to the next process or customer. The best way to improve the overall quality of the product is to constantly improve the quality of the process used to build it. Ultimately, we want to go back into the design of processes (error proofing) and products (Design for Manufacture/Assembly) to anticipate and prevent problems before they occur.

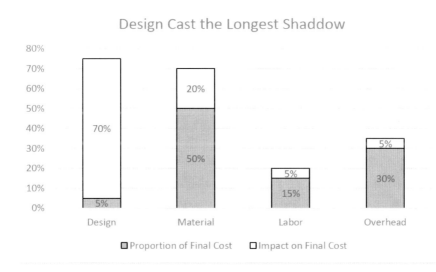

Design Cast the Longest Shaddow

The design process cast the longest shadow as far as the life cycle cost of the product. However, many companies fail to invest the proper time and money during this step of product development.

I am often called in after the product has been launched to help improve the cost. The process I use is called Value Analysis Value Engineering (VAVE). If done correctly, you can get 10-15% reduction in COGS by applying the VAVE method. However, changing design during the manufacturing process after launch is much more expensive than changing it when it is in Concept/CAD. Lots of companies claim to have frozen designs, but if you are changing the product order as it is progressing through the line, you do not have a frozen design; you have what I call design slurry. Even with companies that have done a great job on design, I still manage to get 10% out of COGS following the VAVE process on products that have been in production for years. When the leadership sees these results, they always do a facepalm, because they know they have been wasting margin that whole time. My message to them is they did not know what they did not know. They launched at what they consider the right time. You could also argue that waiting to go to market until the product is close to perfect is not wise. There must be a balance. I think Reid Hoffman said it best when he said, "When you look back, if you aren't embarrassed by the first version of your product, you've launched too late."

GEMBA

Gemba is the real place where the work is being done. Many times, managers try to solve problems while sitting in the boardroom. I have never seen a problem solved by looking at a spreadsheet. It gets solved when someone decides to go and see for themselves to thoroughly understand the situation (genchi genbutsu), so Getcha Boots On! The only way to really solve problems and improve processes is to go to the source and PERSONALLY observe and verify data.

A business owner in South Carolina, Roger Milliken, modeled this behavior very well. Roger had built a very successful textile business and had many sites in the Southeast. No matter how big the company got, he would always personally visit the plants. Often, the visits were unannounced. His reason was he wanted to see how the plants were "really" operating. Afterall, we have all been victims of plant visits for VIP's. These visits are typically announced and there is a great deal of preparation. This has always bothered me. Surely the VP's would think it was strange that their plants always smelled like fresh paint. I admired Roger's approach and I encourage the use of the approach to my clients. The goal is not to "catch" the team at the plant doing something wrong. The goal is to see what is really happening, so you can help solve problems. You can't solve a problem you can't see.

There is a story that I like to tell about Roger that I heard while working at Milliken as a teen. I am not sure how true it is, but it gets a point across, so I think it is worth telling. As the story goes, a new plant manager had taken over one of Roger's troubled plants. A visit from Roger was scheduled about a month after the new plant manager had taken over. The plant manager knew there would be a visit eventually, so he started working on cleaning up the place on his first day, but he did it in a directionally incorrect manner. His idea was to remove the clutter from the plant, but he couldn't put it in the side yards or back yard, because Roger was known for entering the plants at any door and at any time (day or night). The plant manager's brilliant idea was to put the junk on top of the plant. No visitors would see it there, right? Much to his dismay, on the day of Roger's visit, Roger arrived in his helicopter. This didn't end well for the new plant manager. Trying to look good instead of being good, cost him his job.

This idea of having to be present at the process is being challenged lately with the issues concerning Covid-19. The entire world stopped for a while; and we were forced to rethink how we do business. There is a lot of new technology being leveraged to bridge this gap. I have personally embraced the use of MS Teams, Zoom, and WebEx for meetings. I have also embraced the use of MS HoloLens for conducting events with clients.

So far, the results have been great, and I believe there will be a shift toward remote. However, I do not think we will ever fully replace the value of being shoulder to shoulder with the people and fingertips close to the processes. There is an incidental information exchange that occurs when people are face-to-face that you cannot plan for in remote sessions.

There is lots of data in the Gemba. One should think and speak based on personally verified data. Even high-level managers and executives should see things for themselves, so they will have more than a surface understanding of the situation. Data includes what we observe and experience, not what is in the computer or on a spreadsheet. We must build a habit of going to the place where the work is done and looking for information, understanding the full interaction of the system. We need to make decisions based on data rather than making decisions based upon opinions, guesses or feelings. The use of data, past experiences, and experimentations is a form of sense-making.

"A Theory Without Data Is Simply an Opinion."
– Unknown

I do not want it to sound like one should not have their own opinion. One can have their own opinion, but they cannot have their own facts. Facts are facts and are based on data. If there is a lack of data and we make decisions based on feelings, the highest ranked person in the room typically wins. This is called the HiPPO effect (Highest Paid Person's Opinion). When we make decisions based on data, the person with the most data wins, or at least should win. I have personally been humbled many times by line operators who had more data than I. I was happy to concede to the facts. Leaders must analyze and act based upon data. However, do not get caught up in analysis paralysis. This can lead one to never decide on a course of action. Get enough of the data to get to the point where you can leverage your informed intuition.

Speaking with data is extremely important. I was able to leverage this concept against Hertz. I use Hertz rentals exclusively and have for decades, so this is not a slam against them. About two weeks after one of my trips, I got an email from Hertz. It was not the normal email telling me that I owed toll fees, since I occasionally run tolls and let the system charge me later. This time the email was stating that I had damaged a car. At that point, I had been renting from them for over 20 years with zero damage reports. I first opened the email on my phone, so I could not really see the details on the scanned form. All I could tell was that the form had been filled out by hand. I was racking my brain at what the damage could have been. I knew I did not have a wreck, and I did not recall any close calls. Once I got to my computer, I opened the email and was able to see the scanned form. There were multiple views of a car on the form. The top view of the car had lots of dots on it, and below that image it stated "Hail." My first thought was, "I am not sure the renter is responsible for hail damage, or any other acts of God." It turns out that in some circumstances, I could be held liable for the damages. I always wave the insurance. My second thought was, "Was there even a hailstorm during that trip?" This thought prompted me to look up the weather for the week in which I was in the area. Much to my pleasure, there had not been a hailstorm that week. The hailstorm was the week prior. I copied the link to the weather website and sent that to Hertz. I never heard from them again. Once again, data wins!

> "By Simply Ignoring the Facts; Doesn't Change the Facts."
> — *Unknown*

Always doubt the data if you did not personally verify it. I like to borrow Ronald Reagan's famous quote, "Trust, but Verify," when it comes to data. We should make it clear to the person that is bringing the data that it is not that we do not trust them. They should understand that we do this because sometimes people have bad data or have been given bad data without knowing it. This approach also helps combat those times when we think we know but are mistaken. Mark Twain stated, "What gets us into trouble is not what we don't know. It's what we know for sure that just isn't so."

The importance of data does not simply stop at the presence of data, we must use that data to make decisions. Data without insight and action is simply information.

If we trace the path of information to action, we will see there are two "gates" at which the result can be affected:

Gate 1: Our mental models will govern what insights are attained.

Gate 2: Our bias for action will govern whether we respond to the insight.

The graphic below shows the flow of information to action with the gates mentioned above:

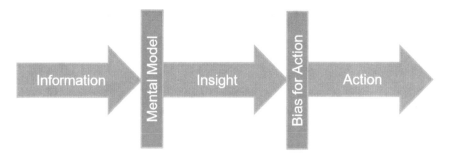

As leaders, we must always be analyzing the information around us to gather more insight and drive action. If there is a concern about mental models influencing the insight, then share the data with other people and get their input. Leaders must have a bias for well-informed action.

While going to the Gemba is the best place to find data, when you are at the Gemba, there are some questions that should be asked. You can't simply walk around in the area. The following questions with commentary from me are from an article written by Jon Miller:

1. What is the standard? If you must ask, you may not have shop floor management tools in place. Hopefully, it will be clear at-a-glance thanks to good visual management. Even if it is clear, this question can be useful to the area team leader or team member to check their understanding of the standard.

2. How do we develop a standard? In cases where a standard is ambiguous or lacking, this question can be the start of a fruitful learning and improvement dialog. Leaders should require standards that are documented, visual, and changing frequently because of continuous improvement.

3. How clear is the standard to those doing the work? Many times, standards, rules, or instructions may be posted as if to say "now we have visual management" when in fact there has been no thorough training of the people in the area to understand these standards. Random audits by asking people about their work, such as "How do you know that the quality is good?" or "How much variation is allowed before you should call for help?" will reveal the depth to which standards have been used.

4. How clear is the standard to those not doing the work? Again, if one must ask, we may not have shop floor management, much less visual management. Leaders should require that they can understand the status of safety, quality, and on-time output in less than 5 seconds each. A truly visual workplace facilitates a 30-minute walk through to give a complete understanding of a snapshot of the business.

5. What is our performance against the standard? Once the standard is clear, this is the first and most frequent question leaders ask when they go see. The response will generally be "on target" or "not on target" but the variation to these responses as well as the off-center replies we sometimes hear to this straightforward question can reveal a lot about how well people understand their standards, targets, and the internal customer-supplier relationship. In all cases, the replies lead to more questions and more learning.

6. Why are we not performing to the standard? This is the classic definition of a problem and a golden opportunity for a leader to practice the 5 why questions to help develop the thinking and

problem-solving skills of their people. Fight the urge to give the answer! Practice being Socratic.

7. Why are we performing above the standard? The kaizen mind thinks that "no problem" is a problem. When we are consistently performing above the standard, we are either working to a false standard or we are using more resources than necessary. Both situations call for creative thinking and continuous improvement.

8. In the case where we are not meeting the standard, what are we doing to meet the standard? This question gives people the benefit of the doubt that they have ideas, containment measures in place, or even full-blown sets of countermeasures underway. The goal of leader standard work is not to solve problems but to understand the situation, help others develop their thinking skills, and then to remove obstacles that may be preventing them from solving the problem. This question enables people to present what is already being done or being evaluated. The soft skill required here is to bite your tongue no matter how bad the idea seems (provided it is not unsafe) and let people try and learn through failure. To do this, you must understand the fact that the difference between a master and a beginner is that the master has failed more times than the beginner has tried. I have been told by some masters that they have forgotten more than I will ever know. Not sure if that is true in my case (I failed a lot), but I could see that being the case for some. Give your beginners room to try so they can fail and remember that failure is a part of life. If you don't fail, you don't learn. If you don't learn you don't grow.

"Find fuel in any failure." — *Michael Jordan*

9. In the case where we may be meeting standards, what can we do to further improve the current condition? This is an open-ended question that can be used as a catch all in any situation, any condition,

any Gemba. Be sure to have at least 1 small improvement in your own mind in case the person you are asking practices their reversing technique on you.

10. How can we make an abnormal condition more immediately visual? Often the reason problems persist is because they go undetected. The role of the leader is to demand ever greater degrees of visual management using quick, low-cost means. Fully electronic display boards linked in real time to dashboards and ERP systems worldwide are almost never the answer, more because they make it possible to avoid going to see than the inherent inflexibility and cost. Pencil and paper have the benefit of almost no learning curve, low cost, and ease of correction.

I have seen some very impressive Andons (lights/displays that show the status of equipment/processes) in my career. However, one that stands out the most is a large jumbo-tron Andon at a machining plant. This company had spent hundreds of thousands of dollars for the display and the interconnection with the equipment. This jumbo-tron was huge. It was on par with a professional sports scoreboard. The intention was that you could see the status of every machining center in the plant from one location. You could also see if each machining center was on target to meet the daily goal. When I first saw this Andon, it was being debugged, but I got to visit it again a few months later, and I could not wait to see it in action. As I walked up to the Andon, I noticed that all the indicators were green. I quickly congratulated the engineer on having all green indicators. He sheepishly responded with, "We were told by management to program it to only show green. They were tired of the customer coming in and seeing everything red. It made them look bad." While they had the money to buy the technology to expose the problems (machine status not green), they had not developed the leadership discipline to respond to those problems.

11. Why do you think I asked you these questions? True learning happens when people practice what is called metacognition: thinking about thinking. When we reflect on the thought process, the questions asked, the answers given, the follow-on questions, and the discussion leading to a consensus solution, we look back and suddenly the whole process makes sense and seems so simple. It is easy to put a fish into someone's bucket of water and call it dinner. That person may not know where to get the next fish. Only when they trace the fish back from the bucket to the hook to the water can they understand what to do the next time. Don't give them a fish when it is your job to teach them to fish.

12. What other questions would you have liked me to have asked? This is the "respect for people" question. Some people speak their mind without hesitation when they see a leader doing their Gemba walk. When a certain level of trust and mutual respect has been reached, it should no longer be necessary to ask this question to draw out the true feelings and concerns of the people on the Gemba. Once an environment has been created where it is safe to expose problems and share ideas freely, the main use of this question is for the leader's learning.

The degree to which a leader can quickly grasp the situation during a Gemba walk largely depends on the quality and variety of visual controls in use. But even with excellent visual management, gaining a deeper understanding of what one is seeing requires thoughtful questioning and listening. This is what I would call a "soft skill" and it is an area in which many leaders who have risen through the ranks due to their keen minds working out problems and their unfaltering delivery of solutions, frankly struggle. Some leaders who have risen from the front lines are more comfortable on the Gemba. Others feel embarrassed that they in fact know so little about what really goes on and are afraid to expose themselves by asking questions. Others have no fear but may waste time asking the wrong questions. Knowing what to ask and how to ask it are completely different things, and any leader preparing to practice standard work should first consider getting some frank input on their soft skills from a trusted advisor.

Another method to help hone one's skills at the Gemba is to practice what is called "Stand in Circle" or "Ohno Circle." This method is said to have originated with Taiichi Ohno, the father of the Toyota Production System (later known as Lean in the US) to help managers understand and "see" waste. People in Ohno's tutelage would jokingly call this circle the "Oh-no" circle. This sentiment was due to him making them stand for hours in one spot, and if they couldn't give him a satisfactory observation, he would have them repeat the process until they could. This approach is a very focused look at how the operator is interacting with the process. It is more detailed than most people are accustomed to doing. The challenge when doing this is to force yourself to practice vu déjà. We have all experienced déjà vu where something seems familiar although we have never experienced it. Vu Déjà is the opposite where we force ourselves to look at a familiar situation as if we have never seen it before.

80% of the purpose of "Stand in Circle" is to build awareness and rewire one's brain to see many problems. 20% of this process is proposed towards actual improvements. The more one can see the hidden or difficult-to-see waste, the more one will be able to help their teams see the same. The process is very powerful.

I was being given a tour at a plant in East TN by their Operations Manager when I noticed how a lady on the line was using an air powered nut-runner. She would put a screw on the end of it, pull the trigger, and at the end she would give it two more turns with her wrist. "Step in Circle" tells us to pay close attention to how the operator interacts with the process, so this stood out to me immediately. I asked the manager to take me over to the lady. I asked her why she was turning the nut-runner two more times. She stated that she had to do that to get the screws to seat completely to the surface. I asked her how long that had been happening and she stated it had been happening, since engineering ordered the new nut-runners. When I asked her if she had complained she sheepishly stated no. She did not see the extra work as too time consuming. In manufacturing, every second counts, but in this case I was not particularly concerned about adding any additional time. I was more concerned about the safety of her wrist over time. The Operations Manager and I continued the discussion with the engineer next. He explained that they had gotten a better deal on the nut-runners, so they were replacing the old ones with the cheaper ones as the old ones failed. Understandably, in the engineer's mind, he was doing the right thing. My advice to them was to spend the extra money on the good nut-runners, so they could avoid carpal tunnel syndrome costs in the future.

I saw another version of the Ohno Circle concept in action at a sheet metal factory in Monterrey Mexico. The owner of the business was very proud, as he should be, of the business he and his brothers had built. He was in his 70's at the time and spent every day at the plant. I was visiting the plant to determine if his company could supply my client with sheet metal. The operation was well organized and seemed to run very smoothly. When I asked him how he managed productivity, he took me to a spot in the plant and pulled out a small piece of paper. On the paper, there were rows for each hour of the working day, and the columns were for each machine. He could see every machine from this spot in the plant. He told me that once per hour, he walks to that spot and takes note of each machine. If the machine is running, he puts a 1 in the box corresponding to the machine and the hour. He repeats this for each machine. At the end of the day, he totals all 1's and divides by the # of machines x the hours worked. This gives him his productivity number. Simple, but effective. On occasion, he would stand in the circle to discern the quality of the processes, but his primary focus was clearly productivity.

If you would like to try the Ohno Circle approach, gather the following tools, and follow the steps below:

- Blank sheets of paper or a notepad.

- Pencil or pen and locate a clipboard or firm writing surface

- Comfortable shoes (you will be standing for 60 minutes)

- Camera is preferred but optional*

Steps for "Stand in Circle" Exercise:

1. Choose a strategic spot in the work environment that allows one to see as much of the process as possible.

2. For 60 minutes, stand and observe — silently.

3. The key is to practice what the Japanese call kizuki; the ability to notice.

4. Write down anything you notice that results in waste - energy, time, a safety concern, abnormalities of any kind, perhaps something that is noticed is not being done as efficiently as it could be. Remember: Focus on the operator interaction with the process.

5. Your task is to find 60 things - that is one every minute including writing time!

The key is to simply observe and write - no need to comment or discuss with others (other than within the necessity of being polite). Describe what you see and why you see these results as waste. Did I mention to focus on the interaction between the process and the operator. Stay in one area and look deeply; it is easy to find 60 things if you flutter around like a butterfly and point out the large obvious wastes -instead, plant yourself like a tree and really see. Sometimes waste can be hard to spot - if you need a place to begin, look for issues pertaining to waste, variation, overburden, safety, quality, environment, or energy losses. Do lights need to be turned off? Perhaps you need better lighting? Is there a counter, carpet, wall, file cabinet, desk area or storage area in need of cleaning? Any work positions with bad ergonomics, awkward access?

Once one has completed the exercise, they should discuss what they have seen with their trainer/coach/mentor and discuss possible quick wins based on some of the items you have seen.

THINK PAST THE FIX

Organizations have become more and more strained for resources, so we must focus our energies in the right direction. I propose focusing our precious time and energy on preventing a recurring problem rather than simply restoring flow each time the problem occurs. We must continue to ask ourselves the 5 Whys (not the 5 Who's) until we understand and discover the root cause of the problem. Some people think you must ask all 5 Why's to conclude a 5 Why session. The 5 Why tool came from Japan, and in their culture the number 5 stands for perfection, so you only need to ask the perfect number of why's. In their culture the number 4 stands for death, so not asking the right number of Why's is not good. Once we have asked the perfect number of Why's we should be at the root cause and at a point we can eliminate the problem's cause and standardize to prevent recurrence. Then we must leverage the countermeasure to any similar risk in the organization.

Most companies do a great job of restoring flow. Restoring flow when the process fails is how companies stay in business. If you were not good at restoring flow, my guess is you would not be in business long, since if you cannot satisfy your customer, someone else will. However, many companies do a terrible job of "thinking past the fix." Thinking past the fix begins after flow has been restored. It is taking the time to answer the following question, "What can we do to make sure this NEVER happens again?!?!" We must do what we know well (standardization) and fix what we know is wrong (problem solving after exposure), since there are plenty of things we do not know that are waiting to be discovered. Allowing things we know is wrong, to continue will constantly prevent us from reaching the level of performance we desire.

VISUAL CONTROL

Due to the complexities involved in business, we can expect to always have problems, so we must use visual controls, so no problems are hidden. We must use simple visual indicators to indicate whether the current condition is to standard or is deviating from the standard. I like to tell my clients that from ten feet and in two seconds, they should be able to determine if there is a deviation to a standard. The team should design simple, visual systems to support flow and pull. There are different visual controls used. Below are some common groupings that we see in our daily lives:

- Visual Indicator - Tells you something (street sign)

- Visual Signal - Gets your attention (brake lights, andon lights)

- Visual Control - Places limits on behavior (yellow lines on two-lane highway)

- Visual Guarantee - Allows only the correct response (concrete dividers on highway). Every time you see where someone has hit the barrier, you know the barrier has served its purpose. This is a perfect example of a process solution that captures unintended mistakes, and in this case, saves lives.

Simply having visual controls is not enough; they must be continually monitored by leadership. Practicing proper visual management will uncover many problems. I often refer to the exposure of these problems as "shining the light on the roaches." How we react to those problems is extremely important. One can have all the visual controls and error proofing tools available in place, but if one lacks observant leaders, the controls will be useless. Leaders must be constantly looking for deviations to the standards. Also ensure the visual indicators are NOT ambiguous. If the control is ambiguous, you would be better off not having a visual indicator at all.

ERROR PROOFING

Another approach to improving quality is called Error Proofing (aka Poka Yoke). The visual guarantee example given above is a form of Error Proofing. Error Proofing is a quality control approach for achieving zero defects. Error Proofing is based on the thought that defects are prevented by controlling a process so that the process cannot produce defects, even when a mistake is made by a machine or a person.

There is a lot of truth to the statement, "If you play stupid games, you win stupid prizes." If someone is doing something purposefully to negatively impact the quality of the product or service, they should win their prize. Even when someone is trying to do the right thing, there will be human factors that allow mistakes to be made. In Error Proofing, we recognize that it is natural for people to make mistakes or fail to notice when an error is made or a machine malfunction. This does not mean that a person is stupid or foolish. If a mistake can be made, it will be made. Leaders who do not understand this typically display a high level of disrespect for their associates. The leaders think they can solve their quality issues by "writing up" everyone. My question to those leaders is, "How is that working for you?" Those same leaders think one can simply inspect quality into the product. When you ask them why they do not stop to fix quality, the answer is, "We don't have time." However, they always have time to make the product for the second time.

The error-proofing approach creates devices to prevent errors and keeps those errors from ever turning into defects. There are three levels of Error Proofing:

Level 1 – Device designed to eliminate an error from happening during the assembly/manufacturing/software process. Do Not Make a Defect!

Level 2 – Device created to catch a defect at the time it happens to prevent passing on to the next station. Do Not Pass a Defect!

Level 3 – Device created to catch a defect after it happens, typically at the next operation, but does not allow it to enter the next station. Do Not Accept a Defect!

Our target is to have as many Level 1 error proofing devices in our processes as possible. If we do our part to design error proofing into our products and processes, we will make it easier for our associates to do the right thing. Remembering that it must be easier to do the right thing than to do the wrong thing.

MANAGING RISK

In aviation, we have saying, "There are old pilots and bold pilots, but there are not many old-bold pilots." This saying is about taking unnecessary risk. Pilots that take unnecessary risk do not often live to be old. I do not want you to get the idea that I do not value risk. I believe the right kind of risk is prudent. For instance, you will not be able to tell if you can swim if you never take off your life vest. That kind of risk, if you succeed, will lead you to becoming better. The risk that I am against is the type of risk that causes you to move away from True North.

> "Nothing worthwhile was ever accomplished without risk and daring." — *Dick Rutan (flew Voyager around the world with no refuel stops)*

A lot of what we have discussed in this habit is reactive. There are also some proactive tools that can be used to improve quality. The two that I have used most in my career at Bosch and as a consultant are Failure Modes Effects Analysis (FMEA) and Control Plans. Both tools should be utilized by a cross functional team. This is another example of not wanting to do things in a vacuum.

The basis of the FMEA is a process flow diagram. Most companies have a flowchart showing the steps which their product takes as it transitions from raw goods to a finished product. This is a starting point, but following the concept of "Trust but Verify," I would always make sure what we think is happening is really happening by personally walking the process flow. The FMEA tool helps us critique each step of that process and uncover potential failure modes, so we can plan corrective actions to either reduce the occurrence of the failure, improve our detection of the failure mode, or reduce the severity of the failure mode should it get to the customer. A numbering system (1-10) is used for each (Occurrence, Detection, Severity) and the product of those three numbers gives us a Risk Priority Number (RPN). Once we have completed this exercise for the entire process flow, we sort the RPN's from highest to lowest, and work our way down the list. In the automotive industry, when I was there, we could not have any RPN's above 120. This number may vary by industry.

When you are developing your plans to reduce the RPN's in the FMEA, you state that there are certain controls in place to manage the risk. The control plan is the tool that documents all the controls that are going to be used, the frequency and size of any checks, and how those checks will be documented. The value of the control plan is when auditing the process. The control plan states what we said we were going to do, and the audit hopefully confirms we are doing it. When Toyota auditors would come to the plant, the control plan was the first thing they wanted to see. They would simply walk the process and ensure you were doing what you said you were going to do. If you were not there was some coaching, and they would recheck during their next visit.

When I was first introduced to these tools it was to prepare for an audit by one of the Detroit 3. The thought was that we must get the 'paperwork' in order, so they would not find anything. Being a good soldier, I did just that and we passed the audit with flying colors. However, it bothered me at the amount of waste expended to pass an audit. It was not until later when I was visited by Toyota that I saw the importance of the Process Flow, FMEA, and Control Plan. From that point forward, I used the FMEA and Control Plan as a method to help further improve my process. When I left Bosch, my product had no RPN's over 90.

Quality has come a long way in the US since the early years of manufacturing. When W. Edwards Deming and others started the journey to improve quality, I am not sure if they knew the movement they would generate within Japan and eventually the world. Quality is the key to winning in today's business world. You cannot produce products with poor quality and expect to be successful. There are many examples that have proven that point. Do not let your company be the next example.

Individual Leadership Reflection:

Obsessing Over Quality

Leader Thinking

Building-in quality is the fastest path to stability and improvement.

I must work "right" to get long-term results

Eliminating the highest recurring problems has a greater impact on stability than only focusing on the largest cost impact problems.

Do we have a problem? No problem. Do we have a repeat problem? Big problem!

If a mistake CAN be made, it WILL be made.

I cannot solve problems that I cannot see.

Leader Behavior

I stop and fix to get quality right the first time.

I go and see.

I speak with data and require the same of others.

I build-in quality through error proofing.

I use visual control so that no problems are hidden.

I step- in-circle and learn to see.

Leader Reflection

Do I think and act this way? If not, what must I adjust?

What are the biggest levers in my area for quality improvement (where should I focus these behaviors)?

End of Chapter GROUP Reflection Questions:

1. Are we progressing on the actions from our last discussion?

2. What was the key learning from the current chapter?

3. As a team, what do we do well as it relates to the key learning?

4. As a team, what do we NOT do well as it relates to the key learning?

5. What do we need to Start, Stop, or Continue doing as a team to improve going forward as it relates to the key learning?

CHAPTER 8

HABIT 6:

CAPTURING ORGANIZATIONAL LEARNING

"If you are not willing to learn, no one can help you. If you are determined to learn, no one can stop you." — *Unknown*

Lots of organizations espouse that they value learning. However, their theory in use is to just get the work done. People are eager to go "do" something, and not give value to discussion and/or reflection. Action without reflection is as bad as reflection without action. We must understand that learning is productivity. I am an action-oriented person, but I believe that action must have direction, or it is wasteful. Reflection and alignment give us direction. We must abandon the ready-fire-aim approach.

Many companies today do not capture the learning that is occurring, so they learn the same lessons repeatedly. The best way to learn is to solve problems. Every time we solve a problem, our business improves. The path to perfection is paved with problems, so we will never not have problems to solve. Our issue is not having enough problem solvers.

The lack of problem solvers is due in part to the flow of problems. There is a right flow and wrong flow of problems that impacts the speed at which we can solve problems. If we have the wrong flow of problems, we simply cannot solve all of them, so we only work on the big ones. This is referred to as "elephant hunting."

Our organizations must be embracing and evolving in innovation and performance. We must consider all "solutions" and decisions to be temporary countermeasures until better solutions are found.

"Is there one decision you can make today that will make tomorrow better?" — *Zig Ziglar*

We become a learning organization through relentless reflection and continuous improvement. As stated, before we must begin the improvement process by creating stability within our processes. Once a stable process has been established, we must identify inefficiencies and solve problems and design processes that require almost no inventory (inventory hides problems). There can be times when you improve a process and there is a certain amount of instability due to the change. This is natural, so you must give the new process time to stabilize before the next improvement. Consider this as a never-ending loop; stabilize, improve, stabilize, improve…

"Inventory is Money Sleeping" — *Unknown*

As waste is exposed, we must have employees eliminate it. As teams are conducting improvement efforts, we must encourage our teams to use reflection both during and after a project to identify the shortcomings. If we do this correctly, the result will be the development of countermeasures to avoid making the same mistakes again. Then we can institutionalize those learnings by standardizing the best practices. However, we must remember that today's best practices must be abandoned if we find a better practice tomorrow.

PROBLEM SELECTION

I am often called in to help solve problems with clients, which I enjoy. What I find a lot of times is they do not have a problem in the sense that the process is creating a problem. They have a different kind of problem. They have failed to create a standard, so what is considered a problem may or may not be a problem depending on whom you ask. Below is a verbal flow that I use to determine what is going on and what are their next steps.

My first question, as you may have already surmised, is, "Is there a standard?" If not, stop and create one. You cannot move forward without a standard. If there is a standard, I ask, "Is the standard universally understood?" Everyone should agree to the standard and be able to apply the standard. If they don't understand and/or cannot apply the standard consistently you cannot move forward. You must now make the standard understandable to and applicable by all. This does not mean simply retraining the people. Retraining someone in something you have already trained them in isn't effective and is often offensive to the person being retrained. Once the standard is universally understood, then I ask, "Is it easy to work to this standard?" If not, provide what is needed to support working to the standard. This may be in the form of new materials, methods, machines, tools, etc. One should never leave a process in a condition where it is easier to do the wrong thing than it is to do the right thing. If it is easy to follow the standard, I ask, "Was this problem anticipated?" I highly encourage the use of Failure Modes Effects Analysis, so this question is aimed at ensuring that document gets updated. This will allow us to leverage our learning from this process to future processes. We want to be more proactive in our approach to not have to learn the same lesson repeatedly. Once we have gotten this far in the process, I ask, "Is the solution to the problem obvious?" If the answer is yes and we have the resources to implement the solution, then we follow the practice of Just Do It. If we do not have resources to Just Do It, the problem is escalated to management to provide those resources. If the solution is not obvious then, we have the beginnings of a problem, and the next question is, "Is the process stable?" If the process is not stable, then we must take actions to stabilize the process; one should never try to improve an unstable process. If the process is stable, then I ask, "Have we consistently (>70%) achieved the standard before? If not, then we may need to completely redo the process with engineering. A process this poor should have never been released to production, which leads to a question concerning how new products and processes are implemented. Assuming the process was >95% consistent when it was released, we need to look at the overall maintenance of the process to determine why it has degraded. If the process is stable, then we apply Core Problem Solving. If that fails, we apply Intermediate Problem Solving, and if that fails, we apply Advance Problem Solving.

WRONG FLOW OF PROBLEMS

Elephants in captivity are trained, at an early age, not to roam. One leg of a baby elephant is tied with a rope to a wooden post planted in the ground. The rope confines the baby elephant to an area determined by the length of the rope. Initially the baby elephant tries to break free from the rope, but the rope is too strong. The baby elephant "learns" that it cannot break the rope. When the elephant grows up and is strong, it could easily break the same rope. But because it "learned" that it could not break the rope when it was young, the adult elephant believes that it still cannot break the rope, so it does not even try!

This is the same effect we have in organizations where we have unintentionally (I hope) trained people to not give input or challenge the status quo. This has led to managers having to solve all the problems. We now must retrain people to embrace the approach of continuously improving the work that they do.

Most managers cringe at the thought of exposing more problems within their organizations. This is with good reason since the old paradigm is that managers are to be the primary problem solvers. This thought process has created a situation in which 90% (the associates) of the organization, delegate problem solving to 10% (the managers) of the organization. This is not sustainable based on the pure volume of work being created by these problems. Add to this the fact that the manager is also getting tasked from above as well. Those tasks from above can come from their boss, corporate, customers, supplier, etc. When forced to choose where to focus, the manager will always give more attention to the request coming from above.

Imagine a manager getting a problem from an associate, but subsequently that manager forgets to handle the issue. The associate then considers the possibility that not only was the problem not important to the manager, but the manager does not really care about them as a person. Assuming the manager did not forget, the manager may attempt to give the associate a solution. In many cases that solution is flawed due to the manager's lack of understanding about the problem or the work wherein the problem lies, and the manager does not have time to spend to better understand the problem. I would hope that we can all agree that those with the most knowledge of the work are the ones who do that work each day. Oftentimes, the associate implements the manager's solution only to be met with a poor result, in which case some managers give the associate negative feedback. In the associate's mind, they are thinking, "I raised a problem, was given an ineffective solution, and got negative feedback." The associate then concludes that surfacing problems is not worth the hassle, so he decides to work around the problems (aka tampering). At this point all problem-solving collaboration has ended. The manager may be thinking, "Everything is fine since I am not hearing problems from the floor. All is good, right?!?!" In this case no news is not good news. No news means his people have given up on him and do not see him as capable or willing to help them, so they have decided to create workarounds to get the job done. Those workarounds lead to product, service, and/or process variation that will eventually be noticed by our customers. The graphic below shows the cycle described above.

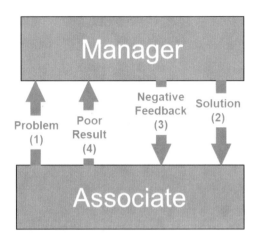

CORRECT FLOW OF PROBLEMS

For the correct flow of problems to work, the leaders must understand the value of being a coach over being an individual contributor in the problem-solving engine. Being a great problem solver IS NOT the goal of leadership. Growing problem solvers IS the goal. I always use the analogy of T-ball coaching to get this point across. The coach of a T-ball team could probably hit a homerun every time from the T. However, that is not his role on the team. His role is to transfer his knowledge to the team members. The team wins by making hits that lead to runs across home base. The coach wins by enabling them to do so.

The best approach to problem solving or process improvement in general is to put the people that do the work in charge of improving the work. It is leadership's responsibility to create space for this to happen. There is typically some very strong organizational memory that has not been aligned with this thinking, so we must help the leaders embrace this new expectation. In this new environment, the managers begin functioning as coaches and the associates become learners. In this approach, the coach, using Management by Walking Around and Visual Management, exposes problems and asks learners to propose a countermeasure. Allowing the coaches to facilitate this problem exposure process assumes the organization has trained the learners to use a specific process (core problem solving) to solve problems.

> "Guessing is cheap, guessing wrong is expensive."
> – *Unknown*

We cannot rely on simply guessing. It is not fair to ask learners to solve problems if they have not been properly trained to find and eliminate the root causes of those problems. The learner makes a proposal using the standard format for the business. The proposal is typically in the form of a problem solving A3. This allows the coach to properly coach and offer critique to the learner on the process and content of the proposal. This coaching is always Socratic (teaching by asking questions) to ensure the coach is not giving the learner a solution. In this case, the coach must be more focused on the process being followed to solve the problem more than solving the problem.

> "Success consists of going from Failure to Failure without loss of enthusiasm." — *Winston Churchill*

The learner takes the coaching and critique and continues with the process of solving the problem. This continues until the root cause of the problem has been found, a countermeasure has been implemented, and the effectiveness of that countermeasure has been verified. The best solutions are the ones that the local team can implement. If we start allowing problem solving on the floor to drive action lists for maintenance and engineering, we shift the problem-solving bottleneck from management to maintenance and engineering.

The graphic below shows the correct problem-solving cycle as described above.

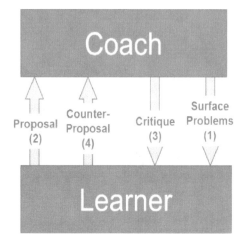

Once we have made the transition of putting problem solving in the hands of the people doing the work to 90% of the organization, or area, then we can deploy a systematic approach to exposing and solving problems at the process level. That process is called Managing Daily Improvement (MDI), which will be covered in the next section.

MANAGING DAILY IMPROVEMENTS

When we focus on something, it improves. This has been proven over time and is sometimes referred to as the Hawthorne Effect. The issue with the Hawthorne Effect is that when management moves away from an area the improvements digress. To institutionalize the Hawthorne Effect, we need a system in place to ensure we are managing the daily improvement of the process. To ensure we are managing daily improvements, we need to have triggers that force problem solving to occur. One method of doing this is referred to as Takt Attainment (takt = selling speed of the product/service). This is a process that requires problems to be escalated when Takt is missed (not meeting the selling speed). This requires us to have first responders (Team Leaders) in place to address problems. Consider the following example from Toyota.

At Toyota they monitor the number of line-stops. At the time I was researching, they had the staff to address 1000 stops per week. If they got down to 600 line stops (line-pulls), what do you think they should do? The normal approach for Western companies would be to reduce the staff to only cover 600 line stops. Toyota's response was to increase the number of line-pulls by making the standard harder to attain. This in turn generates more problems to solve. One of their main goals is to solve problems at a faster rate than their competition. This is their competitive advantage.

Management typically knows where there are big problems in the process. However, one can suffer death from a thousand cuts. Managing Daily Improvement helps us notice the thousand cuts are occurring and allows us to respond. Once you have generated misses (not meeting takt), evaluation of the misses is very important. This evaluation is the beginning of Managing Daily Improvement. Without evaluation of the misses, we are simply collecting data to be used in a history lesson at some point in the future. Those history lessons are in the form of end-of-day, weekly, monthly, or quarterly meetings. At the time of the miss, immediate short-term counter-measures should be put in place to prevent the same issue from occurring on the next takt cycle. Each takt miss should then be captured in a Live Pareto or Histogram. The goal is to narrow what we are willing to work on, since some juice simply isn't worth the squeeze, and we cannot fix all problems at the same time. The Live Pareto is used to determine which item (highest pareto item) warrants the team's focus. We want to focus the team's energy on problems that are known and felt. Solutions to the top takt misses will be in the form of Just Do Its (JDI's), Core Problem Solving A3's (CPS), Rapid Improvement Events (RIE's), or Project A3's. In some extreme cases, the team may need to pull in outside resources to apply advanced problem-solving techniques, but most problems can be addressed at the CPS level. Another important consideration when tracking reasons for missing takt is to account for the times the process is starved or blocked. The importance here is to ensure we know where the bottleneck is in our process. Starved and blocked should always be options on the histogram. If the process is starved, then the bottleneck is upstream, and if the process is blocked the bottleneck is downstream. I typically see less blocked conditions due to the habit of people "pushing" inventory to the next operation. Blocked will show up when we have 1x1 flow or are following FIFO max quantities.

Another benefit of monitoring takt is to see when we exceed takt. When we exceed takt, we need to ask the following questions:

- Did we learn a faster way to do the process? If so, we need to update the standard.

- Did we skip a process step? If so, we need to quarantine the parts.

Managing Daily Improvement, if done correctly, will move the exposure of problems and the solving of problems down the organizational chart to the people closest to the work.

Many times, when it comes to solving problems, there are barriers to gaining alignment. Managers fear losing power/control. Managers got their positions by always having answers. If we have not engaged the associates in problem solving before, the associates may fear responsibility. Associates have inadvertently, or in some extreme cases intentionally, been trained to believe their opinions do not matter. This does not necessarily mean that someone has told the associates their opinions do not matter. We send the message that we do not value an associate's opinion when we fail to include the associates from a specific area in the improvement of their area. We must do improvement work WITH the team, not TO the team.

I am reminded of a workshop conducted in Trenton, NJ. The workshop (Total Productive Maintenance) was focused on equipment improvement and building a sense of teamwork between operators, maintenance, and engineering. The event went very well with great participation and team-work from all groups. During the end-of-event report, we were asking the team to reflect on the event when one of the older gentlemen stood up. He looked at the top officer in the room and said, "I have been working for this company for over thirty years, and this is the first time I have been included in an event like this. For thirty years, you have paid for my hands when you could have had my brains for free." The look on the top officer's face was priceless. It is hard for me to believe a company could have people in its employment who have not been engaged for their entire career, but I assure you this happens frequently. We often do not engage our associates, which ensures there is less alignment and a shallow understanding of the reasons behind the things we do.

Some of the root causes for this misalignment are:

- Management failing to define the business case (reason for action)
- Management failing to gain agreement on the current condition
- Management failing to understand the current condition deeply
- Associates delegating problems to Management
- Associates failing to provide solutions to problems in their areas (dead fish)
- Management failing to gain consensus that the problem is really a problem

The question we must ask ourselves is, "How many of these misalignments exist within our organization, and what are we doing to address them?"

The following is an excerpt from Deming's book "Out of the Crisis":

> *Dr. Ouchi's speech the third day commenced as follows:*
>
> *While you are out on the golf course in the afternoon waiting for your partner to tee up, I want you to think about something. Last month I was in Tokyo where I visited with your trade association counterpart. It represents roughly two hundred Japanese companies who are your direct competitors. They are now holding meetings from eight in the morning to nine at night, five days a week, for three months straight, so that one company's oscilloscope will connect to another company's analyzer, so that they can agree on product safety standards to recommend to the government (to speed up getting to the marketplace), so that they can agree on their*

needs for change in regulations, export policy, and financing and then approach their government with one voice to ask for cooperation. Tell me who you think will be in better shape in five years?

In the excerpt above, Dr. Ouchi is comparing Japan to the US, but the same can be done company to company within the US. The 'government' in some cases is our own internal business bureaucracy. The diagram below shows how the effects of your system and people can impact your overall culture and way of doing business.

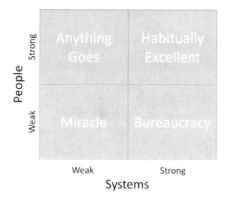

In a business, where there are weak people and weak systems, I call it a Miracle. It is a miracle they even have a business. Their product must be so good that it does not matter. When the people are strong and the system is weak, anything goes. There is not a standard in this case. When the system is strong and the people are weak, they simply let the system run the show, bureaucracy reins. In the case where bureaucracy exists to this level, it is easier to not do anything than to deal with the process of getting things done. What we want is a strong system and strong people. At that point, we have a business that is Habitually Excellent. Being Habitually Excellent makes it easy to do the right thing and creates alignment across the entire enterprise.

SCIENTIFIC THINKING

Have you ever heard the statement, "trust the science?" That is one of the most anti-scientific things you can hear, since questioning the science is how we do science. The best thing about science is it is not based on consensus. It deals with the facts of nature. Many people over the years have attempted to sway scientific thinking based on what a group thinks, but the facts always prevail. Sometimes it may take time for the facts to appear, but they will eventually appear. Consider the fact that there was consensus that the world was flat for many years. Those who opposed this thinking were often killed, so challenging the wrong thinking in your business may be a little scary. You may not get killed, but you could certainly get fired, or "labeled."

The Scientific Method has been around for centuries. However, many organizations still fail to utilize this simple process to improve their business. The scientific method was established in the 1200's by Roger Bacon and was later called the Plan Do Check Act (PDCA) or Shewhart cycle when Deming and his team popularized it within manufacturing circles in the 1950's. I follow the Plan Try Reflect Standardize (PTRS) cycle which is a derivation of the PDCA cycle. Both processes are used to test hypotheses. If you have ever conducted a science experiment, you have used this cycle. The key is to experiment rapidly. We have all heard it stated that we want quality over quantity. In this case quantity of experiments can lead to quality if we are learning and adjusting after each experiment. Consider experimentation an example of economies of repetition that pays off in learning. After all, if you do something every day, you are bound to be good at it.

> "The best angle from which to approach any problem is the try–angle." — *Unknown*

I am reminded of a time when I was a child. My dad gave me a chore to cut the grass while he was at work. He arrived that night to find me sitting under a tree reading. I was reading the operation manual for the lawnmower. You see, I had never cut the grass before without my dad. My plan was to understand everything there was to know about grass cutting and the lawnmower before I started. My dad was not happy with this strategy. He told me to get on the lawn mower and cut the grass. I could focus on doing better each time I cut the grass. He was not looking for perfection the first time. He was looking for shorter grass, and the longer I put off cutting the grass the taller it would get and eventually it would be too high to cut with our push mower. I learned a valuable lesson that day that has impacted the way I design, engineer, and implement processes throughout my career. It is better to DO something and adjust going forward than to do nothing trying to make something perfect.

"I never lose... I either win, or I learn" — *Unknown*

As I mentioned above, I use a form of PDCA called PTRS. I adopted this from Toyota. The reasoning for the adjustment from PDCA to PTRS was to clearly send the message that we are TRYING something, and if it fails, we will TRY again. DO, the D in PDCA, can imply that you are done if the experiment fails. Below is a deeper dive into each of the steps of PTRS.

PLAN: Create a plan to test the hypothesis. The plan should be proportional to cost and risk. If there is a large cost and high risk to safety, quality, delivery, then the plan should be significant. Small decisions lead to small mistakes, where large decisions often lead to large mistakes. If the cost and risk of the "try" is low, then one should simply do it and see what is learned. I have noticed many western companies spend too much time planning and not enough time trying. This is another time when it is wise to know when to ask for permission and when to ask for forgiveness. Sometimes in the process of asking for permission to TRY something, you will encounter someone that thinks their job is to say NO. In those instances, you must be more confident that you KNOW more than the person saying NO.

"A good plan executed violently today is far better than a perfect plan executed next week." — *George Patton*

TRY: The key in this step is to TRY something. I like to call this step "Try-storming." It involves running small tests/experiments to see if our hypothesis was correct. After each test, we CHECK the result. If the result did not meet our expectations, we ADJUST and try again. The key here is to adjust when needed; do not be stubborn, and do not fall for the fallacy of sunk cost. Never let yourself or your team be taken on a Nantucket Whale ride. A Nantucket Whale ride is when you harpoon a whale, and it drags the boat offshore. If you don't cut the cord, you will be taken out to sea, and those seas may destroy your ship and kill everyone onboard.

> "Don't cling to a mistake because you spent a lot of time and/or money making it." — *Unknown*

Mr Fujio Cho (former Toyota Chairman), was quoted as saying, "There are many things one doesn't understand and therefore, we tell them why you don't simply go ahead and take action; try to do something. You realize how little you know, and you face your own failures and redo it again and at the second trial you realize another mistake or another thing you didn't like so you can redo it once again. Consider every failure a sacrifice at the altar of Operation Excellence. So, by constant improvement, or the improvement based upon action, one can rise to a higher level of practice and knowledge." This is the purpose of the PTRS cycle.

> "One validated experiment is worth 1000 expert opinions." — *Wernher Von Braun*

We continue this cycle until we achieve what we set out to achieve in the plan (target condition). Sometimes leaders are stubborn when it comes to adjusting, so we must be relentless to ensure adjustments are made when needed. Although scrapping a project may seem extreme, sometimes it may be necessary. We should avoid throwing good money after bad money. The Nantucket Whale ride may be in your wallet.

"Continuous Improvement is better than delayed perfection." — *Mark Twain*

REFLECT: In this step, we reflect on what went well, what we learned, and what did not go so well, or what we should do differently the next time. This reflection is mainly focused on the improvement process that was used. Of all the steps, reflection seems to be the one most overlooked. It is one of the most important steps in the learning process. If executed properly, the learning is captured, and the process is improved during the next cycle. The key when reflecting is to focus more on the opportunities to be corrected in what you are doing. Spend a little time congratulating the team but spend most of the team discovering what you can do better the next time. Earlier in this book, I stated that not wanting to learn is "Intellectual laziness." Reflective Learning is one of the most powerful ways we can combat this laziness.

STANDARDIZE: Once we have learned something new about our process, we must standardize it to ensure the learning is retained within the organization. This is also the step in which we would read-across any learning to like processes in the organization.

> "Something happened that impressed me very much. During the testing of the 200 looms I came up with various suggestions, and father tried every single one.....Humans come up with a surprising number of useless ideas; when you actually try them out, the ones you thought were good ideas sometimes prove to be unexpectedly useless, and the ones you thought were bad ideas sometimes turn out unexpectedly good. This is the principle that practice is number one."
> — *Kiichiro Toyoda (Founder of Toyota Motor Company and President, 1941–1950)*

The key to PDCA or PTRS is to ensure timeliness in following the method. Organizations must change their paradigms about how long it should take to complete a project. We want to be the "rabbit" (think of the rabbit that is chased during a dog race) that everyone else is chasing. When the project is developed or the idea is conceived, there is a Net Value of the project or idea. As we delay the project or idea, we lose the opportunity it could give us for each day it is delayed (i.e. Opportunity is Reduced (Net Value – (Lost Opp x Days)) We must cut hay while the sun (opportunities) is shining, since the "sun" may not always be shining as bright as it is today. One of my clients told me that they didn't want to take advantage of the additional opportunities in the current year to keep demand up in future years. On the surface, this sounds reasonable. However, if there is a large enough opportunity on the table, the competition may take it, or worse it may entice a new entrant into the market. In that case you have competition (the current) plus more (the new). The future market pie will be divided by more players in your space.

I highly encourage the use of the PTRS cycle. However, I highly discourage the use of the PTAR cycle. The PTAR cycle is Plan-Try-Abandon-Revert back to the old ways of doing things. This is often the approach used by teams that do not really want to change. They are looking for failure as an excuse to go back to the old way of doing things. The old way is comfortable to them.

Another way of practicing the experimentation approach is to use the Kata approach. In his book, "Toyota Kata," Mike Rother does an excellent job of distilling the pattern (aka kata, the root word in Karate) that Toyota follows as they iterate their way toward a target or challenge on their way toward true north. The below diagram given to me by Mike after one of his Kata Conferences shows the idea of Kata in a graphical form:

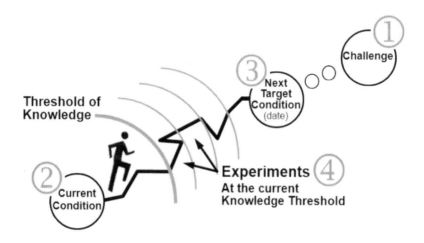

The following questions are used by a skilled coach to guide the learning shown in the graphic above:

1. What is the Challenge?

2. What is the Target Condition?

3. What is the Actual Condition now?

4. What did you plan as your last step/ experiment?

5. What did you expect to happen?

6. What happened?

7. What did you learn from taking that last step / experiment?

8. What obstacles do you think are preventing you from reaching the target condition?

9. Which one are you addressing now?

10. What is your next step (next PTRS experiment)?

11. What do you expect?

12. How quickly can we go and see what we have learned from taking that step?

13. What else do you need?

As the leader, you should set Challenges and Targets that are just outside of the learner's current knowledge threshold. Using this line of questioning helps the learner learn how to think in a manner of continuous improvement. As with any approach, the goal of the coach is to teach the thinking, not solve the problem or tell the team how to get to the target/challenge.

> "One must learn by doing the thing; for though you think you know it; you have no certainty until you try." — *Sophocles*

We see, in some cases, the team does not get the result they want initially, and they abandon the effort instead of adjusting the plan and trying again. This faulty mindset will ensure no continuous improvement success.

HUMBLE BEGINNINGS

If one studies the origins of the most coveted business system in the world, The Toyota Business System, they will find that the genius behind that system can be traced back to an engineer by the name of Taiichi Ohno. I am not sure Toyota would tout that they have the most coveted product system due to their having confidence with humility. This confidence with humility ensures they never fall into the trap of thinking they have "arrived." They are always looking to learn more. In the beginning, Ohno was doing three things in his area:

- Finding a Problem
- Fixing that Problem
- Ensuring It Never Happened Again

From that approach, many tools were developed that now have universal applications.

- A3 Problem Solving: A result of standardizing how teams solve problems to ensure they are getting to the root cause.
- Single Minute Exchange of Die: A result of standardizing the process of reducing changeovers on all processes; not just stamping presses.

- Workplace Organization (5S): A result of standardizing the process to improve the work area to support flow of product by having materials and tools at the point of use. If done properly, it ensures Everything has a place, and Everything is in its place. Sadly, over the years, 5S has become a verb used to explain why something is missing (e.g. I can't find my tools, since they were 5S'd). Housekeeping is not the goal of 5S.

- Autonomous Maintenance: A result of standardizing the process of involving operators in the maintenance of their equipment.

Every Operational Excellence / Continuous Improvement Methodology has the purpose of exposing problems so that the problems can be solved. This leads to continuous improvement in the business. To do this effectively, we must ensure the following are occurring:

- Problem Exposure

- Root Cause Identification

- Countermeasure Implementation

- Repeat (Continuous Improvement)

You will never run out of problems to solve. If any one of these steps is skipped, the business will not be propelled toward the ideal state (True North). Every day, we must ensure we have every person on every process following this Find-Fix-Prevent cycle. The typical pattern I see in businesses is the problem appears (it finds them), they fix the problem (restoring flow), but they don't think past the fix and prevent the problem from happening again. This approach ensures the problem will appear again in the future.

To encourage the teams to keep striving toward the ideal state, we like to continually reinforce the following:

- Every day little up

- Some days big up

- Until you take the first step, it will not be possible to see the next step.

- "Please try."

- "Do your best."

"You don't have to see the whole staircase, simply take the first step." — Unknown

One may find it hard to believe, but I have met with businesspeople who stated their businesses were running fine, and they did not have any problems. In 100% of the cases in which I could visit the business, I found many excesses that were covering up the problems. Those excesses were in the form of excess inventory, capacity, labor, and floor space. Not only were business leaders paying for the excesses, but they were also paying for the problems the excesses were hiding. I have a saying, "No Problem is a Problem." Seeing no problems usually means no one has challenged the business enough to expose the problem. This breeds complacency and lazy processes which will result in associates who are unable to perform at peak when the demand increases.

If your team finds itself struggling to expose problems, I recommend the leadership team create what is called System Pressure. This can be done by doing one or all the following:

- Reduce time (work less time on production, spend spare time on improvements)

- Reduce Inventory (less time stored as inventory between processes)

- Increase Volume (move volume from another area)

- Reduce Capacity (turn off assets (do maintenance) or slow them down (less wear and tear))

Always remember, if there are no problems, that is the problem. How we view problems can be the difference between success and failure.

When we are creating system pressure, we are battling against an effect referred to as Parkinson's Law. Parkinson's Law tells us that any activity will expand to fill the time allotted for that activity. An example would be if you give someone eight hours to do a four-hour task, that task will take eight hours to complete. If not dealt with this can impact many functions and activities across an organization and drive cost up and productivity down. As is the case with quality, this dwindling of productivity is like the boiling of a frog. It will slowly kill the business without you even realizing it until it is too late. Horstman's corollary to Parkinson's law: "work contracts to fit in the time we give it.". If you challenge the system, the system will increase performance to meet the challenge.

> "The problem isn't the problem; your attitude about the problem is the problem." — *Jack Sparrow*

Individual Leadership Reflection:

Capturing Organizational Learning

Leader Thinking

Every production run is an opportunity to learn. Every problem is an opportunity to learn. Every interaction with another person is an opportunity to learn. Leverage the opportunity.

I must initiate engagement by identifying deviations in the Gemba.

The key to learning is experimentation following PTRS. I never lose; I either win or I learn.

One validated experiment is worth 1000 expert opinions.

Problem solving is my improvement engine that propels me along the path to True North.

Leader Behavior

I Socratically engage my team at the point of pain (problem).

I model PTRS

I overcome my cognitive bias through experimentation. It does not matter how eloquent the theory is or how smart the person is that puts the theory forward. If the experimentation doesn't agree with the theory, then the theory is wrong.

My biggest developmental focus for my team is problem solving capability.

Leader Reflection

Do I think and act this way? If not, what must I adjust?

What must I personally do to improve my problem-solving capability and the problem-solving capability of my team?

End of Chapter GROUP Reflection Questions:

1. Are we progressing on the actions from our last discussion?

2. What was the key learning from the current chapter?

3. As a team, what do we do well as it relates to the key learning?

4. As a team, what do we NOT do well as it relates to the key learning?

5. What do we need to Start, Stop, or Continue doing as a team to improve going forward as it relates to the key learning?

CHAPTER 9

HABIT 7:

RESPECTING PEOPLE

"Clients don't come first. Employees come first. If you take care of the employees, they will take care of the clients."
— *Richard Branson*

While IQ (Intelligence Quotient) is important, EQ (Emotional Intelligence) is more important. People are at the heart of what we do, and people will not care about how much you know until they know how much you care. It is also important to understand that you have what is called an "Emotional Bank Account" with everyone with whom you interact. When you do good for them, you are depositing into the Emotional Bank Account, and when you do bad for them, you are withdrawing from that account. We must be conscious to never become overdrawn in any of the accounts in our relationships. Also, the value of a withdrawal is 10x the value of a deposit, so we can become overdrawn very quickly.

One of the key roles in our business to help manage talent is Human Resources (HR). Notice that I said, "help manage." The ownership of HR belongs to every leader in the business, not the HR group. Below are the seven pillars of HR:

Pillar 1: Talent Acquisition (Recruiting, Screening, Hiring)

Pillar 2: Talent Development (Onboarding, Performance Evaluations, Performance Development)

Pillar 3: Talent Management (Performance Management) - Organizational Learning

Pillar 4: Talent Retention (Succession Planning, Surveys)

Pillar 5: Compensation and Benefits

Pillar 6: Safety and Security

Pillar 7: Culture Change (Intentional) - Organizational Development

The HR group should be experts in each of these areas and ensure they are being executed in alignment with the value creation of the business. They serve as the consultants to the leaders in the business.

When an organization begins a journey to continuous improvement, the following tenants that support respect for people must be considered. The organization must:

- Ensure no loss of regular jobs due to continuous improvement projects.
- Make it easy for people to do the right thing.
- Provide a safe, ergonomically sound working environment.
- Provide challenging work.
- Utilize people to their optimal capability (Who they ARE matches what they are asked to DO.)

I have seen, in many cases, organizations' leaders being critical of the associates without first ensuring the leaders, first, are holding up their end of the employee / management relationship. The table below shows what management owes the associate before they [Management] can expect the associates to provide what the associates owe.

Management Owes:	Associate Owes:
• Meaningful Work	• Engagement to operate, maintain, and improve core processes.
• Follow-up when tasks are given.	
• Processes that Work.	• Safely meeting production rates and designated quality levels.
• Tools/Equipment that Work.	
• Standardized Work Instructions	• Follow Standards
• Response to Problems	• Problem Solve
• Problem Solving Coaching	

One cannot expect associates to do their part until management has first done its part!

VITAL WORKFORCE

The team will be the primary driver of our progress along this journey, so how we view the team will determine how successful we become along the way. If we have not spent time developing our associates, the associates may be considered "unskilled." When associates are perceived as unskilled, those associates will be the first to be removed when cost cutting begins. As you may recall from the "About the Author" section of this book, I was personally a victim of this type of approach in my teenage years. The company for which I worked had a lay-off just before Christmas. They called back after Christmas to let me know I could come back to work. My response was, "No, thanks." I could not see myself working for a company that thought so little of the associates that they would lay them off at Christmas. This company still operates in a similar manner today. With the emergence of temporary labor, they have essentially shifted most of their workforce to temporary labor, which only serves to bolster the perception that they view their associates as an expense.

> "In the military, we give metals to those who sacrifice themselves for others. In business, we give bonuses to those who sacrifice others for themselves." — *Simon Sinek*

At the opposite end of the spectrum, we have what is called a vital work-force. This means we view our associates as a crucial part of our competitive advantage. If we see them as a competitive advantage, we will never consider laying them off in times of cost cutting. Instead, we would leverage them to help us get ready for the next business cycle. If your business were down 50% and you had hopes of it coming back, would you sell 50% of your assets? I think not, so why do it to the team? Are they not more important than assets? Along this line of thinking, there are catch phrases going around these days that refer to the team as assets. I would challenge that thinking. They are better than assets. They are talent. Assets can be owned, but people cannot be. The graphic below shows the various mindsets and how those ideals translate to our perception of the team.

NON-BLAMING NON-JUDGMENTAL

Another key to creating the proper environment for continuous improvement is to create an environment in which each member of the team, especially leaders, are non-blaming and non-judgmental. When a problem occurs, instead of assigning blame to an individual or department, we must focus our understanding on what happened and why it happened to prevent the problem from recurring.

> "The measure of success is not whether you have a tough problem to deal with, but whether it is the same problem you had last year." — *John Foster Dulles*

Blaming leads to fear, mistrust, and the misrepresentation of "bad news." If members of the team fear sharing bad news with the boss, they may not tell the entire story when communicating an issue. This will, in turn, inhibit the leader's ability to help solve problems, since they do not have all the relevant information. We must also focus on the issue or problem and not the person. If you have worked with me, you have no doubt heard me use the phrase, "Hard on the problem, easy on the people." I have leaders push back on this by saying, "But, Harold you do not know Jimmy. He is different and no process can be created to prevent him from making a mistake." At this point, I refer them back to the Maynard story where Toyota used Maynard as a test of processes to ensure processes were developed so anyone can run them. I firmly embrace this adage, and if practiced, I believe it creates an open, trusting, and communications-rich environment.

> "Fear is a mind killer." — *Mike McKee*

This trusting environment allows "real issues" to emerge. Surfacing real issues with all relevant information will increase our problem-solving capability. When we give our teams the license to act in this way, we need to be very cautious. When the team is being frank with us, it may hurt a little. The truth hurts. As leaders, sometimes it is easier to believe a lie that you have heard a thousand times, than the truth which you have only heard once. In the case where the business has fallen for untruths, we must get all the liars around the table to find out what is the real truth. Can you handle the truth?

PROBLEM RESPONSE

As we empower the team to improve the business, we must also ensure we rapidly identify problems. Ideally, we want to have a quick response to problems, like the nervous system's responses in the human body. If your hand touches something hot, your body responds in milliseconds. The body's response is to protect itself. In business, the faster we can respond to problems the faster we can protect the business. This allows us to contain cost and be able to determine the root cause accurately. The further we get in time from when the problem first occurred, the less likely we are to be able to solve that problem and the more costly the problem will be. In some cases, when a problem has reached our customer, we resort to "creative writing" to appease them. This is due to too much time having passed since the defect was produced. We literally may not know what happened or how to find out what happened.

Our ability to solve a problem is indirectly proportional to distance (time and space) from the problem. Time is of the essence when we are trying to contain problems. When it comes to business performance, reliance on data review on a monthly, weekly, or even daily basis is not sufficient. When we are discussing the previous month's performance, it is like performing an autopsy. The questions we are asking are, "Why did the patient die?" If we have the correct problem response system in place and are better at taking vital signs continuously as close to real-time as possible, the question can then become, "Why is the patient sick?" If we know the patient is sick, we can take measures to cure the patient.

One of our main business-improvement focuses must be to expose problems, so those problems can be resolved. Listed below are four of the most used methods used to help expose problems:

- Visual Management Tools
- Live Pareto / Alarm Levels
- Production Control Board / MDI
- Andon / Line Stop

Earlier I explained that leaders must check the health of the system. The items above are part of the system and must be monitored to ensure they are being used. However, if they are used by the process operators, but not responded to by leadership, they are useless, and we have disrespected the people by asking them to do something that is not important enough for us to check.

ESCALATION POLICY

Exposing the problem is only part of the equation; we must also respond to the exposed problem. One method to ensure proper problem response is to have an escalation policy. This policy provides the structure, the expectation, and the permission the team will need to 'escalate' up through the organization when a problem arises. Many teams have spent little to no time developing their plan for when a problem arises. We should have a response plan BEFORE the problem arises. We have plans for fires, tornadoes, and hurricanes even though those events rarely happen. We have plans, and we run drills to practice those plans. When was the last time you practiced responding to the process when a problem arose? We must raise the urgency in the minds of leadership to respond to problems. If we considered all deviations from the standard to be "EVIL," we will put such a plan in place. Unfortunately, most companies consider deviations from the standard as NORMAL. This is what is referred to as Normalized-Deviations from standard, and these deviations have simply blended into the environment over time.

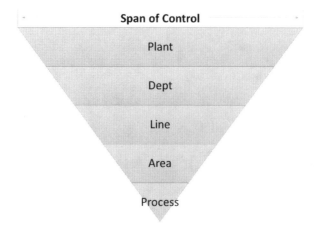

The graphic above shows how the span of control increases as you rise in an organization. As time passes after a problem has been escalated, the level in the organization getting involved is higher. The reason is the higher up in the organization you go, the more span of control you have, which allows you to pull in resources and remove barriers. What may be a feat for a process level person, can be the stroke of a pen for a President. The key to proper escalation is to ensure flow is restored and root cause corrective action is implemented. The leader is responsible for ensuring this escalation process is followed. Escalation also ensures the top leaders are not laboring under the delusion that things are going well at the process level when they are not going well.

A great example of an escalation policy was demonstrated during a tour of the Fuji Plant in Greenwood, SC. A team from Bosch was benchmarking Fuji to see their improvement process. Fuji has lots of machines and the products move very fast. These machines run in a dimly lit manufacturing area since they make a light sensitive product. During the tour, one of the machines stopped as indicated by the Andon light turning red, and very quickly all the machines stopped. The room was full of machines with red Andon lights at this point. Fuji did not have lots of inventory in their system, so at this point the entire process was stopped. The tour waited to see what would happen next. Soon after the machine stopped, a light above the problem machine came on. This made it very easy to see where the problem machine was located. After a few seconds, there was a group of people running toward the machine. One of the tour participants stated that it was odd that they could run in the plant. The tour guide's response was, "You can only run for fire and downtime." The response team that ran to the machine quickly got the machine started and all but one of them returned to the office. The one that stayed behind was with the machine operator. Another tour participant asked the tour guide why they were still there. The tour guide responded with, "They have restored the flow, and now they must do Root Cause Correct Action (RCCA) to ensure whatever caused this stoppage never happens again.

Any response to a problem is better than no response at all, but we should also consider having a standard response. The example above is what I would call a world-class example of problem response. Most companies consider restoring flow to be the only response to problems. However, this will only build the organization's ability to be heroic. Our challenge will be to restore flow and then move into identifying the root causes of the interruption. Most companies do a poor job at identifying root causes. As mentioned above. failure to identify causes of these stoppages stems from the belief that deviations from the standard are normal.

As we begin solving problems, we should target solving the problem at the lowest possible level of the organization. Most problems can be solved with simple tools that anyone can use. This is referred to as core problem solving. This method is best deployed on acute (special cause) problems where there is an assignable cause, and it must be deployed in a timely manner. Advanced statistical problem-solving tools are only needed to solve the most complex situations. This approach relies heavily on the analysis of data. This advanced method is best deployed on chronic (common cause) problems, where there is a constant level of variation that is not acceptable to the customer. I would also propose that if the lower-level approaches cannot solve the problem, we should leverage advanced problem-solving techniques.

Common cause variation in a process not only impacts quality to the customer, it also decreases process capability (aka CpK). Anytime we have reduced capability in the process, we cannot run it at the desired speed for fear of creating or sending defective products downstream. Some companies simply ignore this and "sort it all out" at the end of the process. It should go without saying this is a horrible strategy. I always tell clients to think of their process capability as a car (the car width is the width of the process distribution) and their process tolerances as the width of a tollbooth. If the width of the car is the same width of the tollbooth and you are exactly in the center of the tollbooth (CpK = 1), how fast do you think you can drive through that tollbooth? The answer is not very fast. You must slow down to ensure you do not hit the mirrors. Hitting the mirrors is analogous to going out of the specification range for the process. Assuming I have worked to improve my process capability (CpK => 1.66), and the variation is narrower, it would be like riding a motorcycle through the center of that same narrow tollbooth. Now I can go at a much faster speed with no worry of hitting the mirrors.

I have mentioned two methods (Core and Advanced) to solve problems thus far. There is another method between Improvement Ideas and CPS that I call Quick Kill. It is a precursor to CPS and is not as rigid. However, if the quick kill is not quick and does not kill the problem, we must move to CPS. The third method is called 8D. I consider it an intermediate method between Core and Advanced. It is a systematic approach that was developed by Ford. We were required to follow this method at Bosch when we sent defects to them. This method was eventually widely adopted in the automotive industry. I consider it a great approach when you must have the formality of sharing your findings with a customer or outside auditor. With that in mind, I recommend the 8D approach for all EHS and Customer Quality issues. I would also recommend you coach your suppliers on the use of the 8D for any supplier quality issues. However, it would not be wise to train every employee in the business on all the methods of problem solving. This would be considered over-processing from a training standpoint, which would be wasteful. Lastly, but not least, is the process of getting improvement ideas for free. I believe 100% of the organization should be engaged in providing ideas to improve the business.

Below is my recommended training percentage by level of problem-solving method/complexity.

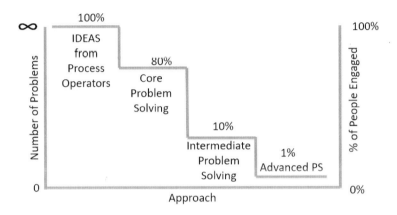

As these methods are deployed, we will begin solving more problems and coming up with better countermeasures. We will need to validate the effectiveness of these countermeasures, standardize those countermeasures across our other processes. As we improve the processes, we are showing respect for the team.

Jeffery Liker, in his book The Toyota Way presented some principles which align perfectly with the habit of Respect for People.

- Use only reliable, thoroughly tested technology that serves the team and processes.

  - Using technology to support people, not to replace them; understanding that humans will always be needed for what they are good at, which is problem-solving, intellect, judgment, flexibility, and unique "artisanal" tasks. There will be an increase from 1 to 1 (man to machine) to 1 to many, but never 0 to many.

- Understanding new technology is often unreliable and difficult to standardize and therefore endangers flow.

- Rejecting or modifying technologies that conflict with your culture or that might disrupt stability, reliability, and predictability.

- Implementing quickly a thoroughly considered technology if it has been proven in trials and it can improve flow in your processes.

When I was with Bosch, I inherited a project from a previous engineer that was focused on upgrading our robot system. The robot system was used to place adhesive and lids on the Anti-Lock Brake units. I had not been involved in the project planning phase since it was handed off to me after that phase had been completed. However, I wanted to be present for the installation. The installation started at the end of 2nd shift one Friday night. The plan was to have 3 shift coverage to get the installation completed over the weekend. I came in early on Saturday to check progress. They had already taken the old robot out and installed the new robot. Their next step was to swap out the control system. They looked like they had it under control and were on schedule, so I let them continue. I came back in early on Sunday morning, and the engineers were struggling to get the new robot to run. I stayed with them to see if there was anything I could do to help. I asked if they had seen the problem on any other installation, and one of the engineers said no they had not, since they had never installed this type of robot system before. It was a new robot and control system, and we were going to be the first ones to use it. The way she said it made me think she thought that was a good idea. Having had my butt handed to me by some of my customers for missing deliveries, I did not like the idea of using untested technology at all. I immediately made the unpopular decision to rip the new robot out and put the old one back in. Why would I make such a call? See Jeffery's principle above. If that robot is not running or runs poorly, it will be the team working weekends to make up for it, and I was not going to let that happen on my watch.

Another quick story was of a laser in Honduras. I was visiting the plant about once per month at that point. Before then, I had spent a year and a half setting up the factory for flow, but now I was in coaching mode with them. They got a deal on the laser and had purchased it between one of my visits. The laser in question was used to lase logos onto wooden blocks for some customers. You basically had to be an engineer to run it. One day when I was working to stabilize the process, I looked at the back panel, and there is where I saw the problem on the nameplate. It was serial number 00001. You never want to be the one to get SN00001.

When it comes to technology, it is either a push (new technology looking for a problem to solve) or a pull (a problem that requires technology as a solution). As leaders our job is to ensure it does not ultimately negatively impact the people it is meant to help.

Let us continue with Jeffery's principles…

- Grow leaders who thoroughly understand the work, live the philosophy, and teach the philosophy to others.

- Grow leaders from within, rather than buying them from outside the organization. I would only modify this to include an 80:20 split to encourage outside hires 20% of the time which should introduce "fresh eyes" and new thinking to the business. A good example of having to get "fresh eyes" in the business is when GM tasked its current engineers with reducing the weight of their vehicles in response to the oil embargo in the 70's. The current engineers were so ingrained in their thinking that they could not conceive of weight savings. GM had to get young engineers that did not know they could not reduce the weight. The results were significant weight reductions in GM's new vehicle models.

- Leaders must be role models of the company's philosophy and business procedures.

- A good leader must understand the daily work in detail so he or she can be the best teacher of your company's philosophy.

- Develop exceptional people and teams who follow your company's philosophy.

  - Create a strong, stable culture in which company values and beliefs are widely shared and "lived out" over a period of many years.

  - Train people to work within the corporate philosophy to achieve results. Work tirelessly to reinforce the culture continually.

  - Empower people to use the company's tools to improve the company.

  - Teach individuals how to work together in teams toward common goals.

- Respect your extended network of partners and suppliers by challenging them and helping them improve.

  - Treat your partners and suppliers as an extension of your business.

  - Challenge your outside business partners to grow and develop. It shows that you value them. Set challenging targets and help your partners reach them.

From my experience, most suppliers are willing to work with you if you treat them with respect. During one of the few full weeks, I was home during my consulting career, I got a call from the CFO of one of my clients. He asked me what I was doing the next day. I told him I had plenty to do, but I would make time for him, since the sound of his voice communicated urgency. He stated that they had a supply issue with a part that was being purchased through a distribution network. The distribution company said everything was on backorder, and they couldn't get the part for months. This was a big deal, since my client had 20 of their products already sitting in the lot waiting on this part, and two months would be 30 more in the lot. My client had located the OEM of the part. However, the OEM would not answer their phone. The CFO needed to know if they were still in business and if they could order parts directly from the factory. I knew my client had enough volume to justify direct buys, so I agreed to go pay the plant a visit. The plant was only an hour west from where I was living at the time. I scoured my network and found a contact that lived near the plant and had a contact inside the company. My contact stated that he could get me lunch with the Engineering Manager. I told him that was great and had him tell the Engineering Manager what I was looking for from his company. I needed 200 of their tanks and I needed them fast; they could name their price. My contact relayed the message and responded back later telling me that the Engineering Manager canceled the lunch. My contact also told me that that Engineering Manager said there was zero chance of me getting tanks, since they were months behind on orders to their current customers, and their current customers' products costed $200K. I held back the fact that I was putting this tank on a product that costed $2M. I guess I was too aggressive with my request, and I had blown my opportunity to speak with someone at the plant. I had to help my client, so my plan B was to drive to the plant the next day and sit in the parking lot. I arrived at the plant at 7am. I had some other calls, so I was on conference calls while there was no activity at the front door of the plant. However, when someone would walk from their car to the entrance, I would tell my caller to hold-on a minute and ask the person walking up to the plant a question. To the first person I saw, I asked what they did there, what their name was, and who was the GM. He told me his name, he was an engineer, and the GM was Jimmy Carlisle (pseudonym). I thanked him and let him go on his way. To the second person I saw, I asked if Jimmy Carlisle had arrived yet. He stated no he won't arrive until around 8am, but I noticed where he had looked to make his assessment of whether the GM was there. I surmised that was the GM's normal parking spot. To the third person, I stated, "I see that Jimmy Carlisle isn't here yet (pointing to the empty parking spot), what is he driving these days?" The person responded with, "A white Lincoln." I stated, "I thought he had a white Cadillac (I had no idea what he used to drive)." The person stated, "Well, he used to drive a Cadillac, but he traded it for the Lincoln." [that was pure luck]. Now, all I had to do was wait for a white Lincoln with a guy named Jimmy Carlisle to pull up into that parking spot. As 8am approached, in drove a white Lincoln and it pulled into the spot. I got out of my truck and approached the guy that I assumed was Jimmy Carlisle. It was Jimmy. I introduced myself, told him that I had driven over from Knoxville that morning, I needed 208 (4 per week for 52 weeks) pieces of a part that they made at that plant, and I would pay 10x what they normally sell for. He said, "Well, Harold I wouldn't normally do this, but I don't normally get approached by a guy in my parking lot wanting to buy parts. Come to my office and let's see what we can do." We went to his office, and he called in his senior staff [minus the Engineering Manager, and I didn't tell them I had reached out to the Engineering Manager] and told them to figure out how they could get started on my 208 tanks. Within an hour, my client was on the way to being set up as a customer and we had parts the following week. Before I left Jimmy's office, I thanked him for making the deal happen so quickly, and he thanked me for not mugging him in the parking lot. It turns out that was the first thought that came to his mind as I approached him. Now that the deal was done, I had a few hours to kill, since I promised my contact who lived in the area that I would have lunch with him. To kill time before lunch, I went to a nice coffee shop to get some work done. While at the coffee shop, I got a text from my contact asking if the Engineering Manager could join us for lunch. I said, "Certainly, and let him know that I have a story to tell him." When I arrived at the lunch location, the Engineering Manager met me at the door. He said, "Harold, I owe you an apology." He had obviously heard of my visit to the plant that morning. I responded with, "No you don't. If you had not canceled on me, I wouldn't have had the balls to go sit in the parking lot." We had a great lunch, and I made another friend.

Concerning the selection of suppliers…

> "It is unwise to pay too much but it is also unwise to pay too little. When you pay too much, you lose a little money; that is all.

When you pay too little, sometimes you lose everything, because the thing you bought is incapable of doing the thing it was bought to do. The common law of business balance prohibits paying a little and getting a lot – it cannot be done. If you deal with the lowest bidder, it is well to add something for the risk you run. And if you do that you will have the money to pay for something better." – John Ruskin

I have had two bad encounters with my customers that have stuck with me my entire career. One is with whom I will call Company A and the other is with whom I will call Company B. The Company A encounter was probably deserved but could have been handled differently. The Electronic Control Unit (ECU) that goes into the Anti-Lock Braking System (ABS) is very complicated and not easy to manufacture. It was so challenging that even though Company A bought the rights to make it, we still made it for them. However, we had let the quality of the product slip, mostly due to a chemistry change in the gold pad material that was 100% out of our control, but Company A did not care. They bought the part from us, not our supplier. The peak of the problem was when Company A sent Joe (may or may not be a pseudonym) to see us. He showed up at the conference room with two things in his hands: a 2x4 and a brown paper bag. He laid the 2x4 on the table and said it symbolized what was about to happen, and for the next two hours, he figuratively took a 2x4 for our A%#. We were filming the meeting since we wanted everyone in the division to feel our pain. However, at the end of the beating, I meant meeting, he made us turn off the video. He then pulled out a competitor's (a Company A subsidiary at the time) ABS unit. He told us it was a drop-in replacement for our unit, so we had better get our act together. He said they paid more for Bosch products because of the quality, but he was not getting the quality. I learned what it was like to work under extreme pressure during that time, but we got our act together!

The Company B encounter was not as dramatic, but it did give me a bad impression of Company B from a supplier point of view. One of the

Company B supplier development coaches set up an improvement event on one of my lines. To learn as much as we could, I told my team to share everything they could with the Company B coach. The team had a great time and learned a lot; the issue was what happened at the end of the event. The Company B coach reported the potential savings and stated that they wanted half of that savings now, and we could have the other half after we implemented all the changes. Some of the changes were very long-term and others may not even happen. That was the last time I allowed Company B to come to one of my areas to "help."

"Good artists copy; Great artists steal." — *Picasso*

Company B had not always had that approach, and I am sure they have tempered that approach recently. Believe it or not, but Company B was a big part of Toyota's start in the automotive business. Toyota visited Company B's plant in the 50's to benchmark their processes. There was no shame in what Toyota was doing because Company B had set the standard for productivity in the industry at that time. Toyota took what they learned from Company B and redesigned their entire manufacturing process. They were grateful to Company B and planned a 25-year reunion to bring the original team back together. One of Toyota's comments after the visit was that they could not believe that Company B had not improved / changed what they had been doing in the last 25 years. Toyota had started from a position behind Company B, but by continuously improving they eventually surpassed them.

"Train people well enough so they can leave. Treat them well enough so they don't want to." — *Sir Richard Branson*

As we grow and develop our people, we should consider a lesson nature has given us concerning bonsai trees. A bonsai tree will only grow as large as the pot in which it is planted. As leaders, we determine the size of the pot for our teams. If we limit the individual or team, it is our fault; not theirs.

A discussion around Respect for People would not be complete without discussing some of the reasons people leave companies. Based on the Department of Labor's statistics, the TOP 3 reasons people leave their jobs are outlined below:

#1 Reason – Immediate Supervisor

- Lack of accountability
- Favoritism
- Lack of communication
- Lack of credibility/has not earned respect
- Lack of the knowledge/skill to do the job properly

Countermeasures:

- Build leadership of the Front-Line Managers (FLM's)
- Ensure leaders are in leadership positions
- Grow leadership intentionally (own this yourself)
- Pay for performance/ focus on go-getters (we will discuss later)
- Perform evaluations and develop plans for everyone
- Ensure FLM's are engaging people in problem solving

#2 Reason – Performance Acknowledgement

- Inability to see how they can make an impact
- Belief that they are being paid unfairly for their work
- Belief that poor associates receive similar pay as excellent associates
- Inability to advance and learn new skills

Countermeasures:

- Pay for Performance/ focus on go-getters
- Engage people in problem solving

#3 Reason – Work Environment

- Poor physical conditions (noise, temperature, danger, disorganization)

- Poor cultural conditions (firefighting, repeat problems, lack of problem response)
- Unhelpful fellow associates/ lack of teamwork

Countermeasures:

- Problem response system
- Engage people in problem solving
- 5S (Workplace Organization)
- Safety management

Leaders have a huge impact on whether the team feels respected or valued. Leaders must be present with their teams setting the expectations. When leaders neglect to inspect that which they expect, they have abdicated their roles as leaders in the organization.

> "Leader Standard Work is about discipline, sustainment, and accountability. Expecting Discipline, Sustainment, and accountability without Leader Standard Work is a fantasy."
> — Mike Rother

Hajime Ohba (Vice President and General Manager at Toyota Production System Support Center Inc.) stated, "Checking = Respect." He always said, "When you tell people that it is important to do something, but you show them that it isn't important enough for you to check it, then they feel you have lied to them and they feel disrespected. Eventually they stop checking not because they are lazy, but because they know (from your actions) that it is not important."

At the start of this book, I gave a warning that I was going to be very hard on leaders. This is true, but I also think that if I am to be hard on them, I should give clear guidance around developing leaders that can be Habitually Excellent and support Habitual Excellence in the business.

DEVELOPING LEADERS

Leadership shouldn't be seen as something we have to do it should be seen as something we get to do. Therefore, we must have leaders that see leading others as a privilege, not a right or a chore. Furthermore, since leadership is the number one reason for people leaving a company, we should spend a good portion of our time developing leadership. I firmly believe that once people know what needs to be done, they will do it. Now that the team has learned the habits it takes to become excellent, we will address the development of leadership.

When it comes to developing leaders within the enterprise, the top officer must be responsible. A leader who is truly Character-based is much more predictable and trustworthy. A leader that is Personality-based (putting on a front) can get away with it for a while, but when the heat is on, the true character of this leader will surface.

To avoid this, we must understand what Leadership is and is not, and be able to see leadership in others. Leadership is NOT being a manager. Leading and managing is not one and the same; cost and time are managed, and people are led. The table below shows a comparison of management and leadership:

Management (Vital)	Leadership (Vital)
• Doing things right	• Do the right things
• Urgency (Eisenhower Quadrants 1 & 3)	• Importance (Eisenhower Quadrants 1 & 2)
• Speed	• Velocity (Speed and Direction)
• Bottom Line (Egg)	• Top line (Goose)
• Efficiency	• Effectiveness
• Methods	• Purpose
• Practices	• Principles/Habits
• Work IN the System	• Work ON the System
• Climb the ladder quickly	• Is the ladder leaning against the right wall?

In the case of the entrepreneur, they don't worry about climbing the ladder. They want to own the ladder.

Leadership is NOT being an entrepreneur. There is a large misperception that all salespeople and entrepreneurs are leaders.

Leadership is NOT being knowledgeable. Knowledge and intelligence can take you places, but it will not make you a leader.

Leadership is NOT being a pioneer. Just because somebody is out in front of a crowd does not mean they are a leader. To be a leader, one must be out in front AND have people intentionally following their lead and acting on the vision.

> "A vision without action is a dream. Action without vision is a nightmare." — *Unknown*

Leadership is NOT having the top position. The number one leadership myth is that leadership is based on position.

Leadership IS influence; no more, no less. To have influence you must operate at a certain level of leadership. A weak leader cannot lead strong leaders. To lead strong leaders, one must be a strong leader themselves. If you are a strong leader and have had to work for a weak leader, you know what I mean here.

Bad News! You currently have a personal brand. Your personal branding is what people say about you when you are not in the room. Your influence today is dictated by the example you have set up to this point. If you think people are not watching, and do not care or even know the example you set, you are sorely mistaken. People in positions of authority are always living in the fishbowl in the middle of a packed stadium; everyone is watching from all sides. The higher the position the larger the stadium in which the fishbowl is set. If you have not turned positional authority into leadership influence, you have a long journey ahead of you! If you do not develop these habits, you will not have influence and you will NOT be followed. If you are in a leadership position, not having people want to follow you makes you ineffective. You can't have a leader if there is no team.

Having influence down the organizational structure is important, but there are also times when you need to influence up in the organization. When you find that you cannot directly influence the position above you, you should find the influencer of that position and work to influence them. I call this influencing the influencer.

You must also understand where your influence lays to determine where to focus. The graphic below shows the relationship between your circle of influence and your circle of concern.

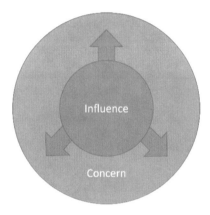

The key is to focus on that which you can influence; not that which you are simply concerned. As a leader, you only have so much leadership capital to expend with your team, so spend it wisely by focusing on what matters most and what you can control. Don't waste your capital on trivial items in the business or with the team (e.g. policies that don't matter in the long run). As you focus on what you can influence, you will grow your circle of influence which in turns grows your circle of concern.

Good News! Leadership can be learned. While there are aspects of leadership that are nature, most leadership ability is nurtured by having a strong mentor-mentee relationship in place. Once you learn the principles and habits of good leadership, you must practice them and apply them to your life. Develop these habits and apply the principles and people WILL follow you.

The beginnings of good leadership require no talent. As proof, below is a list of 10 things that one can do with no talent:

Effort	Being Coachable
Body Language (Yes, People Notice)	Do Extra / Go Beyond
Energy	Be Prepared
Attitude	Be Ontime
Passion	Work Ethic

"Don't judge a man by where he is, but by what he had to overcome to get where he is." — Booker T. Washington

LEADERSHIP TRAITS

"People come to work to succeed, not to fail. It is the leader's responsibility to lead them to success."
— Norman Schwartzkopf

If a leader is wanting to be effective, they cannot "mail" it in each day. The leader must demonstrate qualities and characteristics that support the long-term effectiveness of the team. There are many traits for which we should expect in our leaders. Below are a few that I think are the most important:

Dependability

The perception of being trustworthy and capable of being counted upon by your peers, direct reports, and leaders.

The use of the word perception is intentional here. Perception is reality, so if the perception is you are not trustworthy, you must own changing that perception.

Professionalism

A favorable impression in appearance and conduct created by exhibiting a courteous, conscientious, and generally business-like manner in the workplace.

Courage

The mental or moral strength to venture, persevere and withstand difficulty. The drive and the desire to meet new challenges head on. Afterall, fortune favors the brave. Richard Branson once stated, "The brave may not live forever. but the [overly] cautious never really live at all."

Decisiveness

The ability to make decisions promptly and to express them in a clear, concise, and confident manner. Especially when others are not being decisive. Understanding the risk of inaction.

Empathy

The action of understanding, being aware of, being sensitive to, and vicariously experiencing the feelings, thoughts, and experience of another of either the past or present without having the feelings, thoughts, and experience fully communicated in an objectively explicit manner.

Endurance

The mental or physical ability to withstand hardship or misfortune that often comes with being a leader.

Enthusiasm

The genuine expression of strong excitement and emotion which inspires action of one's team.

Initiative

The beginning of action in the absence of tasks or responsibilities.

Integrity

Honesty of character and soundness of moral principles.

Judgment

The process of forming an opinion or evaluation by showing insight and understanding, accompanied by comparison using all the available data and information.

Justice

The ability to be impartial and consistent, using facts – not personality, to determine action.

Knowledge

The condition of knowing something with familiarity, which includes the job, the tools, and the people, that one works with. The higher in the organization you go, the less you will need to know about technical things and the more you will need to lean on leadership. The old saying that knowledge is power is flawed. Knowledge is potential power. If that knowledge is not put to work or shared with others, then it is wasted potential.

Tact

A keen sense of what to do or say to maintain good relations with others or avoid offense. One definition of tact that has stuck with me over the years is, "being able to tell someone to go to hell and have them look forward to going."

Unselfishness

Not being concerned excessively or exclusively with yourself (law of sacrifice).

Loyalty

The distinguishing characteristics of truth and trustworthiness towards one's peers, direct reports, and managers. Loyalty also means sticking with those that stuck with you when no one else would. There is an old saying that communicates this very idea. The old saying is "Don't forget who brought you to the dance."

How do you stack up against what I have covered so far? The key is to know your capabilities and always seek self-improvement. Work very hard to be strategically, tactically, and technically proficient. Develop a sense of responsibility and ownership among your team. Ensure your team makes timely decisions. You should set the example here. Know your team and look out for their welfare. Ensure you keep your team informed. Take responsibility for your actions and the actions of your team. Tasks can be delegated, but responsibility is held by the leader. Never abdicate your responsibility. Ensure that assigned tasks are understood, supervised, and accomplished. Train your team together. Only delegate tasks to the team according to their capabilities. If you are not satisfied with their abilities, work to improve it.

The best way to manage is to assign objectives and allow the person the self-control to achieve the objective. When we see issues with delegation and/or micromanagement, we know there is an issue with a lack of trust in the abilities or integrity of subordinates or a manager's need for control. The corresponding reasons for this are the leader's failure to train subordinates or the leader's needs to feel needed, respectively.

> "Never be a prisoner of your past. It was simply a lesson; not a life sentence." — *Unknown*

If a leader does not trust members of the team or does not see them as worth training, then the leader should question why those people are on the team.

True delegation can lead to empowerment. The levels of empowerment are:

Level 1: Wait until told

Level 2: Ask for instructions

Level 3: Bring recommendations

Level 4: Do it and report back immediately

Level 5: Do it and report back routinely

Level 6: Simply do it (True Empowerment)

Our goal is to create a team where we can consistently operate at level six. Having members operating at lower levels will keep the leader busy managing and not leading.

LEADERSHIP PHILOSOPHIES

Now that we have covered the traits (who the leader is) of a leader, let us look at some leadership philosophies that will be at work when leadership has been properly developed. Consider these philosophies as "what the leader does."

"How you do anything is how you do everything." — Unknown

Set Direction

Create a compelling directionally correct vision that is understood and shared by all.

Initiate Action

Have the attitude of "If it is to be, it is up to me." Initiate action within yourself and others.

"Determine never to be idle. It is wonderful how much can be accomplished if we are always doing." — Thomas Jefferson

Organize Systems

Ensure that solutions interface with other countermeasures into a holistic system that does not require a hero to sustain it.

Hustle

There is a story about two frogs that found themselves in a bucket of milk. Strange I know but stick with me here. There is a moral of the story, I promise. One of the frogs was lazy and only jumped a few jumps. That frog eventually sank below the surface of the milk and drowned. The other frog had hustle and refused to give up, so he kept jumping. Eventually, the milk was churned into butter from his constant jumping. His hard work had paid off and his reward was being able to exit the bucket with his life.

Success is at the intersection of hard work and preparation. Never be out-worked, out-hustled, out-prepared, or out-cared; EVER! Always ensure you "get it" and "show it". Consistency is key. No one has ever changed the world working 40hrs per week.

Study while others are Sleeping
Work while others are Loafing
Prepare while others are Playing
Do while others are Daydreaming

My personal approach is, "I will out work and our learn anyone." This stems from growing up with nothing and having to work to get what I have.

"A great leader fills the gap between what was and what can be." — *Unknown*

Being a great leader requires sacrifice. Many people today want to climb the corporate ladder because they believe that freedom and power are the prizes waiting at the top. They do not realize that the true nature of leadership is sacrifice. When you become a leader, you lose the right to think about yourself.

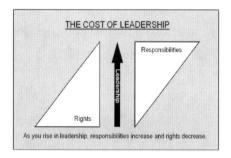

"We don't believe that rank has its privileges; we believe rank has its responsibilities." — *Unknown*

Enable Effectiveness

Make it easy for people to do the right thing. Give people what they need to be successful. Practice Line Back as a leader – provide support, take away waste.

Value Time

You are expected to contribute 100% while at work. Efficiently use your time to meet company goals. Spend sufficient time in quadrant 2 (important, but not urgent items) to be effective long-term. Develop ways to save time in the processes and with people and teams. Our time is limited - never waste it. Time is the one thing of which we cannot make more.

Empower People

Do not wait for others to give you a solution. Empower yourself to solve problems. Do not do everything on your own. Utilize your teams and resources effectively. Take extreme ownership in your area. Develop others so that they can do it on their own the next time.

Avoid Waste

There is a lot of emphasis put on eliminating waste in a process, but the best thing is to never let that waste get into the process. This approach is a design imperative, so when designing processes, one must ensure the waste is designed out. This applies to product as well as process design.

Eliminate Waste

Scrap, rework, process downtime, extra movement, too many people, poor workflow, poor organization, lack of cycle time balance, etc., all contribute to waste. Identify and eliminate waste in your area. Look for those hidden factories that are covering up problems.

Be Innovative

Find creative solutions to problems. If we have always done it a certain way and it still has problems, then we must find another way to do it. Challenge yourself and others to find many possible solutions, then choose the one that makes the most sense. Take calculated risks to find new ways to achieve success. Think outside of the box.

Continuous Improvement IS Our Future

Competition in business is fierce. We must continuously improve just to keep-up. The fact is the competition is improving more and improving faster. If we want our business to thrive, we must have EVERYONE committed to continuous improvement. Be active in continuous improvement and focus on projects, rapid improvement events and just-do-its that improve our key measures. Expect and Lead Improvement with every person, on every process, every day.

Use Your Head

Make sound decisions based on data and logic while considering the impact on others. Find the root cause of problems. Think about the big picture (embrace the total system). Focus on systems. Think beyond the fix. Think long-term.

Abundance Mentality

Understand that there is enough recognition to go around for everybody. Everyone is good at something, and everyone can bring something to the team that nobody else has. There is plenty to do and plenty of benefits to getting them done. Share information and recognition with others. Let us get to the top as a team!

Build Trust

Confront people with whom you have a conflict (mutual learning). Do not discuss other people's shortcomings with anyone but that person. Do not spread rumors. Do not Gossip. I define gossip as a negative discussion about someone in their absent that isn't aimed at helping that person improve. Get all the facts. Ensure that everything is communicated. Also, be careful whose toes you step on today, since they may be connected to the butt you have to kiss tomorrow. Take people out to lunch that you would not normally take to lunch.

> "Everyone likes to eat, but few want to hunt." — *Unknown*

Be the Hunter

In this age of global competition there are two kinds of companies: the hunters and the hunted. We want to be hunters. Find ways to give us a competitive edge. Take initiative to make improvements without being asked or prompted.

Respond Quickly

Procrastination is the grave in which opportunities are buried. By procrastinating, you only compound the problem. Do not procrastinate. The largest nation today is procrasti-nation; do not add to its population. Get things done as they are identified. Learn to prioritize. Consistently meet deadlines. Communicate your commitment to the team.

> "It is a capital mistake to theorize before one has data. Insensibly, one begins to twist facts to suit the theories, instead." — *Sherlock Holmes.*

Communicate Honesty

As Lord Kelvin said back in 1883; when you cannot express your knowledge in numbers, your knowledge is of a meager and unsatisfactory kind, so you must Speak with Data. In this age of blatant "Fact-Free Decision Making", you can stand out if you have facts when presenting your point. Your data does not have to be perfect, but we would rather be approximately right than precisely wrong. Focus on the situation, not the person. Give your peers continuous feedback, both positive feedback and constructive feedback, often referred to as constructive criticism, on development needs. You too must be able to accept feedback. Use mutual learning.

Process Yields Results

We cannot improve things by just hoping they will get better. Hope is not a strategy. We must implement systems, tools, and processes which will lay the groundwork for future positive results. Avoid problems by doing things right the first time (equipment and product design/ process capability). We must focus on the root cause of our problems. We must solve the problems correctly the first time. A strong process will yield long term results. Focus on WHAT the problem is (not who). Ask WHY five times; not the 5 Who's.

Lead by Example

Remember "If it is to be, it is up to me!" Do not dwell on what others are doing (or not doing). Focus on yourself. Always win with integrity, so you can sleep with yourself at night. You cannot win if you are not right within. Do the best job possible and encourage others to follow.

> "Wrong is wrong; it doesn't matter who is doing it. Right is right; even if no one is doing it." — *Dabo Swinney*

Set the example in everything you do at work or outside of work. For example, I don't know of one successful person that leaves their shopping carts in the middle of a parking lot. If you are too big to do the small things, then you are too small to do the big things.

Make it Happen

I was very fond of the moniker given to me at Bosch. They would call me "Make it Happen Chapman," and I worked very hard to have that never be a false statement. Do not wait for others to solve your problems. Find out what you need, get what you need, and do it yourself. Get help from your teammates, resources, and managers. Overcome obstacles by attacking problems from different angles. Follow-up regularly with those that must help you. Be the power sponsor, by removing barriers and adding resources to ensure the right things are getting done.

> "Some people want it to happen, some wish it would happen, others make it happen." — *Michael Jordan*

Be Fair

Use the golden rule (Do unto others as you would have them do unto you). This does not mean "Do unto others as they have done to you." Assume that, like you, everyone is here to try to do a good job. Seek win/win solutions to all problems. Rigidly follow policies. If a policy is not fair, follow it while trying to get it changed; do not simply violate it. If you as a leader violate rules, what message does that send to your team?

Commit to Quality

Strongly focus on the long-term quality of the product. Understand that it is critical and that our work can improve lives. Create and lead teams and initiatives that improve quality. Communicate quality issues to all involved. Use analytical problem-solving tools and communicate solutions with Core Problem Solving A3's. Become an advanced problem solver and focus on high-impact quality issues.

People Make Quality

Understand that the ultimate responsibility of quality lies with people; the people that design, build, deliver, and install our product or deliver our service. Solve quality problems by getting all the people involved.

Lead Situationally

Practice situational leadership and understand that it is an adaptive leadership style. Leaders must take stock of their team members. This requires them to not practice a one-size-fits-all leadership style. The leader must weigh the many variables in their workplace and choose the leadership style that best fits their goals and circumstances individually.

Welcome Mistakes

The first thing you do when you find yourself in a hole is to stop digging. If you make mistakes, admit them, and adjust accordingly. Making mistakes is not the issue. It is how we deal with those mistakes that is the issue. Losers make mistakes and then make excuses. Winners make mistakes and then make changes to ensure the same mistake doesn't happen again. An old mentor of mine once told me, "If you are going to be dumb, you better be tough." Everything happens for a reason, and sometimes that reason is we are not wise and make bad decisions. In those cases, we should adjust our thinking process to prevent bad decisions in the future. However, sometimes mistakes are made when we take initiative to make things better. There is a risk to all change. If we are not making mistakes, we are not changing. If we are not changing, we are not improving. Do not be afraid to take calculated risks. Fail fast and fail forward. This is yet another time when you want to know whether to ask for permission or to ask for forgiveness.

> "Good decisions come from experience. Experience comes from making bad decisions." — *Mark Twain*

If our goal is to solve problems, then not exposing problems and thinking there are no problems becomes the problem. I was told a story about a young plant manager that was tasked with running the engine plant that supplied the Toyota plant in Georgetown KY. He was very proud of the fact that he had not impacted the main plant since he started as plant manager. That was until he got a call for the main plant to report to a meeting with Fujio Cho, who was the Chairman of Toyota at the time. Fujio was concerned that the plant had not been impacted. Did that mean that the engine plant had too much inventory, or was working around the problems? Fujio Cho assured the young plant manager that it was OK, and even expected, to impact the plant if the problems being exposed were solved. It was implied that if he impacted the plant for the same reason more than once, indicating they were not solving the problems, it would not be OK.

Treasure Defects

Congratulate associates who find quality problems. Every defect tells a story. It is an opportunity to improve our process and eliminate future defects. Problems should not be hidden. Rather, communicate it to everyone and use it as a tool to improve our processes.

Learn Continuously

Understand the need to always learn more. Value learning. Grow with technology and company initiatives. Continually seek to learn new methods that will improve our processes. Examples include going back to school, getting familiar with new computer software, volunteering for projects and learning as you go, reading books, asking people what you can improve about yourself and taking on new leadership responsibilities. Ensure that you never stagnate. Every day should be a growing experience for us all. We owe it to the team to be on the cutting edge. Never let your team out-learn you. Most CEOs understand this very well and read at least one book per week.

Deal with Conflict

Understand the need to deal with conflict to ensure it does not grow and create larger HR issues later. Not dealing with conflict is lazy leadership and adds to the Management Debt. Focus on the situation, issue, or behavior, not the person.

Manage Performance

Provide recognition (positive and negative), establish accountability, focus people on development, and provide a venue for two-way communication on career aspirations, leader's style, and supporting processes and systems. Managing high performers is easy, but there is a time when a person's performance is not up to par. In those instances, the leader must develop a Personal Improvement Plan (PIP). The PIP is their last chance to correct the behavior or performance issue before being terminated. This philosophy works closely with the next philosophy.

Manage Progressive Discipline

Create and/or follow a progressive discipline process that ensures we are correcting or managing-out bad performers/behaviors from the business. However, always remember to praise publicly and punish privately. At Bosch, when we knew someone was going to the boss's office to get "punished privately," we would jokingly say they were going to the "woodshed." If you grew up in the country like we did, you knew exactly what that meant. The only time I correct someone publicly is if they have shared bad thinking and others heard it. I want to ensure the bad thinking does not spread.

I cannot tell you how many times I had to deal with a poor performer longer than necessary, because the leader before me did not document the performance issues of the poor performer. I am prepared to terminate quickly upon arriving in the department, but their past reviews show no performance issues and there are no progressive discipline steps that have been taken. From an HR group point of view, it may seem that I am the issue, since I am constantly trying to terminate people that have glowing reviews from the past. However, I was fortunate to have an HR group that concurred with my assessment 100% of the time.

JOHARI WINDOW

Your team must be willing to give you feedback. Therefore, you must surround yourself with people that you trust to give you feedback. How you respond to that feedback will determine if you continue to receive feedback.

The Johari is a quick tool to manage information about YOU and perceptions of you as a leader. The model was created by "JO"seph Luft and "HARI"ngton Ingham. Thus, the name Johari. The goal is to increase your ARENA. This can be done by receiving feedback on your blind spots as well as self-disclosure of items to others that others do not know about you. Being approachable and transparent are keys to closing the unknown gaps within yourself.

Respect for People and great leadership go hand and hand. The habit of having Respect for the team is extremely critical in any endeavor. I hope this chapter helped shed light on what it means to have this habit.

Individual Leadership Reflection:

Respecting People

Leader Thinking

Respect is not about being nice, but about being transparent. Never let your kindness be taken for weakness.

Hard on the process; easy on the people.

Dealing with performance issues is a key lever to build credibility with my high performers. Without credibility, I have the leverage of a toothpick.

I own the development of the team. I do not abdicate this responsibility to others. HR is there to help not own it.

Leader Behavior

I practice mutual learning (compassion, transparency, and curiosity)

Everybody on my team knows exactly where they stand with me.

I have a development plan for myself and for my team (training them together) and a customized individual plan for each person.

Leader Reflection

Do I think and act this way? If not, what must I adjust?

What is the biggest thing I can do now to improve my credibility as a leader with my team?

End of Chapter GROUP Reflection Questions:

1. Are we progressing on the actions from our last discussion?

2. What was the key learning from the current chapter?

3. As a team, what do we do well as it relates to the key learning?

4. As a team, what do we NOT do well as it relates to the key learning?

5. What do we need to Start, Stop, or Continue doing as a team to improve going forward as it relates to the key learning?

CHAPTER 10

GET THE TOP TEAM RIGHT

"You must have teamwork to make the dream work."
— John Maxwell

It amazes me at the amount of patience a company can have when it comes to dealing with poor leadership. I have heard, and agree with, this being called long-suffering. The amount of damage a poor leader can create in a very short period is devastating to any team, so my advice is to deal with poor leadership swiftly. That sounds harsh, but it is the truth. However, step one in "swiftly dealing with the issue" should be an attempt to rehabilitate the leader. This may be a painful process, but something about your promotion or recruiting processes allowed it to happen. You now get to deal with it. In the case where someone is promoted through the ranks, it is much more cost effective for the business to have the behavior corrected due to the experience the person holds. I often ask my clients how long it takes to replace a 30-year employee. The typical response I get is related to their backfill lead-time. In reality, it takes 30 years to replace a 30-year employee, since that employee has spent 30 years in your business. This is not the same as a 30-year employee with 1 year of experience 30 times. In either case, if there is an attempt to salvage the leader, and no improvement is seen, it is your duty to send them packing. Do it for the sake of those having to work for them.

THE LEADERSHIP FLYWHEEL

In his book, "Turning the Flywheel," Jim Collins challenges us to find and maximize what it is that we do that makes us successful. He uses the analogy of a flywheel. In the beginning a flywheel is hard to turn, but as you keep adding energy to the flywheel it starts building momentum to the point where there is eventually a breakthrough, and the flywheel simply develops seemingly unstoppable momentum. You can develop a flywheel example for many different parts of your business. The key is to understand what actions will drive the next action until they eventually loop back to drive the original action. Below is what I consider to be a Leadership Flywheel:

DO WE HAVE THE RIGHT LEADERS?

Have you surrounded yourself with good leaders or poor leaders? Are your leaders leading or simply managing? You nor anyone on your leadership team should practice "Pigeon" leadership. This form for leadership is when the leader flies in, craps all over everything and then leaves. Real leadership can only be exercised by an individual or a team of individuals who has a vision and the ability to motivate others to execute that vision.

As mentioned previously, if you have leaders unable to do both, you need to address this immediately. If you have successfully selected and developed the right people for your staff, the staff should all be able to leave and become world-class consultants in the function in which each staff member leads. Your staff should be experts in their fields, and they should know this is your expectation.

Your staff drives the culture of the business. To ensure our target culture stays intact as we grow, we must promote from within as much as 80%. This will require formal succession planning for key positions. If we have done the correct planning in the succession planning process, we should have our future leaders in the plan. We do not want those future leaders in our succession plan to leave, so we need to ensure they are compensated according to the value they provide the business, not just their title. Our HR processes (including promotions, reviews, and bonuses) must be aligned with this new way of thinking.

"When we promote someone, the organization should applaud." — *Debbie Croft*

When setting up incentive programs for your staff ensure they align with the new thinking you are developing. If we say one thing and incentivize another, we will get what we incentivize. The following is an approach to ensuring we have the "right people" on our team from the start.

RECRUITING NEW MEMBERS

We have often noticed that companies hire for technical expertise over value and cultural fit. This leads to hiring people for what they know and then firing them for who they are. We should always hire those people who fit into our culture and value system. If we have created solid processes, we can quickly close the gap in knowledge.

> "Leadership is the ability to abandon one's ego to the talents of others." — *Max Dupree*

While I think time is the scarcest resource we have, I think performing associates is the second scarcest resource we have. Notice that I used the word "performing" associate. Performing is the focus on having process associates that get the right things done efficiently and knowledge associates that are effective (ensuring the right things are done). There is nothing more wasteful than getting the wrong thing done no matter the efficiency. We should always be looking for talent and then recruiting that talent when it is needed. Some companies hire talent even when they do not have a position open, because they know the future war in business is going to be for talent. Also, the right talent will find ways to add value regardless of position. As leaders we must be talent scouts. As stated above, our goal should be to promote and recruit talent from within as much as 80% if the talent is present. We encourage going outside at least 20% (maybe more if we do not have a strong bench), so a culture fit is ensured during this process.

One of my clients had a huge talent gap in his engineering group. This was a major issue for the business since engineering was a key part of the sales and engineer-to-order process. He was hesitant to hire the needed talent since it would require him to pay that talent more than his salary. I reminded him that his total compensation should be his measuring stick, not just his base salary. If he hires the right talent, he will get bonuses that will far outweigh the cost for the talent (Tim Cook did this at Apple when he hired Angela Ahrendts). This logic rang true to him, so he hired a head of engineering and gave him a salary that far exceeded his own. The Human Resource department thought this was crazy. However, the Engineering Manager proved to be one of the most valuable players on the senior team, and the company's Earnings Before Interest, Tax, Depreciation, and Amortization (EBITDA) began to reflect that value as did the General Manager's bonuses. There are times when you must hire-up in both talent and salary. Don't let pride or corporate policies blind you from making the right decision.

While we may occasionally hire outside the company for higher positions, our Front-Line Managers (Team Leaders and Group Leaders) should be promoted from within to ensure job knowledge is present. A Front-Line Manager will find it hard to lead team members in jobs the manager has never performed. A common approach would be to promote from within while following one's external screening process.

Since the outside hires are typically at the higher levels of the organization, the wrong hire can have a huge negative impact on the culture. Again, a general rule of thumb is to create development processes so robust that we can hire from within 80% of the time or more. However, we look for outside talent 20% of the time to ensure we introduce new thinking and fresh eyes in the business. Also, never be afraid to hire-up (someone smarter than you).

"If you are the smartest person in the room, you are in the wrong room." — *Unknown*

As important as recruiting talent is, retaining that talent is even more important. We must avoid the "Brain Drain" that can occur if we don't take care of and respect our talent. On the flipside, if you take care of your talent, they will take care of you. As we develop the team, there will be those looking to steal the company's talent. We must incentivize the high performers in an organization to keep them from leaving. One way to keep people from leaving the company is to instill a sense of ownership within them.

How does one create ownership thinking within all their employees? There are many ways to do this, below are only a few:

- Profit Sharing / Distributions
- Goal Sharing
- Stock Options

- Stock Grants
- Employ Stock Ownership Plan (ESOP)

Profit sharing / Distributions is when you share a % of the profits with the entire organization.

Goal Sharing is when you set certain goals for the business and any improvement beyond that goal is paid out as bonuses to the team. This is a self-funding type of incentive plan.

Stock Options are where the employee has a right to exercise their options at a certain point in the future. If the business improves over that time, they will have a gain. In the case where the business does not improve, the options are worthless.

Stock Grants are where actual stock is granted to the individual. This is seen as compensation and the receiver of the grants must pay taxes on this compensation, which is why most employees prefer Stock Options.

ESOP is where the owner(s) of the business sale the business to the employees. If done correctly, this can be beneficial to the seller and the buyer. There are also some great tax advantages to the business for being an ESOP.

Some venture capital groups require top leaders to buy stock to show that they have some skin in the game. This is another method of ensuring an ownership mentality in the business. However, it is not always practical at the lower levels of the business.

Taking care of all associates at all levels is extremely important to the longevity of a business. If only the top leaders are taken care of it can lead to a kleptocracy and drive resentment of the working level.

All companies should have a capital plan that rewards good performance as well as builds the business. One simple method is to split the net profit capital into two categories:

1. 20% goes to reward performance.
2. 80% goes to invest in growth.

The "reward performance" portion of the net profit is given to the team for getting those results. Do not underestimate the power this incentive will have on the business's ability to improve performance year over year.

The "invest in growth" portion is used in many ways to advance the vision and mission of the business. The growth focus should be on growing better; not simply growing bigger.

Some pitfalls to avoid when incentivizing the entire workforce:

- Individuals working against each other.
- Departments working against each other.
- Undue pressure on the customer
- End-of-quarter financial games

The best way to avoid these pitfalls is to ensure the incentives are tied directly to the net profits of the entire business; not just sales, not just engineering, not just one division. This type of incentive plan ensures everyone is helping each other improve the overall business.

There is an old saying that states, "You can't make a man understand something if his salary depends on him not understanding it." This statement is as true today as it was when it was first spoken. I will give An example of incentives gone wrong that was seen in a large automotive company. T

he department heads were charged with reducing the manufacturing cost in each of their areas. Their personal bonuses were tied to their department's ability to reduce cost locally. To make a car, you basically, stamp it, weld it, paint it, and stuff it. The issue in this example was with the relationship between the "Weld It" and the "Paint It" departments. Without warning, the paint department started having paint flaking issues. A quick study of the issue by the paint engineers showed that the flaking was primarily around the weld joints. The engineers went upstream to find out if anything had changed in the welding department that could have contributed to this issue. They soon discovered that the welding department had changed the welding flux used to weld the joints in question. This new flux was creating issues in the painting department. When this problem was escalated to the department heads, the welding department head stated that the new flux was helping them reduce their cost, so he was not going back to the old flux. The painting department's costs went up (well beyond the savings of the flux) as a result. This is a classic example of violating the habits of excellence.

Sharing profits with the team that helped generate the profits is a no-brainer to me. If you have people on your team that you would not share profit with, then you should ask yourself, "Why are they on my team?"

When you have properly incentivized the entire company, you will have all your employees thinking of the business as if it were their own business. This level of ownership will help drive the right decisions deep down in the organizational structure.

SCREENING

Screening tools that are well-developed will ensure that the selection process is world-class. Below are some common tools and their uses:

- **DISC/Myers Briggs/Predictive Index/Enneagram:** Used to determine a person's temperament or personality type. Different types of personalities perform better at different positions. While there are no "bad" personality profiles, personality profiles do show areas in which a person may want to focus for improvement based on the individual's current or targeted position.

- **Change Style Indicator:** Used to determine if a person is an originator, conserver, or pragmatist when it comes to change. Again, there is no good or bad style. However, it does give insight as to how the person will deal with change.

- **Wonderlic:** Used to determine how fast a person can learn or process new information. This test is used by the NFL to test quarterbacks, since they must process loads of data and respond quickly. Quick witted people score highly on this test while deep thinkers tend to score lower. However, these different types of people are typically working in different areas, and there is value in both styles.

Personality, Change Style, and Speed are only three aspects of the recruiting process. We also need to consider if a prospective person will be a fit for the culture. This can be done by having the team members with whom the new person will be working conduct the interview. Team members should ask questions that will ensure the new person is a fit. It also gives the team ownership once the person is hired. During this interview, the psychometric testing will be validated using open-ended questions including role plays and case studies.

TECHNICAL CAPABILITY

While culture fit is the most important aspect, technical aptitude is the second most important if we are hiring for a highly technical position. We must develop some method to test the person's technical aptitude for the given position. For example, if we are hiring for a position that deals with electronics, we would target someone with an electronic background or degree. If we target someone with a mechanical background or mechanical degree, the learning curve could be prohibitive. In this case, we would select someone with an electrical background and then test that person's electrical aptitude. There are technical aptitude tests out there, or you may want to create your own.

HIRING PROCESS

Dee Hock once said, "Hire and promote first based on integrity; second, motivation; third, capacity; fourth, understanding; fifth, knowledge; and last and least, experience. Without integrity, motivation is dangerous; without motivation, capacity is impotent; without capacity, understanding is limited; without understanding, knowledge is meaningless; without knowledge, experience is blind. Experience is easy to provide and quickly put to good use by people with all the other qualities."

Below is what I believe to be an effective hiring process. This is only one of the many processes I have seen and/or developed, but this process has proven to be quite successful in the consulting industry.

Pre-testing

- Resume review
- Psychometric testing (online or electronic)
- Technical exam (timed)
- Video of person teaching a topic related to the position.
- Phone screen (focus questioning on any areas of concern in the above items)

Interviewing

- Candidate completes a case study dealing with a topic in the industry
- Group interview with peers and managers
  - Questions aimed at resume's statements
  - Questions aimed at gauging values' fit
- Proctored psychometric testing
- One-week tryout (in some cases this is not possible)

Note: The one time I skipped the one-week tryout, I regretted it.

ACHIEVE COMMITMENT

Now that we have the team assembled, we must ask, is there a sense of commitment to each other among your staff members? If asked, would each member of your staff identify the staff as his or her first team, or would the department over which they manage be your staff member's first choice? In most cases, the answer will be the latter. Managers see the functions over which they manage as their team. The managers hire and mentor their people, and the managers' direct reports tend to be the ones the managers spend most of their time with at the office. Consider this possibility when a manager keeps an office with his or her team rather than keeping an office with the staff. This separation is a sign that the staff has not achieved commitment as a team or maybe even to the direction of the business. An uncommitted staff does not have a shared sense of purpose to drive a higher-level strategy. With the lack of a shared sense of purpose, the manager will seek to optimize the function, which is in direct violation of the habit of Embracing the Total System.

I am speaking specifically of commitment here, not interest. There is a difference between interest and commitment. When you are interested in doing something, you do it only when circumstances permit. When you are committed to something, you accept no excuses, only results. For those that like making excuses, we must remove their excuses to get at the real problem. We need leaders that are committed, and all-in for the change that is coming. While I do not recommend this approach, I do want to bring attention to an extreme example of getting a team to be all-in. In an effort to send the message, "We will succeed or die," Cortes burnt/destroyed his ships. His team had no other choice other than to succeed or perish. Cortes created intrinsic motivation, with extreme extrinsic action. There is some debate about whether this happened or not, but I think it makes the point I am trying to make regardless.

GROUP ACCOUNTABILITY

One thing a company can do to create accountability within the team is to do what we refer to as a Stop-Start-Continue exercise as a group. We covered this tool in the strategic alignment section as it pertains to strategic alignment. However, we can also use it with our staff. This is when the team sits together and tells the other members of the team the following:

1. Things the department or department head is doing well and should continue doing.

2. Things the department or department head should start doing because it would positively impact the team member, the department, and the company.

3. Things the department or department head needs to stop doing because it negatively impacts team members, the department, and the company.

This exercise can create anxiety for some members of the team, but at the end of the exercise everyone on the team knows what everyone else is thinking, what needs to be done, and who needs to be doing it. The final step is for each member of the leadership team to create an improvement plan for him or herself and have everyone hold them accountable to the result.

> "THAT'S NOT MY JOB"
>
> THIS STORY IS ABOUT 4 PEOPLE. EVERYBODY, SOMEBODY, ANYBODY, AND NOBODY. THERE WAS AN IMPORTANT JOB TO BE DONE AND EVERYBODY WAS SURE THAT SOMEBODY WOULD DO IT. ANYBODY COULD HAVE DONE IT, BUT NOBODY DID IT. SOMEBODY GOT ANGRY ABOUT THAT, BECAUSE IT WAS EVERYBODY'S JOB. EVERYBODY THOUGHT ANYBODY COULD DO IT BUT NOBODY REALIZED THAT EVERYBODY WOULDN'T DO IT. IT ENDED UP THAT EVERYBODY BLAMED SOMEBODY WHEN NOBODY DID WHAT ANYBODY COULD HAVE DONE.

> "We [Leaders] are often guilty of protecting people from the consequences of their actions." — *Unknown*

The accountability should be in real-time, but one can also make it part of the staff meeting conversation to ensure people are following through on their commitments.

Another extremely important form of accountability is one of holding each other accountable to achieve the results of the strategic plan. Assuming the team has been involved in developing the plan together, no excuse should be acceptable for failure to execute the plan. Accountability starts with Purpose! Missing targets and ignoring results is unacceptable. If the strategic plan is not important enough to enforce, why spend the time to create it?

"Accountability has its emphasis on the future: Doing what you said you would do within the time frame you agreed to do it." — *Unknown*

GOOF-OFFS vs. GO-GETTERS

Here's a question for all leaders concerning poor performers: "If an employ quits today and you wouldn't hire them back tomorrow, why is that employ is still working for you?"

Have you ever heard someone say, "As long as that guy has a job, I don't have to worry about being fired?" This statement usually comes from a low performer. This low performer is looking at the lowest performer as a measure of how much they can get away with before being fired. Allowing this to happen in a team will result in a very low performing work team. If we have differing levels of performance on the team, which we always will, then a certain level of differentiation must occur. If we do not practice the art of differentiation, we risk losing our highest performers.

There is a concept called Focus on the Go Getters that I have used for many years. This concept is the basis for building and maintaining a high performing workforce. The premise is that three groups of people exist in every organization. Group one is most of the associates. They are competent and will do what is expected of them. Group two (Goof Off's) is typically the lower performing five to ten percent of the organization. These people often quit but remain on the payroll. They have a huge impact on the culture, since the culture is often defined by the worst behavior you as a leader are willing to tolerate. They will do as little as possible. Group three (Go Getters) is the top performing five to ten percent of the organization. The Go Getters will give us 100% every day without having to be managed. We could not run the business without the go getters, and we should overpay them. Each group is watching how we deal with the other groups. Always remember that your culture is defined by the lowest performance and worst behavior that you allow. The competent (middle group) will trend toward Goof Offs if they can do so and remain with the company. It is the path of least resistance, and this results in an overall lower performing team.

The Go Getters are watching how you deal with the Goof Offs. If you do not deal with the Goof Offs, the Go Getters will think you are blind or even worse, they will think you do not care. In either case, the Go Getters will try to do less, but it is not in their nature, so they continue to work hard and just lose respect for you for not dealing with the issue of the Goof Offs. The Go Getters may even leave the company/department if a better opportunity presents itself. The net result of this is a further shift toward low performance.

> **"When your good ones are leaving, look at the leadership."**
> — *Unknown*

On the other hand, if we deal with the Goof Offs by placing the proper heat under them, the competent (middle group) will work to get away from the heat, and the Go Getters will respect us for addressing the Goof Offs. Those that were close to the Goof Off group will be grateful we didn't fire them and therefore will work harder. If we do not actively live this philosophy, we will slowly create a team of mediocre performers. At that point, our chances of becoming world-class are so remote, we will kill ourselves trying to get there and lose some high performers in the process. You're always punishing somebody – make sure you're punishing the right people. When you don't deal with the Goof Offs, you are in essence punishing the Go Getters.

There comes a time in a team's evolution when the bottom ten percent is fully competent and there is no need for the "heat." We have experienced this situation often and enjoy the accomplishments produced by such a team. Do not continue to chop when you do not need to.

I have stated many times that you should attempt to rehabilitate if possible. You have two choices, rehabilitate, or replace. You should never move a problem, deal with it. I have had many cases where the rehabilitation approach has paid off for me. One was with a lady that fell into complete depression. She was a model associate before this incident. I had not heard from her in two days, and Bosch's policy at the time was to terminate if an employee was a no-show and no-call after three days. I knew she was struggling with depression, so I reached out to one of her family members who also worked at Bosch and had them check on her. It turned out she had locked herself in her house over the weekend and still had not come out. This was now Tuesday. They were able to get her to come out and I worked with HR to get her a leave of absence so she could get things back in order. She did get things back in order and worked at Bosch the rest of her career.

Another example was with a guy I called Paint Chip. Not very professional of me, but I was a young manager at the time and can claim some level of ignorance. So, how did he get that nickname? During the first few days of him working in my department, I noticed two things about him. One, he could not hold a coherent conversation, and two he always had paint on the tip of his nose. I finally went to my second shift group leader and stated that I think the guy is huffing paint. He said what guy, and I said Paint Chip. He is the guy that always has the paint chip on his nose. Well, that nickname stuck. His behavior eventually got to the point where we had to have him drug tested. He failed the drug test, which was no surprise to me. Back then, Bosch had a two-strike rule. If you failed the drug test once, we would pay for your rehabilitation, but if you failed again, you were fired. He went to rehabilitation, and never failed any of the retests. He turned out to be one of my best associates. I have other examples where we gave people second chances, and they failed the retest. I had no problem letting them go. I would like to think that I never actually fired anyone. They fired themselves. I simply did the paperwork for them.

I had one guy get so mad at me because I "did his paperwork" for him for having a flat tire that made him late for work. I explained to him that I was not firing him for the flat tire. He had allowed his absences to creep up to the point where the flat tire put him over the limit. If I thought you were playing the attendance system, you can bet I had my eye on you, since I did not appreciate you disrespecting your team members by not being there each day. The best performing employee is useless if they are not present.

When at Bosch, I got moved around a lot. One pattern I noticed was the types of people that would put in for transfers when they announced my next department. I would always look at the transfer list to ensure there were no go-getters on the list. However, I was perfectly fine with the goof-offs leaving before I got there. My thought was they would eventually get caught by another leader that cared about managing performance to create a high performing work team. If not, our paths would cross again, and I would have a chance to deal with it myself.

CHEMO NEEDED

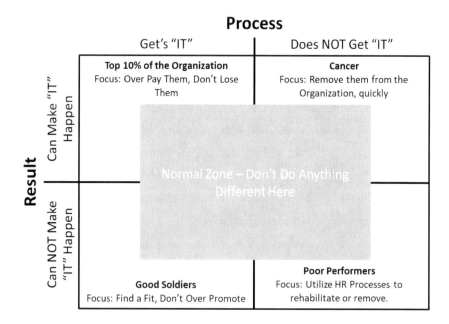

Jack Welch, former CEO of General Electric, detailed a model with four quadrants (See Figure Above). It shows a contrast between those who "Can Get It Done" through others, those who "Can't Get it Done" through others, those who "Do Get It," and those who "Don't Get It." "It" in this case would be your company's vision, principles, habits, philosophies, and strategic plan.

> "If the flock is headed in the wrong direction, replace the Shepard; not the flock." — *Unknown*

The Group that Can Get It Done and Do Get It are the real leaders. They are the top 10% of the organization and as such, should be overpaid and happy. They are the Go Getters of leadership and are valuable to the organization. They are the ones an organization must keep.

If the organization loses them, HR, incentive, and leadership practices need to be reviewed. At this point, one needs to consider whether performance is being appropriately incentivized and whether he or she is continually dealing with poor performers. Keep in mind the number one reason people leave organizations is due to the direct supervisor's failure to hold people accountable. This is also true at the top. Holding top leaders accountable may ruffle some feathers, but great leaders understand that sometimes doing the right thing means pissing people off. If you want to make everyone happy, do not be a leader; sell ice-cream.

The group that Cannot Get It Done and Does Get It are our soldiers. These soldiers need to have a place that suits them. While all good leaders were once good soldiers, not all good soldiers will make good leaders. With that in mind, there are a lot of people in this group that are not leadership material. In fact, they do not want to be leaders, so they should not be placed in leadership positions in which they will fail. I have often seen great engineers promoted to management without the leadership skills or desire to be a leader. In those cases, a valuable engineer is lost, and a terrible manager is gained. In many cases this person is fired and not demoted. This type of engineer can get things done on his/her own but not through others and that should be acceptable. If the position was accepted solely due to the pay increase, we may have an issue with pay scales within the non-leadership ranks. I have seen the same problem play out in operations where the top operator gets promoted to group leader and does a horrible job at leading. Not only did they lead poorly we also lost a valuable operator.

The group that Cannot Get It Done and Do Not Get It are the poor performers. HR processes are designed to deal with these people. There are typically three types (wise, fools, evil) of people you will deal with in this group, and each will require a different approach. The wise in this group will immediately close their gaps and will not be an issue in the future; the fools will need to have consequences linked to the needed change (they may or may not change and will need to be fired); the evil ones should simply be fired (don't waste your time). These folks are typically Goof Offs. They must be removed from the teams, or they will contribute to the loss of the Go Getters.

The final group from Welch's Quadrants is the group that Can Get It Done and Do Not Get It. This is a company's worst nightmare. This group of folks has shown results but do not embrace the company's vision, principles, habits, philosophies, and/or strategy. They get things done, but the way they get things done is out of sync with the values of the organization. The Can Get It Done and Don't Get It leaders have people listening to them and doing what they say. These people can do a lot of harm to an organization. This group is considered CANCER and must be removed from the organization immediately. As the leader, you must be the CHEMO. The longer the delay, the more damage these people can do to the culture of the organization, which will, in turn, delay a successful start to becoming world-class.

PROMISE YOURSELF A ROSE GARDEN

When it comes to building a great team, there is a lot we can learn from a rose garden. The rose stalk can only support so many buds, so as the gardener, we must make a choice. We can either let the entire rose bush die, or we can take steps to save the rose bush by pruning it. Below are the types of pruning that are often required to save the bush:

- Remove the dead buds

- Improve to best or remove the sick buds
- Remove the less than best buds

The reason for this pruning is to make room for the best buds to grow. Pruning is a necessary activity for growth. Pruning is the job of the gardener. It does not take much imagination to realize the analogy here. The bush is the business, the buds can be members of the team or products, and the gardener is the leader. While it may not be fun to prune in your business, it is necessary to save the jobs and livelihoods of those working for you.

TEACHER

> "Teachers don't teach for the income; they teach for the outcome." — *Unknown*

The spirit of a teacher should be at the heart of every great leader. Every one of us can recall that certain someone in our lives, personally or professionally, who poured into our lives and helped us become the person we are today. With that being said, if we have people in leadership roles who cannot teach, we cannot expect them to develop their people well. We must have leaders who understand our principles, habits, and philosophies and TEACH them to others. One of the longest living legacies we can achieve is passing on our knowledge to those we teach. Teaching is a huge responsibility and takes a lot of work. As teachers our stance must be to understand that if the student has not learned, then the teacher has not taught. It is our responsibility to ensure learning is occurring. That is not the role of those being taught. Another key to keep in mind is the Law of Primacy. The Law of Primacy holds that the side of an issue presented first will have greater effectiveness in persuasion than the side presented subsequently. So as the teacher, we must ensure we are teaching the right concepts from the beginning.

> "The best teachers teach from the heart, not from the book." — *Unknown*

We must promote teachers, not those leaders who get results based on pure brute force. Teachers ensure that we are spreading our knowledge and becoming more of a learning organization.

WAYS OF LEARNING

I teach that there are three main ways to learn or teach new skills: Hear-See-Do, Mutual Learning, and Socratic Method. In Hear-See-Do, I tell the team about what can be done, so they HEAR it. Then I show the team examples of what has been done, so they SEE it. Finally, we all roll up our sleeves and help the team DO it in their processes. Getting the improvement work done requires a team who is willing and able to do the work. I call this the DO CREW, and there must always be a DO CREW if we are going to get things done. That DO CREW should not just be hourly or staff folks. We, as leaders, must get in there as well. We do not want to do transformation TO the team, but rather do transformation WITH the team.

As part of the DO step, I also ensure I am transferring the learning to the team, so I follow the I DO, WE DO, YOU DO method. In the I DO step; I lead the entire process of DOING. I do this to model the behavior of the leader during the process. In the WE DO step, I co-lead with a client representative that has been selected to lead the process in the future. And finally, in the YOU DO step, the client representative leads and I serve as a coach to them. At the end of this three phase process, the client representative will have enough grasp of the process to continue without me, and they will become more and more adept as they lead more implementations.

The basis of mutual learning was developed by Chris Argyris in the mid 1900's. Chris referred to his research as theories of action (or theories in use), double loop learning, and organizational learning. These theories have been refined over the years to be applicable on a larger scale. Most notably in the form of Skilled Facilitator Training where the method Mutual Learning is taught. In this method, we learn from each other. We take the approach that everyone is a teacher in that we all have understanding to share with one another. The motto is, "Let us LEARN and move forward TOGETHER." Roger Schwarz, studied with Chris and is a pioneer in developing the application of Mutual Learning. Roger has written many books and articles on the subject. In his book "The Skilled Facilitator," Roger discusses the assumptions that are held by those who practice mutual learning, opposed to those who practice unilateral control. Those Mutual Learning assumptions are and are NOT:

> *I have information, so do other people.* **NOT** *I understand the situation and those who disagree do not.*
>
> *Each of us sees things others do not.* **NOT** *I am right and those who disagree are wrong.*
>
> *People may disagree with me and still have pure motives.* **NOT** *I have pure motives and those who disagree with me have questionable motives.*
>
> *Differences are opportunities for learning.* **NOT** *My feelings and behaviors are justified.*
>
> *I may be contributing to the problem.* **NOT** *I am not contributing to the problem.*

Roger also covers 8 rules that help govern how teams should behave when together. Those rules are:

Rule 1: State views and ask genuine questions.

> The key here is to have a balance between advocacy and inquiry. If you over advocate for your ideas, the team will think you are not open to their ideas. If you over inquire about what they are thinking, they may think you are tricking them by not sharing your thoughts.
>
> If you can put "you idiot" at the end of your question, it may not be genuine.

Also, be very careful with the use of sarcasm in your questions or statements. The root word of sarcasm is sarkasmós, which means to tear the flesh, which is what you are figuratively doing when you are being sarcastic.

There are times when someone will say something to you (or at you) that is not genuine. I call these "gifts," and it is up to you to decide if you want to open that gift at that time or not. I highly recommend you eventually open the gift. Otherwise, you and that person will miss an opportunity to learn together.

Rule 2: Share all relevant information.

The key here is to share everything you know pertaining to the situation even if it does not support the direction in which you want to go.

If there is information that would impact the decision, which you cannot share due to confidentiality reasons, please let the team know that as well.

Rule 3: Use specific examples and agree on what important words mean.

It is hard to troubleshoot a hypothetical situation, so only bring up real examples.

If a word is used that may have different meanings across the business, take the time to clarify what is meant by that word in that instance.

Rule 4: Explain reasoning and intent.

The trap we fall into here is asking for information, without sharing our reasoning and intent. In the absence of knowing, the person being requested to provide information will draw their own conclusions as to why the information is needed. However, the conclusion is typically not favorable. We also tend to assume negative intentions.

The example I use here is that of a boss sending an email to a subordinate asking, "Can you please send me a list of what you do each day?" In this case, the subordinate will naturally think, "Oh no, my boss thinks I don't do anything all day." The response from the subordinate will be from a defense posture. However, if the boss were to share her reasoning and intent, the request may go like this, "I think you are one of the most productive people on my team, and I would like others to learn from your example. Can you please send me a list of what you do each day?" Not only will the subordinate not feel attacked, but they will also probably spend a lot more time on sharing details with the boss.

Rule 5: Focus on interest; not positions.

The key here is to not take a position on a topic. Once a position is taken, it is hard to back down. The higher up in the organization one is the harder it is to back down.

The example I use is of a window. If two associates are sharing an office, and one wants the window up and the other wants the window down, we have an impasse. A window cannot be open and closed at the same time. Some would state that they should compromise and leave the window half open/closed. This would be a lose-lose. Neither party got what they wanted. We often call this a compromise, so a compromise is really a lose-lose. However, if we take the time to understand the interest behind each of the positions, we may find a solution that satisfies both sides. For example, if one of the associates were concerned about the wind blowing papers off their desk and the other associates wanted to feel the breeze, the solution would be location within the office, not the position of the window.

Rule 6: Test assumptions and inferences.

We naturally assume we know someone's intent or infer (based on historical data) what is meant. As stated above, we typically lean toward the negative when doing this. If this happens, one should paraphrase what they think they heard to ensure no assumptions are being made.

That dialog would go something like this:

When you said or did, "X." I thought, "Y."

Was that what you meant?

This a very simple dialog that if followed could clear up a lot of misunderstandings in our business and personal lives. Also, remember to not hold a grudge, hold a conversation. The issue may be a result of a misunderstanding.

The drawback to not testing assumptions is the person will begin telling themselves stories that may or may not be true. As time passes, these stories become their truth.

Rule 7: Jointly design the next steps.

The team must agree on what the next steps are once a decision has been made.

There should also be a cadence of accountability after the meeting to ensure the next steps get completed on time.

Rule 8: Discuss undiscussables.

It is hard for a team to have a productive discussion when there is a proverbial elephant in the room. Mature teams can discuss what is often considered undiscussable. As the leader, you should notice the elephant and start the discussion. If needed, the Start-Stop-Continue exercise mentioned earlier in this book can be used to help expose the elephants.

By following these rules, you ensure the team has as much information as possible to help facilitate the decision make process. As a result, you can expect higher quality decisions, better working relationships, shorter implementation times, greater personal satisfaction, increased commitment, and increased learning. Your job as a leader is to ensure the rules are being followed on a consistent basis.

The below graphic shows the difference between double-loop and single-loop learning. Single-loop learning is often referred to as Unilateral Control.

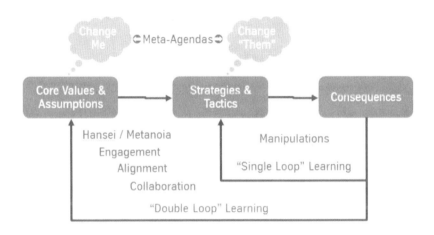

I would say Roger and his team are some of the bests I have seen at teaching the skills of facilitation as it relates to being more mutual learning focused (double loop learning) and less unilateral controlling (single loop learning). I make it a point to send every one of my clients that is interested to his one-week intensive facilitator training. It is one of the best workshops I have ever attended, and I hear the same from everyone that I send.

Finally, there is the Socratic Method. I covered this method in detail earlier in this book, so I will only briefly touch on it here as it pertains to leadership. This method involves teaching someone something new by asking questions that lead the learner to an answer. By having that person discover the answer on his/her own, the lesson is forever embedded in his/her mind.

Socratic questioning is one of the most powerful teaching tools. In his book, "Toyota Kata," Mike Rother details the process that Toyota uses to coach their teams toward continuous improvement.

Below are the Socratic questions he distilled from his study of Toyota:

- What is the Challenge?
- What is the Target Condition?
- What is the Actual Condition now?
- What did you plan as your last step/experiment?
- What did you expect to happen during your last step/experiment?
- What happened during your last step/experiment?
- What did you learn from taking the last step/experiment?
- What obstacles do you think are preventing you from reaching the target condition?
- Which one (obstacle) are you addressing now?
- What is your next step (next PTRS experiment). What do you expect to happen?
- How quickly can we go and see what we have learned from taking that step?
- What do you need from me?

This line of questioning helps the person being questioned frame their thinking toward a continuous improvement mindset. There will always be a challenge. The challenge should be just outside of what the team thinks is possible based on their current knowledge. There will be many target conditions to get to the challenge. There will be many obstacles between us (the current condition) and the target condition. The key is to keep dealing with one obstacle at a time until we reach the target. Then set a new target until we reach the challenge.

Our leaders must embrace these learning and teaching models, and they must demonstrate these models daily to their team members. One of the best things a coach can say is, "I don't know, what do you think?" There is a chance no leader has ever asked the team member that question. Questions are powerful. If we look at the word question, more closely, we will see the word 'quest' embedded in the word. When we ask **quest**ions, we allow the person being asked to go on a journey in their thinking. This is opposed to giving answers which ensures there is no journey.

How we ask these questions is very important. Do not ask questions where the default answer is "no action." If one has a default 'no action' question, we risk not explaining something to some of those who may benefit from it.

Examples:

- Raise your hand if you HAVEN'T heard of BTS (Build to Schedule). – Default is no action.
- Raise your hand if you HAVE heard of BTS. – Default is to explain BTS. If they do raise their hand, a good follow-up step could be to have them explain it as they know it.

Good Sentence Structure for Mutual Learning:

- State your view, give your reasoning. Then ask a genuine open-ended question of the person with whom you are having the discussion. And always remember, if you can put "you idiot" at the end of your question and it makes sense, it may not be a genuine question.

ALIGNMENT

Yet another benefit of teaching is the alignment that comes within our teams once our expectations are clearly communicated. Teams will do what is expected of them in most cases.

I am not a big fan of many things Fredrick Taylor espoused, but one thing he and I do agree on is the fact that wasted human efficiency is one of our largest unaddressed wastes. Below is a quote from him on this topic:

"We can see our forests vanishing, our water-powers going to waste, our soil being carried by floods into the sea; and the end of our coal and our iron is in sight. But our larger wastes of human

effort, which go on every day through such of our acts as are blundering, ill-directed, or inefficient, and which Mr. Roosevelt refers to as a lack of" national efficiency," are less visible) less tangible, and are but vaguely appreciated. We can see and feel the waste of material things. Awkward, inefficient, or ill-directed movements of men, however, leave nothing visible or tangible behind them. Their appreciation calls for an act of memory, an effort of the imagination. And for this reason, even though our daily loss from this source is greater than from our waste of material things, the one has stirred us deeply, while the other has moved us but little."

Fredrick's statement is correct. Our goal is not to simply work people harder. It is to ensure there is a steady rhythmic work pace that is progressing the product or service along the path to the customer. However, too often we pay our team members for attendance rather than performance. Members are working to appear busy but are not productive. When the boss is coming, statements such as "Get busy. The boss is coming," might be heard. This is the result of years of bad management telling the employees to stay busy. If the work the employees are doing is not going to add value to the current item or the next one in line, the personnel should not be doing it. Allowing people to simply stay busy rather than productive will result in piles of inventory between processes. This is overproduction. Over production is the worst form of waste since it creates all the other forms of waste.

The inventory created also covers up other problems in the business (see graphic below).

The countermeasure to Overproduction is to implement pull systems between each process. The best pull system is one by one flow, the first compromise from one-by-one flow is sequential pull (aka FIFO lanes), and the second compromise from one-by-one flow is supermarkets. The challenge that most companies face is they compromise on sequential pull or supermarkets and do not continue to work toward one-by-one flow, or worse they never implement pull systems at all.

PROBLEM-SOLVING

One of the most important skills we can teach our staff is effective problem solving. It is critical to introduce a structured problem-solving method in such a way that 100% of the organization will understand and practice it from the very beginning. This will always begin at the top and include the top leader. Once the top administration has demonstrated proficiency, they can, in turn, train the next level. This process will continue until everyone in the organization is using a standardized method to solve problems. The leaders in the organization from Team Leader to CEO are expected to coach and hold others accountable to this process.

This structured problem-solving method will encourage the use of the Plan Try Reflect Standardize (PTRS) cycle, which was discussed earlier. It ensures we are constantly trying to improve our processes.

We perform mini experiments daily, hourly, and even after each cycle. Failure is a chance to learn as much as success is. It is acceptable to let the team fail (within reason, of course) if a valuable lesson is learned in the process.

"Truth discovered is far better than truth imposed."
– Dan Erskin

Are you willing to let your team fail, so they can discover the truth? How have you responded in the past when the team has failed? Have you ever heard the saying that failure is not an option?

"Good Decisions Come from Experience, Experience Comes from Failure." — Tim Broughton

Failure should be a lesson. The key is to let those lessons make you better; not bitter. Failure is not the end; failure is the beginning if there is a lesson. Let failures be lessons learned; not simply lessons acknowledged. Lessons learned means you will change your approach going forward to reduce the chances of failure in the future. Lessons acknowledged means you will not change and are likely to make the same failures over and over. If when you fail, you see yourself as a victim, you will never be as successful as you could be. You cannot be a victim and a victor at the same time. Never be victimized by failure. Failure helps build our mental muscles. Failure is the chance to begin again; just more intelligently. Humans are antifragile. This means we get stronger when pressure is applied. It is from where the saying, "What doesn't kill you makes you stronger" comes. It is easy to see this at work in our muscles, but the same is true with our brains. Learning is a form of pressure for our brains. Too many people acknowledge failures, but do not learn from them. If you are not failing, you are not learning. You are not pushing the limits; you are taking the easy route.

"Be sure to never snatch defeat from the jaws of victory."
— *Unknown*

We must be constantly learning from and improving our processes. The first attempt at PTRS in an area will begin with the CHECK to see if there are standards. The results of that check will determine our action. We will act to create standards if standards are not present, solve the problems keeping us from achieving the established standards, or raise the standards currently in place to ensure continuous improvement. Some people like to jump straight to improvement without fully understanding the current condition. As we mentioned before, we cannot have improvement without standardization. If no standards exist, Standardization IS Improvement.

"Failure is a bruise; not a tattoo." — *Unknown*

Embedding a systematic problem-solving method into our culture is the single most important thing we can do for the business. By doing this, we engage the minds of the people working for us to solve our problems. I love when people approach me and tell me that the solution to a work problem came to them while doing something at home. We do not ask them to do that thinking at home. It is a side benefit of engaging their minds in a manner that challenges them mentally. As stated earlier, one does not have to be trained in advanced methods of problem-solving. You can solve 95% of your problems using the simple 12 Step process. The 12 Step process is as follows:

1. State the Problem (What? Where?)
2. What is the Standard?
3. What is the Actual?
4. Clarify the Problem?
5. Set a target/challenge.

6. Implement Immediate Temporary Countermeasures

7. Analyze the root cause.

8. Develop countermeasures.

9. Implement Countermeasures

10. Evaluate both results and process.

11. Standardize successful processes.

12. Reflect and Knowledge Transfer

When we deploy problem-solving, it is tempting to just do a blanket training session and send people out to begin problem-solving. This will generate a lot of activity without ensuring the process is followed. Remember, Process Yields Results! The problem-solving process is no exception. We also do not want to just train them without allowing them to experience the process in a real application. Also, be sure to consider the gap from knowing to doing when conducting training; do not let too much time elapse between training and application. I always tell my mentees that learning a new tool is like riding a bike. I can speak to them for days in the classroom about how to ride the bike, what to check on the bike, and the maintenance of the bike, but I cannot teach them balance. The only way for them to learn balance is to go RIDE that bike. The proper way to deploy problem-solving is to start at the top (you will regret not following this approach if you choose to ignore it).

> **CFO asks the CEO:** "What if we invest in training all of our people and they leave?"
> **CEO Responds:** "What happens if we don't and they stay?"

Follow this simple process:

1. Outside Sensei Trains and Coaches the Top Person (Plant Manager, CEO, etc.)

2. Top Person demonstrates use and competency in the process in front of a Panel Review (Sensei)

3. Top Person Trains their staff on the process and conducts a Panel Review

4. Outside Sensei Trains on Sponsorship

5. Top Person Demonstrates competency in sponsoring and coaching their teams.

6. Process is repeated down to the process level team members.

Note: As we move out of the leadership roles (leaders are expected to be trained), we should consider making the training on a voluntary (off hours) basis to ensure we are getting those people that want to learn. The thought is the company provides the training on their dime, and the employee takes the training on their time.

In a mature improvement environment, Management will conduct problem solving activities on the System, the Group Leader will conduct problem solving on the process, and the operators will conduct problem solving on the tasks. Management's engagement in Problem Solving is not negotiable. If there is a manager not willing to engage, we need to provide coaching, and if they still do not engage, we need to find a replacement.

As in life, there are some things in business that are considered closed-handed issues. Closed-Handed issues are not debatable, and I recommend that leaders following the company's direction on continuous improvement be a closed-handed issue. There are also open-handed issues that are open for debate. For example, what font or format is used on forms within the continuous improvement environment. However, I have seen companies spend more time on font than on dealing with passive aggressive leaders not embracing the company's improvement philosophy. Don't waste your leadership capital on open-handed issues.

At the Team Member level (manufacturing, function, or service) the measure of success is the amount of voluntary problem solving we have occurring in the organization. We can "make" people do whatever we want based on pure authority. A truer measure of a leader is if that leader's people are willing to help improve the company without being "made" to do so. This will uncover some interesting dynamics within your organization. A strong authoritative leader that gets results based on force and fear will not fare well in this arena unless they change their style of leadership.

Another benefit of solving our own problems versus buying a solution is that the solutions we develop internally may not be known in the industry and therefore making it a competitive advantage. Known solutions can be purchased by our competition. This makes the solution less of a competitive advantage. Also, if we work with a vendor to develop the solution, you can bet that same solution will be out for sale to our competitors within weeks.

Another thing to consider with vendors is to never let them know more about your process than you do. I witnessed this almost kill a company that was a long-term client of mine. I had worked with this client a few years earlier but hadn't heard from them in a while. The team caught on to lean quickly and was extremely capable to move forward on their own. The next time I heard from them was when they had purchased a company that was a key part of their product flow. The company electropolished 80% of the products that my client produced, so my client decided to vertically integrate this part of the process into their business. On the surface, this was a wise move. However, they very quickly realized the process was extremely unstable and was at risk of killing the whole business. After I got the call, I spent a week in the new business trying to figure out what was going on. Toward the end of the week, it occurred to me that they had a small line that always ran good parts, but the large line always had trouble running good parts. I asked what the difference was between the two lines, other than the obvious size difference. The plant manager at the time, stated that they were using a different chemical in the large line. The chemical in the small line was the old chemical. I asked why they had changed chemicals, and I was told that the salesman told them it would run better. At that point, I asked "Well how's that working for you?" My next call was to the salesman to have him come to the plant ASAP. When he arrived at the plant, I asked him why he thought the chemical would run better, and where else he was running it.

He stated that he wasn't running it anywhere else. It turns out my client was the first one to run it. This not only broke the "don't use untested technology" concept, it also was reckless on the part of the salesman. At that point, I was fuming. I told him that we were switching back to the old formula that day and he needed to get the new stuff out of the plant. He didn't want to do it, but that is what was done. The line improved, was eventually collocated at my client's first location, and we now have a fully automated version of that line at my client's second location. My client has staff that now understands this process better than anyone else in the industry. The moral of the story is never let your supplier or vendor understand, or act like they do, the technical aspects of your business better than you do.

> "Be Polite, Be Professional but have a plan to kill everybody [competitors] you meet." — *General Mattis*

Competitors can copy your process, your product, and steal talent. However, they cannot copy your culture. I propose that the true competitive advantage should be one's culture. I recommend that the culture be one that is based on 100% of the team being focused on exposing and solving problems. We know that people naturally support and ensure the success of a solution of which they were a part of developing, so it is our job as leaders to ensure the teams have a safe environment to develop their own solutions.

To get a team moving in this direction, we must allow the team development process to unfold. When developing a new team or redeveloping an older team, we must consider the stages that all teams go through. Those stages are:

Forming

Storming

Norming

Performing

In the Forming stage, the team will cautiously explore boundaries of acceptable group behavior. There may be feelings of confusion—they may not know what role they play on the team. Members will be very polite and demonstrate superficial relationships, as they do not know each other well enough to move beyond that yet. They need to work to determine what is expected of the team, and of the role they play on the team. Productivity will be low since the team hasn't done any real work yet, but morale is still high—they are excited to start something new and haven't had any conflict. Members will try to define where they fit on this team compared to the existing authority of their "regular job" or of other teams they are on.

The Storming stage is the most difficult stage. If a team doesn't work through it, the team will not recover and never reach its potential. Conflict naturally occurs… In fact, if conflict doesn't occur, you might start to wonder why it is not occurring. Numerous surprises within this stage, especially when team members realize that the task is a mountain and not the mole hill as originally thought. Conflict also emerges, often fueled by the fact that the teammates become better acquainted and feel more comfortable confronting or disagreeing with each other. Afterall, an environment where it is not safe to disagree in is not an environment focused on growth; it is an environment focused on control and/or manipulation. By taking time to discuss disagreements, you may find that some debates are violent agreements. One of our biggest communication problems is we often don't listen to understand, we listen to reply. Each side simply hasn't taken the time to carefully listen to the other side when in fact they agree on the issue at hand. Through these debates, true LEADERSHIP emerges. This leadership may often be different from who was "appointed" the leader in the Forming stage. The key is to work through this stage. Many teams quit during this stage. It is critical to remember that Storming is a necessary transition. A team cannot Norm if it doesn't Storm.

In the Norming stage, a sense of group cohesion develops. The team members use more energy on data collection and analysis as they begin to test theories and identify root causes. The members accept other team members and develop norms for resolving conflicts, making decisions, and completing assignments. Norming takes place in three ways:

- As storming is overcome, the team becomes more relaxed and steadier. Conflicts are no longer as frequent and no longer throw the team off course.

- Norming occurs when the team develops a routine. Scheduled team meetings give a sense of predictability and orientation.

- Norming is cultivated through team building events and activities.

In the Performing stage, the team has developed relationships, structure, and purpose. The team begins to tackle tasks at hand. The team has demonstrated that it can work effectively and cohesively. The members of the team may occasionally surface feelings that remained unresolved from the storming phase.

The leader of the newly developed team must have patience as the team works its way through these phases. The issue is we live in a "download it now" society when certain things must be grown. Great teams are grown; not downloaded. These phases are very normal and if allowed to occur, will create a much stronger team bond, leading to the unity that we desire. Team development is an organic process, so trying to rush it is like trying to pull on a plant to make it grow faster; if you pull hard enough you will destroy the plant and the very thing you are trying to create. Be patient!

The most important thing you can do as the leader is ensure you have the right team in place to lead the business or enterprise to the next level. It is your job to get the top team right.

End of Chapter GROUP Reflection Questions:

1. Are we progressing on the actions from our last discussion?

2. What was the key learning from the current chapter?

3. As a team, what do we do well as it relates to the key learning?

4. As a team, what do we NOT do well as it relates to the key learning?

5. What do we need to Start, Stop, or Continue doing as a team to improve going forward as it relates to the key learning?

CHAPTER 11

THE JOURNEY

"Determination = FFOYF + 1; Where: FFOYF = Fall Flat
On Your Face" - Unknown

We all need help at some point in our journey. I cannot tell you how many times I have pointed out what was obvious to me, but not so obvious to the client team. This is not that they are not smart. I have the pleasure of working with some of the smartest people on the planet. It is because they have become numb to it. I too have had this happen to me in my own business. I occasional have consultants help get me out of the numbness. Yes, even consultants use consultants.

THE QUESTION: WHERE DO I START?

This is a question that befuddles many executives. In fact, 70% of companies who have embarked upon an improvement are dissatisfied with the results they have achieved (McKenzie & Bain study). Millions of dollars are spent each year by companies hiring consultants, creating Continuous Improvement departments, attending training and seminars, doing Kaizen Events (which is an oxymoron. Kaizen means continuous and Event is a point in time), moving equipment, and implementing improvement tools. Yet most companies who do this are not happy with the return on investment. Why is this? The biggest reason is the misconception that Continuous Improvement is nothing more than a set of tools. Part of the fault lies with the term "Lean Manufacturing." That term was coined to market the Toyota Production System (TPS) to western manufacturers. In addition, much of the early teaching on the subject in the USA was focused on the implementation of Lean Tools. If we had kept the original name (Toyota Production System, now called the Toyota Business System), it would have clued us in to the fact that what we are talking about here is a System (a holistic system), not a collection of independent tools.

Another problem is that western managers are not in the habit of deeply understanding problems. So, when they began to look at Toyota, they took a very superficial look at what Toyota is doing. What they tend to see are the surface things: a clean, well-organized shop floor (5S), low levels of inventory (pull systems), lights and sounds indicating when problems exist (Andon), a focused workforce (standardized work); you get the picture. So, the typical westerner is going to think it is a matter of tools and endeavor to learn and implement the tools, not understanding that each tool is a counter-measure to a specific problem (this is a profoundly important point). Instead of understanding this, many companies set out to solve Toyota's problems, by simply implementing the same tools, in their plants. They may not have the same problems as Toyota, so this can often be ineffective. In effect, they are trying to solve Toyota's problems in their plants.

One example of this happening was with an engineer from a competitor of Toyota. Toyota will give anyone who comes to their plant a tour. This engineer toured the plant and noticed how Toyota was using line-side inventory in the radio installation station. There was every type of radio available at the station. When a car showed up in the station, the installer would simply get the radio required and install it. The warehouse would simply replenish these radios as they were consumed. In manufacturing, this process is called a supermarket (adapted to manufacturing by Japanese companies based on the US Supermarket System), but the concept can be used for many different product-based businesses. A few years go by, and the same engineer toured Toyota for a second time. This time he saw a totally different material presentation method being used at the radio installation station. This time he saw carts in what is called a FIFO (First In First Out) lane feeding this station. This confused the engineer, so he quizzed one of the tour guides (who are actually very knowledgeable of the manufacturing plant) and stated, "The last time I was here they were using a supermarket for the radio installation station, and now I see they are using a different method. Which one is the right way?" The tour guide responded with, "Well, it depends on what problem you are trying to solve." We did have inventory stored line side. However, the variety of radios available to be installed increased to the point where we could not store inventory lineside, so we had to move it to the warehouse, and we now kit the radios along with some other items to the line via that station. These kits are in sequence with the cars coming down the line and are electronically triggered to be kitted and delivered when the car clears a certain station." The difference between the competitor's engineer and Toyota's engineer was the Toyota engineer understood the problem being solved each time and the competitors engineer was simply copying the solution that the Toyota engineer developed. This is exactly what I mean when I state, "Don't solve Toyota's problems in your plant. You may not have the same problems."

FALSE STARTS

I often see remnants of past improvement initiatives, which I refer to as Kaizen Debris. It shows that at some point in the past, someone was doing the right things, but for whatever reason, they stopped. This is typically due to lack of leadership discipline to sustain the system. From their superficial understanding of continuous improvement, several false starts can be initiated. One of the common false starts is the idea of a "model line" or "focused factory." Typically, the train of thought runs along these lines: "If continuous improvement is nothing more than a set of tools, and I do not have experience with those tools, then I'm going to pick a small area where I can apply the tools and learn to be proficient with them. Then I will expand what I learn to the rest of the factory." On the surface this seems perfectly logical. However, continuous improvement is not a collection of "tools"; it is a system for management (more on this later). The problem with the model line concept is that once you get to a certain point, you start to have two very different systems running concurrently in your plant, which causes all kinds of conflicts and inefficiencies. All supporting systems (logistics, maintenance, management, engineering, accounting, human resources, shift structure, union contracts, supply chain management, etc.) are set up to support traditional manufacturing and most often do not adequately support a model line. This causes the model line to perform poorly. Because the model line conflicts with the existing support systems, continuous improvement gets a bad reputation within the organization. Another false start is to attempt to implement improvement through Kaizen events. Typically, this involves picking a specific area and implementing a specific tool (cellular manufacturing, SMED, 5S, etc.). A number of these events are executed throughout the year and improvement is "sprinkled" throughout the organization. The idea is that as you plant the improvement "seeds" throughout the facility, Improvement will begin to grow.

One problem here is that of planting the right seeds in the wrong soil. The culture of a traditional mass manufacturing organization is not the kind of environment that will nurture the proliferation of continuous improvement. Quite the opposite, such improvements are difficult, if not impossible, to sustain and the area improved slowly degrades until it eventually runs like the rest of the plant. Another problem is that an area is picked, and a tool is picked, but the problem (if there is one) is not understood. Many Kaizen events solve problems that do not exist. We are answering the wrong questions. Another potential pitfall with Kaizen events is that you solve a problem, but it is not a high-leverage problem, so that it yields minimal bottom-line results. Still another false start is to designate (or even hire) a Continuous Improvement Coordinator (some firms even create entire departments of improvement specialists). I am not against hiring this position, since the current team is often too busy focusing on being good today instead of being better tomorrow. There is a need to create a position or group to start focusing on tomorrow. However, such specialists are not cheap. A competent, experienced practitioner will command a six-figure salary per year.

Getting the right experience is not cheap. There is an old tale concerning a company that called a repairman to help them with a machine that had been down for days. The company was desperate, since they had already tried everything they knew to fix the problem. They finally broke down and called in the expert. The expert walked in the plant, approached the machine, looked it over for a few minutes, pulled out his hammer, and hit the machine. The machine then came to life. The expert left and said his invoice would follow in a few days. When the invoice arrived, the company could not believe the cost. They were offended. There was a single line item on the invoice that read, "Fixed Machine: $10,000." The purchasing department pushed back and stated they could not believe that hitting a machine with a hammer cost $10,000. They phoned the expert and asked if he could resubmit the invoice, since they thought hitting a machine with a hammer should not cost $10,000. Afterall, he had spent less than an hour in the plant. The expert told them to tear up the old invoice, and he would resubmit the invoice. A few days later, the company received another invoice. This time the invoice had two line-items on it; one read, "Hit Machine with Hammer:

$10." The other line-item read, "Knowing Where to Hit a Machine with a Hammer: $9,990." The company paid the invoice.

Many companies are not willing to pay for this experience, so they find a cheaper option.

Expectation vs. Reality

There is always someone who will do it cheaper.

The saying, "you get what you pay for" is very true in these cases. A good improvement practitioner should be able to cover their salary per year in multiples with the savings they generate.

BEGINNING THE JOURNEY

Now that we have someone or even a department in place, what do we do? A fatal flaw is, this person in charge of improvement is usually a middle manager, 1-2 levels removed from executive management on the organization chart. This individual is given the task to "implement improvement"; however, the rest of the organization is still managed in a traditional way, by "functional silos". In some extreme cases the function groups have become insular. So, this middle manager and their department of specialists are trying to "swim upstream" against the prevailing corporate culture - trying to change an organization which lacks the same expectation and/or desire to change. The result is that it takes monumental effort on the part of the manager and their specialists and an extraordinary amount of time to implement improvement. Executive management gets frustrated because of the slow pace and low return on investment. The middle manager and the team of specialists get frustrated at the organizational barriers to implementing change and the lack of support from executive management in removing them. The rest of the organization gets frustrated at the team of specialists that keeps trying to get them involved in annoying projects that do not help them meet their goals and that takes away their "real work."

The TOP leader's job is to design the corporate character of the institution. The type of cultural change required to effectively implement improvement cannot be led from middle management, it must be led by executive management. The improvement specialist must be on the staff at the right hand of the executive leader.

Yet another type of false start is to attempt to audit your way to improvement. This approach involves creating an audit, then auditing each department at some frequency. Generally, some amount of contingent pay for most or all employees is tied to the results of the audit scores. There are myriad problems with this approach. The primary pitfall is the fact that it is impossible to create an all-encompassing audit that perfectly fits every situation (even within one facility). The audit will be well-suited to some areas/products and poorly suited to others. However, since pay is tied to it, employees will do whatever is within their power to get the desired audit score. Very often managers will adopt the practice of looking at the audit, seeing where the most points are available and focusing in that area. It may be an area that yields little if any bottom-line results. So, the audit score improves, but business results do not. Toyota would never spend time on such activities. A few months ago, a large manufacturing plant held their annual plant-wide meeting. One key performance measure after another was reviewed. All measures were below goal and were trending negatively. The plant is projected to lose money for the year. However, at the end of the presentation the Vice President stated, "On the positive side, we did meet our target score on our Continuous Improvement Assessment." What an alarming message! Universally, plant performance was poor, but the score on the assessment was on target. Sadly, such disconnects between audit scores and tangible results are common. One must ensure we have a common language of performance across the business to ensure this does not happen. I prefer to assess to a maturity model approach rather than the audit approach. The maturity model helps us agree on what good looks like and the assessment to that model helps the local team understand their current condition. The maturity model simply tells you where you are along the path of maturity, and you are expected to improve over time at your own pace and in the areas that will have the most impact on your business. The maturity model assessment should never be used to compare sites or divisions. The results are for the local team, not corporate. A proper maturity assessment should gauge the business's current condition in all eight types of flows that were covered previously and the culture that supports those flows.

I have encountered many examples of where an audit drove the wrong behavior. One instance that stands out to me was a manager that was preparing for an audit from corporate. The audit would give extra points for having a supermarket (every variety of part available when needed) in the process. The manager approached me about how he should go about implementing a supermarket in his process. I was puzzled by this, since the process was already one-by-one flow (the best option for flow in a process). The move from one-by-one flow to a supermarket would be directionally incorrect, so I asked him why he would want to implement something that would take him in the wrong direction. He pulled out the audit document and showed me that he could get 5 extra points for having a supermarket, and the 5 extra points would help him with his bonus. We did not implement a supermarket. He had to find another way to get his extra 5 points, and I worked with corporate to change the audit to prevent this specific occurrence in the future. However, the nature of audits can drive this type of behavior, and it is impossible to catch all the loopholes.

AVOID THE SHOTGUN START

Probably the worst type of false start is the "shotgun approach". Using this approach, you take all improvement tools and apply them one at a time to the entire organization. The idea behind this approach is that if a company copies all the Tools from Toyota, then they will get results comparable to the results that Toyota gets. Unfortunately, the typical result is that every department gets, for example, a pull system, regardless of whether there is sufficient stability to implement a pull system and regardless of whether there is a problem that indicates the need for a pull system. A lot of time and money get invested in solving problems that do not exist.

I have seen companies spend hundreds of thousands of dollars implementing Improvement Tools without knowing the answers to the following basic questions:

What problem are you trying to solve?

What results do you need/expect?

How much will it cost?

What is the return on investment?

It is possible to spend a lot of money and realize minimal results using this approach. The root cause of all these ineffective approaches to implementing improvement is the lack of fundamental understanding of what improvement is… a system for managing all aspects of the enterprise.

PLANNING THE JOURNEY

"Everyone has a plan until they get punched in the mouth"
— Mike Tyson

HOSHIN WHAT?

While we covered the practical implementation of Hoshin (in the form of Strategic Planning) earlier in this book in chapter covering Habit 3 – Embracing the Total System, I wanted to revisit here again with more of the theory. Many organizations who are years into their Improvement Journey have never heard the term Hoshin Kanri, yet it is the heart of the Toyota

Production System. Hoshin Kanri helps ensure that an organization works on the right things to get the expected results. That sounds attractive until I mention that an organization usually needs to turn their entire approach to managing upside down; product development, back-office business processes… Indeed, the entire enterprise needs to be managed differently. Can you get results without it? Sure, albeit limited results. As an example, Single Minute Exchange of Die (SMED) is a process by which one can reduce the amount of time spent changing from one product or service to another. The value in reducing this changeover time is to allow more time to produce more products, conduct more changeovers, or perform more services. SMED will work as a stand-alone process. A mass manufacturer can use SMED to reduce changeover time and therefore make more parts on the same equipment, amortizing the capital cost of the equipment over more parts, thus reducing cost per piece. However, with Hoshin Kanri, it might become evident that it is more important to use the changeover time reduction to reduce batch size and change over more often, leading to greater flexibility to meet customer demand and lower inventory carrying cost. So, the tool without the holistic approach of Hoshin Kanri can get some results, but likely will not lead to the best result and the greatest return on investment. There are three basic components of Hoshin Kanri. The first is setting goals. When setting goals for the team, the goal cannot be too big to achieve nor too small to inspire. The second is creating a detailed plan to meet the goals, and the third is putting in place a system to ensure the detailed plan is executed in the planned timing, with the planned results. For a detailed explanation of these steps refer to the chapter on Habit 3.

THE TYPICAL APPROACH

Instead of using Hoshin Kanri, what typically happens in traditional companies is that plant level goals are established for a variety of areas. Many organizations do a good job of "deploying" those goals down to most levels of the organization, but rarely do they make it all the way down to the individual level. In fact, it is most often very difficult to even understand how an individual employee's goals support the plant's goals. Therefore, there is no comprehensive, detailed plan outlining how goals at all levels are going to be met. Very rarely is there a system in place to ensure that the plan is executed on time with the desired results.

As an example, let us look at how financial goals are typically handled. Financial goals are usually stated in a business plan or budget. Numerous accounts have a yearly spending target. If all accounts stay within the spending target, the business should meet its profit goals. Each month, the status of each account is reviewed, and any variances are reported. Managers take action to bring accounts in the red back in line, usually through draconian measures. Therefore, in many companies you cannot order office supplies or go on any business trips during the last couple of months of the year. This is also why many arbitrary cuts are made in areas such as labor and inventory leading to quality and delivery issues. I refer to this as the 4th quarter evaporation routine.

The problems with the above method are manifold. First is the frequency of review. As stated earlier, if you measure progress monthly, it is equivalent to a doctor doing an autopsy asking, "Why did the patient die?" In contrast, if you measure progress daily, or every hour, or every cycle, it is equivalent to a doctor checking a patient's vital signs asking, "Why is the patient sick?" If you only check progress once a month, chances are that by the time you detect a problem, you will be so far removed from it that either you will be unable to accurately determine its cause, it will be terribly expensive to fix, or both.

"A goal without a plan to achieve it is a fantasy."
— Unknown

The second problem is that of monitoring progress towards goals without having a proactive plan for how to meet them. There are always gaps – areas where you know it will be a challenge to stay on target. Communicating those gaps is not sufficient. Once identified, a proactive plan must be developed for how to close those gaps and the plan must be executed relentlessly to ensure that the gap closes as planned.

Without this type of planning, it is difficult to answer questions such as:

- Which projects are most important?
- Where do resource limitations exist?
- Where do I have excess resources?
- What is the value of each initiative?
- Are all my initiatives and projects aligned?
- Do I have any duplication of effort?

The third problem flows from the first two. When you do not have an "early warning system" and you do not have a plan for closing gaps, you are going to end up in a position where your only alternative is draconian cuts. These draconian cuts often lead to a business cutting into the capability (the muscle) of the business in the name of cost savings. In continuous improvement we look for cost reduction by removing waste from the value-added process.

Many companies, to control cost, begin strict cost cutting efforts. For example, have you experienced 4th quarter spending, hiring, and travel freezes? When this occurs, they make many short-sighted decisions and eventually negatively impact the business's capability to deliver. As a consultant, I too have fallen victim to this 4th quarter evaporation (referring to my schedule) routine due to clients canceling my work to "cut" costs.

When I contrast the difference between cost cutting and cost savings, I use the following analogy. If my wife asked me to lose 20 lbs, I could cut off one of my legs. I will have satisfied the request. However, I may not be able to run again. It may turn out that since I lost the weight quickly, my wife would want another 20 lbs. Well, there goes my other leg. On the other hand, should I decide to diet and exercise, I could lose 20lbs and improve my running speed. In this case, I met the goal and improved my capability at the same time. As leaders, we must do the same in our businesses. This is the key difference between Continuous Improvement and traditional accounting-driven cost reduction. Accounting-driven measures tend to cut costs, sometimes quite arbitrarily. Continuous Improvement focuses on elimination of the waste that causes the cost, and then removes the resources that were in place to cover up the waste. The former can cause you to remove some value-added resources. The latter always removes waste.

It is never a good idea to cut into the capability in the name of cost cutting.

LEADING THE JOURNEY

Leaders don't force people to follow them, they invite them on a journey. The first step here is to set the direction of your company. To do this, you define your Current Condition, which is a description of where your organization is right now. Next, you define an Ideal Condition that describes where your company will be in 100 years (consider this the IDEAL condition which is one step below TRUE NORTH). Then, you must establish what defines success for your organization in the short term (6-12 months). This is called the Target Condition. The Target Condition should be defined by slowly compromising from the 100-year plan; not an incremental improvement from the Current Condition. Each of these "Conditions" is defined by a gap (the difference between current and the target), key performance indicators to measure the gap and/or the results, and a list of problems/opportunities expressed in dollars. Now you have a road map for your business. You know where you are now, where you want to be in the long run and where you plan to be in the short term. As you travel on the path from the Current

Condition through the Target Condition toward the Ideal Condition, you want to travel in a straight line to get to the Ideal Condition as quickly as possible. This creates a compass heading toward True North. A lot of companies are committed to the route on which they are currently. However, it does not matter what route one is on if they are headed in the wrong direction. True North helps us set the right direction. Efficiently moving in the wrong direction is one of the worst things one can do as a business. The habits in this book will be a huge help when setting direction. Now you can define what your goals are. Usually, they have something to do with areas such as ES&H, profit, customer satisfaction (quality, delivery, and cost (in that order)), service to the community, and employee satisfaction. You set goals in each of these areas and establish key performance indicators (KPI) that you will use to track progress toward meeting those goals. This process explanation is highly simplified. When done right, it could take a full month for a solid, thorough assessment of the current condition.

ESTABLISHING THE PLAN

Now that you have established KPI's and have set goals for each one, it is easy to assess the gap between the current measure and the goal. Once the gap is understood, you can begin to identify projects that can be executed to close the gaps. Here is where the tools of continuous improvement come in. Now that you understand your problems, probably at a deeper level than ever before, you can (with help from a Trusted Advisor) and with much greater accuracy identify which Improvement Tools should be used. Each project should be clearly defined with a business case, a description of the current condition, a description of the target condition, an action plan for achieving the target condition, expected timing, and expected results as measured by the key performance indicators. You will need to establish more than enough projects so that your plan over-performs compared to the goals. We want to under-promise and over-deliver. The reason for this is that there is always significant uncertainty in estimating the results of each project and you want to be prepared in case the results of some of your projects do not meet expectations. This activity takes place at each level of the organization, beginning at the executive level, then senior managers, then managers, then junior staff. At the end, every individual, department, product, and function should know their goals, the plan to meet their goals, and how their goals contribute to meeting the overall goals for the business.

ESTABLISHING THE TRACKING SYSTEM

Now that you have a plan, the real work begins. Tracking should take place frequently, with short review meetings. Focus should be on the action items in each project that are not on target in terms of timing and results. If projects fall behind significantly, a recovery plan is required. The goal is the goal. A relentless attitude is necessary and failure to meet project timing and results targets is not acceptable. Afterall, this is the plan that the senior leadership team has committed to achieving. It is the project leader's task to keep all actions on track and to report any barriers to management. It is management's task to remove barriers, coach the project leader, and provide necessary support/resources. It is not fair to the team if top leaders expect their teams to reach a goal if they are not willing to provide resources and/ or remove barriers.

Below is a simple graphic showing the basic layout of a project plan.

Team		Timing
Business Case	Action 1	
	Action 2	
Initial Condition	Action 3	
	Action 4	
Target Condition	Action 5	
	Action 6	
Key Performance Indicators	Action 7	
	Action n	

PROCESS YIELDS RESULTS

Now you have an Improvement Plan that will generate significant results if executed properly. Your Improvement Plan driven by the Hoshin Kanri planning process will generate far greater return on investment than the more haphazard methodologies I have seen used in the past. The activities of deeply understanding the Current Condition, then charting an Ideal Condition and Target Condition ensures all levels of the organization understand the implementation and how they contribute to it. The implementation becomes how you run your business, not a separate activity. The process forces your organization to adapt to support the transformation from the Current to the Target condition. You will eliminate many superfluous and counter-productive projects and initiatives. Your projects and initiatives will be well aligned. Resource problems are easier to identify up-front and proactively correct. You will always know where you stand, what needs to be done, where the problems are, and what the most important thing to work on is. Is this Orwellian Utopia? No. You will work harder than you ever worked before… and you will achieve results that are more satisfying than any you have ever achieved. I still believe that if you work hard and do good things you will be rewarded. If your company doesn't reward hardworking and the doing of good things, you may be working for the wrong company.

"It is not enough that we do our best; sometimes we must do what is required." — *Winston Churchill*

TRUSTED ADVISORS

A fighter does not know that his balance is off a little or he would correct it. The champion golfer does not know that her grip is a little too tight, or she would correct it. Any system of aid for champions must include a method of detecting unexpected areas of improvement. If champions need aid, then us mere mortals may also need aid at times but be careful whose advice you take. The thing worse than any enemy is bad advice.

Along those lines, there may be times during your journey when you need help. Do not feel bad about that since all of us need help at many points along our journeys. We all need to be surrounded by trusted advisors. In my career as a consultant, both as an internal consultant as well as an external consultant, I have worked with teams in many different types of engagements. The attitude of those teams varies greatly.

Below is a list of some of the group attitudes that I have encountered:

- The local team that is genuinely interested and engaged in change.
- The team that thinks they are doing well enough and does not need to change.
- The team that thinks they can do it themselves without the need for outside support.
- The team that is only "doing" it because the corporate executives are making them do it.

Anyone helping a team would prefer the first attitude. Which team do you suppose has the most success, historically? Not a difficult question, correct?

Sometimes you and your team will find yourselves in an Echo Chamber. This means you are yelling out what you eventually want to hear back. You are literally talking to yourselves. You must work to break the echo chamber. A trusted advisor and help get you out of your echo chamber.

THE NEED

Many companies have resources in their business with transformation experience, but for whatever reason, they cannot seem to get things done. Sometimes "a prophet can do no good in his hometown."

A few years back, I had been recommended to a business by one of their outside advisors, which surprised me, since I knew there were people at the company that could do what I would be doing. When asked why I was recommended, the advisor explained that he always recommended using consultants for the critical items. In his opinion, once someone is hired, the sense of urgency that is caused by using 'expensive' consultants is lost. Therefore, the consultancy ends up bringing more value. Since the consultant is being paid, the work gets priority. While some businesses believe that they do not need consultants, I argue that everyone benefits from highly experienced support and coaching. Even the best athletes in the world have coaches to help them become better. There is value in having that outside accountability and follow-up to help one focus on "being better tomorrow" versus simply just "being good today." I have also utilized consultants for items with which I am not an expert, such as Customer Journey Mapping and Social Media Marketing. Having experts in these areas come alongside me helped shorten my learning curve.

The key is to hire consultants that aren't afraid to roll up their sleeves and get to work. Consultants that sit in conference rooms (when not teaching) always drove me nuts. Working hard, in a tangible way, for your clients always pays off, and often in ways you don't expect. For example, I was at a client location for an improvement event week, and there were some very high-ranking VP's scheduled to visit the site. The site had been bought by a larger company, and I was already on edge not knowing the new owner's proclivity for consultants. The GM of the site instructed me to keep my head down during the visit. He didn't want to lose my help. He even recommended that I not wear my company shirt, as to not stand out in the plant. I did as I was told. I spent the day working with a team on retrofitting a machine that we had redesigned during one of our improvement events. I was carrying tools, and shafts through the plant and doing as much of the work as I could to get the improvement implemented. I made it through the day without being noticed, at least that was what I thought anyway. The next day the GM approached me and stated that the highest-ranking VP had seen me and asked who I was. I quipped back that I did exactly what he told me to do. I even wore a t-shirt that day. I then asked, "Why did he notice me?" The GM stated that the VP saw me carrying one of those large shafts on my shoulder through the plant while other members of the client team were following behind me. The VP asked, "Who's that guy carrying that shaft?" The GM, not wanting to lie to the VP, told him that I was a consultant. The VP returned with, "That's the kind of consultants we need in all of our plants." Needless to say, I didn't get kicked out of the plant as expected. This led to many more years with this client and other companies within the larger company. You never know who's watching, so always be on your "A" game.

THE FALLACY OF INDUSTRY OR SEGMENT EXPERIENCE

A pitfall companies often make is that they assume when selecting a consultant, they need a consultant with deep experience in their industry. This is not always the best approach. Often, industry insiders suffer from the "curse of knowledge" within their industry or with their product. The curse of knowledge is when one knows too much about or has been too close to the topic and may overlook opportunities for improvement.

> "If you want to learn about water, don't ask a fish"
> – Chinese Proverb

Sometimes it is good to get an outside set of eyes to look at your business. There are industry-wide paradigms that exist. Often, the consultants that are the best fit do not possess those same paradigms. Remember, processes are processes. People that are trained to analyze and improve processes do not need to be experts in the process that they are reviewing. In fact, having deep knowledge of the process is often a detriment to the analysis process.

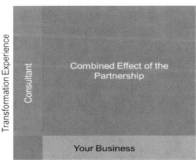

The graphic above shows the combined effect of partnering with the right consultant. The consultant should have proven experience in transformation processes. The experience of the consultant should be more than what the client currently possesses, otherwise, the consultant will not be respected by the business leaders. That same consultant should understand the organizational, cultural, and technical aspects of the change that is needed. When we put the transformation knowledge of the consultant and the product/ process knowledge of the team together, we get the combined effect which leads to transformation and breakthroughs in thinking.

"Knowledge + Experience = Wisdom" — *Unknown*

The value of experience was well explained by a close friend of mine. He was having issues with his oldest Son not wanting to listen to his advice. In a conversation with his oldest son, my friend asked if his son thought he was smarter than his younger brother. The older son stated that he was a lot smarter. My friend then proceeded to ask why his son thought that he was smarter. He asked, "Was it because he was born smarter?" The oldest son stated "no". "Then why are you smarter?" probed my friend. The oldest son argued that he was smarter because he was older and had more experience. My friend questioned, "Are you telling me that experience makes you smarter than your brother?" His son replied, "Yes." My friend continued to ask, "If you are smarter than your brother because you have two more years of experience, do you think I am smarter than you because I have had 20 years more experience?" Silence! At the age at which his son was at the time, it was not typical to think dad is smart. This same example applies to the value a consultant can bring a business. A good consultant will have many more years of experience in conducting transformation in many different environments. Simply conducting transformation in one industry or company can limit the value of the experience.

THE CONSULTANT AS A CATALYST

Often, there is no impetus to change, so the presence of an outside consultant can provide that catalyst for change. The consultant should also serve as an unbiased party for the change initiative. It should also be understood that the consultant is there to help everyone, not just management. This requires you to get a consultant that can transition from the boardroom to the design-room/toolroom/shopfloor with ease. True consultants have the abundance mentality and seek to grow others versus taking the credit for themselves. A good consultant knows that a paid invoice is their recognition, so all additional recognition goes to the transformation team. While I do encourage the use of well selected consultants, I would warn you to stay away from insultants; they are more about their ego than your success.

As I stated earlier in this book, the elements of the transformation process are: Organizational, Technical and Cultural. The right consultant will not be limited to only the technical aspects of change. While technical change is the easiest to implement, the real changes to support that technical change is organizational and, even more importantly, cultural. Organizational and cultural change is what enables the technical changes to be sustained. I often see the most pushback when attempting to change the organization and culture.

DISCUSS THE UNDISCUSSABLES WITH LEADERSHIP

Consultants must be honest with the leadership. They must tell the leaders what they need to hear, not always what they want to hear. Leadership tends to be far more apt to listen to the consultant than the employees that report to them. A great consultant does not tell the top leaders what they want to hear even at the risk of being asked to leave the business. Consultants can also tell you what your team is afraid to tell you. You may not think your associates are afraid to tell you things, but I can assure you this is a normal occurrence in any business. We can also say what the CEO is thinking but cannot say. At times, we have served as the mouthpiece, if it was aligned with the long-term direction of the transformation, for the CEO to the rest of the organization.

Some will choose to struggle through the transformation process on their own. Doing this is better than doing nothing. Afterall, there is a hidden cost to doing nothing. However, if you want to accelerate learning and improvement, you should find a consultant that you can trust and make them part of the transformation process. This person should have the ear of the top leader at the site as well as the C-suite.

TRANSFER OF KNOWLEDGE

The goal of a consultant (internal or external) should not be to create dependency for their services. The goal should be to transfer as much knowledge as possible to the team. Confucius stated, ``I hear and I forget, I see and I remember, I DO and I understand." A true consultant will embrace this and ensure Hear, See, Do is followed with their clients. The more people we can expose to Hear-See-Do the faster the culture will shift. We must also ensure leadership is developed as part of the process or it will not get sustained. A recap of the Hear, See, Do approach is as follows. In the Hear step, we teach them the theory behind what will be implemented. This theory must be practical theory, not untested theory. The next step is See. Show them examples of where it has worked. These examples may be inside their company, from a like company in the same industry, or from a completely different industry. Finally, it is time to Do. This is our call to action; our time to practice what we have learned. This is the point where we follow the I DO, WE DO, YOU DO model discussed in the previous chapter.

What you have probably realized by now is the journey never ends, so I recommend you enjoy the journey. There is a lot to see and admire along the way, so do not miss it.

End of Chapter GROUP Reflection Questions:

1. Are we progressing on the actions from our last discussion?

2. What was the key learning from the current chapter?

3. As a team, what do we do well as it relates to the key learning?

4. As a team, what do we NOT do well as it relates to the key learning?

5. What do we need to Start, Stop, or Continue doing as a team to improve going forward as it relates to the key learning?

CONCLUSION

FINAL THOUGHTS

At the changing of guards, the outgoing CEO gave the new CEO three numbered envelopes. He told him when he thought he could not take any more, to open an envelope. After about six months, the new CEO had reached a point where he thought he could not take it anymore. Then he remembered the three envelopes. He reached inside his desk and opened the first envelope. The note inside stated "Blame it on the last guy." So that is what he did. This bought him another 3 months. At the end of those 3 months, he was frustrated again. He opened envelope number 2. It stated, "Restructure." He restructured the company, which bought him another 6 months. Once it was clear the restructuring was not going to fix his problems, he opened the third envelope. It stated, "Make 3 Envelopes."

It does not have to be like this. If we understand and practice the habits that have been proven over time, we can all expect to be highly successful in whatever we do. I encourage you to embrace these habits and ensure your leadership team lives by these habits daily.

SUMMARY OF APPROACH

The goal of developing these habits is to create people, structure, and a culture that is continuously improving. The result is a system to identify problems and to solve problems utilizing all team members:

Where...

> Problem = A deviation from standard.
>
> Standard = A challenging target condition that we cannot always meet (so continuous improvement is included in the thinking).
>
> A standard could be for cultural, organizational, or technical work.

The work can reside in the...

> Manufacturing Value Stream (flows from Raw Material to Finished Goods)
>
> Design Value Stream (flows from concept to launch)
>
> Business Value Stream (flows from order to cash)

We will need to utilize ALL the team (hourly and salary) to expose and solve the problems in our processes or there is no chance of becoming Habitually Excellent as a company.

While every enterprise may not have a pure profit motive, the goal of every enterprise (profit or non-profit) is to have the cash to execute the vision and mission of the company. I believe the fastest way to generate cash is to improve the flow of the product(s) and/or service(s) to the customer. A deeper understanding of flow would be to look at the collective movement of matter, conveyance of information, and transfer of energy to create the product and/or service. Our goal would be to examine all of these to look for ways to improve them to allow us to provide a quality product and/or service at a faster pace, more flow.

To briefly demonstrate this concept, I will use pizza, since most people understand the pizza making process. Before you arrive at or call the pizza place, the owners have purchased all the ingredients to build your pizza. The total lead-time (order to cash) for the business starts from the moment they order those raw materials and ends when they receive your payment for product that was made with those same raw materials. Your wait lead-time (build to order) starts when you place the order. Now back to the Pizza

Palace; you place your order for the pizza (information), that order gets transmitted to the pizza maker (information), the pizza maker makes the pizza (movement of matter and human energy), the pizza is moved to the oven (movement of matter, and human energy if the pizza maker moved it), the pizza is cooked (electrical/gas energy), the pizza is boxed and delivered to you (movement of matter, and human energy if the pizza maker moved it). As stated above, the time from when you placed your order until the time you received the finished pizza is referred to as order lead-time. To improve customer satisfaction, our goal is to reduce that lead-time and therefore improve the flow from order to receipt. The business satisfaction comes from reducing the order-to-cash flow time, which includes the order lead-time. The faster you can do this the faster you can convert a raw material order into cash for the business. I state all of this to make the point that our ultimate goal is to improve flow.

To improve flow in all areas, we must have a culture and organization setup to tackle the three enemies to flow: waste (finding the least waste way), overburden (finding the least burdensome way), and unwanted variation (finding the least variant way while still giving the customer what they want).

We address the waste (discussed previously using the acrostic of DOWNTIME) using what is referred to in the many industries as Lean tools. These tools were developed by Toyota and others in the automotive industry. Toyota has been held up as the model for Lean and for good reasons. The results achieved by Toyota during the oil embargo of the 70's raised the eyebrows of some researchers at MIT. The researchers visited Toyota, wrote a book ("The Machine that Changed the World") about what they learned, which is the first time the word LEAN was used, and the rest is history. An entire industry around Lean Manufacturing Consulting was born. At the heart of Lean is subtracting (removing wastes from our work) not adding (adding work to the team, or simply working harder). If you find that Lean is adding work to your team, then you should question the practitioner's approach to Lean.

I can remember a visit to one of my clients where the local leadership team was excited to show me what they had done with lean on one of their lines. A tour of the line quickly revealed that they had not implemented lean at all. They had simply taken the operators chairs away, removed the inventory, moved the machines closer together and given them a new more challenging goal. They had done nothing to improve the situation by solving problems. They had not earned the right to take the chairs, remove the inventory, move the equipment, or challenge the team to produce more. Before I could catch myself, I blurted out, "You guys are not doing lean manufacturing, you are doing mean manufacturing." Luckily, that did not get me kicked out of the plant, and we were able to implement lean the correct way on that line. The team had the best of intentions, they were simply misled by their current thinking around lean.

We address overburden using the tools and approaches in the body of knowledge referred to as Theory of Constraints (TOC). TOC systematically focuses efforts, energy, and attention on the "system constraint." This constraint, or bottleneck, restricts the output of the entire system and at the same time represents the primary leverage point for improving it. Finding and eliminating constraints is the key to unlocking performance. Like the weakest link in a chain, every system must have a bottleneck or "CONSTRAINT" which governs its output. A machine, supply-chain, the market, or even shelf space might serve as the constraint. So could resources, orders, internal policies, regulations, or cash. TOC uses the following steps:

1. Identify the System Constraint

   a. The part of a system that constitutes its weakest link can be either physical or intangible.

2. Decide How to Exploit the Constraint

   a. We want it working at 100% for 100% of the time.

   b. How much of a buffer do we need to protect it from being starved?

3. Subordinate Everything Else

   a. Plan production to keep constraint working at 100%

   b. May need to change performance measures to "rope" upstream activities. Roping upstream activities is slowing them down to pace only at the place of the constraint. Otherwise, the upstream processes will overproduce.

4. Elevate the Constraint

   a. Determine how to increase its capacity

5. Return to Step One, But Beware of "Inertia"

   a. At this point, the bottleneck has most likely moved. If the bottleneck isn't in the plant, then it has moved to the market. Go to the market and work on that constraint.

   b. Don't overproduce the demand; work on creating new demand.

This approach was developed by Eliyahu M. Goldratt. He used a novel, "The Goal," to describe the approach. This book was mandatory reading for any MBA in the 80's and 90's. This book is still very popular today, and I highly recommend you read it.

The final enemy to flow is Variation. There are different types of variation. One type is the type that is created by variants in your product offerings. This type of variation is not going down but is going up as customers become more accustomed to getting what they want, when they want it, and where they want it. At Bosch, we had a saying when dealing with our internal customers, "You can have it Fast, Cheap, or High Quality. You pick which two you want." That may have worked back then, but today's customers are not accepting of that approach. They want all three. In the early days, Ford stated that you could have any color car you wanted if it was black. If you try that today, you will not have many customers. The challenge is to provide as many variants of your product to your customer while having as few variants in your manufacturing process. A great example of this can be seen in the home paint industry. There is no way even the largest big box improvement store could profitably stock every color that an end user would want, so the paint suppliers partnered with the retailer to customize the paint at the point of sale. Now the paint company only sells a few versions (Flat, Glossy, Satin, etc.) of white. The color is adjusted at the very end of the process. This is referred to as late-stage differentiation.

Another great example of holding the in-process variants low and creating the variants at the end of the process is Duck Donuts and Krispy Kreme. Duck Donuts makes the donuts on-demand and adds your toppings in real time. The donuts are fresh (cooked to order) and 100% customized for you. Krispy Kreme is a higher volume operation, but they have done a great job of localizing production to serve the local market. Krispy Kreme is more of a cook to stock operation. However, the cooking and stocking is done in the same location, which has allowed them to use the "Hot Now" sign to drive impulse buyer behaviors. In both cases, there is very little inventory at the store front.

The impact of allowing unneeded variation can drive a company to go out of business. Imagine the complexity of McDonalds had someone from Marketing convinced them to allow customers to pick the % lean of their meat each time they order. This would be an extreme example of "Have it Your Way" to help make the point. The customer could be like, "You know I think I will try 85% today, since I had 84% yesterday." There is not a discernible difference between 84% and an 85% lean, but since they can choose, why not? % Fat is not a value driver. It is a choice that if given a chance the customers could randomly jump from % to %. Now someone looking at the data may say, "Wow, we provide this variation, and the customers are responding." The guy at the grinder having to adjust the % per burger would be driven crazy, or should he decide to grind ahead, the inventory of each percentage stored prior to the grill would be astronomical, and spoilage would increase as a result.

If we examine the word customer a little deeper, we will see that "custom" is the root word. We should not be surprised that the customer will always trend toward more variety. There is truth to the old saying, "Variety is the spice of life". A customer: customs or customizes, what they want. The only time they do not do this is when the system with which they are dealing will not allow it. However, if given the choice, they will choose to customize. The company that can satisfy this desire to customize while maintaining their cost and delivery time, will be able to win in the new economy. The company that tries to do the former without the latter, will be out of business.

You are probably thinking that your product is more complicated than paint or food, and you are probably correct. However, there is an entire science around Modularity. To achieve modularity, one must create a modular architecture for the product. A modular product architecture is a strategic means to deliver external variety (to the customers) and internal commonality (to the manufacturing organization). I have seen it applied to complex products including Industrial HVAC, Semi-Trucks, Automobiles, etc. If you are troubled by the amount of product variation that has crept into your products, plan on rethinking your product line or launching a new product line, you should consider Modularity.

Another type of variation is seen at the process level. We address this type of unwanted variation by using what we call variation reduction tools. The two main approaches used are Six Sigma and Shainin®. Six Sigma was developed by Motorola in the 50's and later popularized by GE. Shainin® was developed by Dorian Shainin in the aerospace industry and adopted in the automotive industry, which is where I was exposed to it. Both approaches are very good. I personally use a modified approach that includes what I consider the best of both approaches. The key is to find the source of the variation as quickly as possible and kill it.

Variation also shows up in the form of work content variation and unleveled workflow. This can be driven by many different reasons. The goal is to level load the work volume and content, so the fast flowing products are never slowed down by the slower moving products in the business. It is analogous to you waiting in line for a kid's meal, when the car in front of you has ordered combo meals for the entire office.

Once we have removed (or reduced) these enemies to flow (waste, overburden, and variation), we can standardize the new process and ensure those standards are being followed by using Leader Standard Work, or layered audits.

A key to supporting these approaches is ensuring we have the cultural enablers in place. There are three main enablers are:

- Visual Management
- Leadership Engagement
- Problem-Solving Capability

We use Visual Management, so the problems are exposed, Leadership Engagement at the process level, so they see the problems being exposed and increased Problem-Solving Capability because we have trained our process level operators to solve problems. Leadership simply coaches them, removes barriers, and provides resources.

The last section in the approach is the tools. We select the tools needed to help with all the above. The key is to not start with the tools. As mentioned before, starting with tools (technical) without any cultural or organizational focus will lead to short team gains but long-term failure.

By the time we get to the point of using a tool, the leader should be able to explain the following:

- Why are we using this tool?
- When to use the tool? Are we ready for the tool?
- How to use the tool?
- How does the tool fit into the bigger picture?
- What are the leader's behaviors before, during, and after the use of the tool?

The leader should also realize that they cannot implement the tools at a faster pace than they can support for sustainment. The leader must earn the right to implement each tool.

Another important flow that must be considered is relationship flow. Kimberly Evans at Relations Research and Danny McCall in his book "Work is a We Thing" have explained relationship flow better than I have heard it explained before. Kimberly describes flow as being the point where a person's ARE (who they are) and their DO (what job they are doing) match. In this condition, the person will experience high levels of satisfaction in their work. Kim's exact definition is "Accurate alignment of role functions and environments (DO) with the associate's qualities and needs (ARE)." This supports my statement early concerning hiring people for what they know and then firing them for who they are. Kimberly goes on to explain when a person's ARE exceeds their DO, they will experience boredom, restlessness, and/or lack of purpose. At the other end of the spectrum, she describes when a person's DO exceeds their ARE: they will experience toxic stress, low self-esteem, and/or become overwhelmed. Being bored or stressed can lead to people leaving the company. When a person is in flow they are more of a Human Being (gratified) vs. a Human Doing (simply going through the motions). As we consider flow in the product and information, we must also pay very close attention to the relationship flows.

The graphic below shows the ARE-DO Flow region:

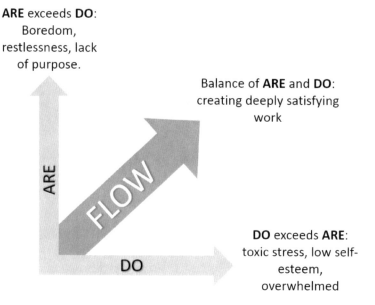

ARE exceeds **DO**: Boredom, restlessness, lack of purpose.

Balance of **ARE** and **DO**: creating deeply satisfying work

DO exceeds **ARE**: toxic stress, low self-esteem, overwhelmed

One's flow region will change over time, so Kimberly and her team have developed some very practical ways to measure relationship flow across multiple relationship structures. Another great resource for understanding flow is the book, "Flow" by Mihaly Csikszentmihalyi. His work on flow also served as the basis for Kimberly and Danny's research.

We started this book with a challenge to you to focus on all elements of change. As a reminder, those elements are:

- Technical

- Organizational

- Cultural

We also attempted to deepen your understanding of the habits that if followed, will engrain true continuous improvement in your organization leading to Habitual Excellence. As with most habits, if done correctly the immediate payback is often unpleasant, but the future payback is pleasant. The opposite is true for bad habits. The following is a quick recap of the habits.

Acting Long-term will require you to make decisions that may hurt in the short term but will set the business up for long-term success. As the leader, you must resist the urge to look good over being good. You must constantly push the team toward True North and provide the resources and remove the barriers along the way. You may not even experience the positive impact of your decisions due to the long-term nature of the decisions being made, but as a leader, you must set up the next generation of leaders for success. Remember, great leaders plant trees under which they will never sit.

Valuing the Customer and ensuring they feel that value. Find ways to 'wow' your customer. Treat them as if you could not survive without them, because you cannot survive without them. As the leader, you must ensure all support functions in the business understand that they are there to support the value providers that are within the business. The customer is paying for this value and nothing else.

Embracing the Total System to ensure all the pieces of the puzzle are working together like a symphony and not in isolation. One of your main focuses as the leader is to ensure alignment between all functions in your business with the purpose of executing a common set of goals aimed at achieving the company's reason for existence. There must be no insular functions within the company.

Focusing on the Process with the understanding that the process drives results, and you cannot get consistent results without having, knowing, and improving the process. Standardize the best way to perform the process and provide ways to ensure the standard is maintained and improved over time. Provide system pressure to ensure continuous improvement.

Obsessing Over Quality when it comes to your processes, product, and/ or service. The quality of the product or service is directly correlated to the quality of the process that produces the product or service. You must also ensure there is a culture of quality within your organization, not simply the tools (the science) of quality.

Capturing the Organizational Learning that is occurring with every product produced and every service delivered to ensure we are growing collectively as a business, not just a few smart individuals getting things done. You must also ensure everyone in the organization is trained in how to solve problems, so you are not reliant on heroic efforts when things go wrong.

Respecting People and ensuring they feel valued and not treated as a disposable part of the business. You must ensure you and your leadership team have a non-blaming and non-judgmental attitude toward your team. People are the lifeblood of the improvement strategy for any business. As leaders, we must give them meaningful work and support them in improving that work.

True North is a big part of ensuring there is never complacency in a business, or in life for that matter. We must be constantly striving to get better. In my opinion, a good target for True North for business is to build products for a market with labor and raw materials in that market. A good example of this being developed is the current trend of Farm-to-Table restaurants. With the understanding of this level of True North, and a desire to get closer to that True North, this book can be used to help enterprises all over the world.

My goal has always been to help others improve their businesses. Hopefully, what you have learned here, can help me with that goal. If you have learned from what you have read in this book, I ask that you recommend this book to at least five other people, or better yet, make it required reading for your organization. Also, feel free to reach out to me directly at mentor@stabilem.com.

If you are serious about making long lasting change within your organization, I recommend you partner with a trusted advisor that understands change management on a very deep level. Then begin the journey to becoming Habitually Excellent.

I am honored that you took the time to read this book, and I wish you the best in your journey forward. As you move along this journey remember to always honor what has already been done in the past. I would like to believe that the current team has done the best it could with their current level of understanding. The journey is long, and it should never end, but there will be many celebrations along the way. Godspeed!

End of Book Reflection Questions:

1. Are we progressing on the actions from our last discussion?
2. What was the key learning from this book?
3. As a team, what do we do well as it relates to the key learning?
4. As a team, what do we NOT do well as it relates to the key learning?
5. What do we need to Start, Stop, or Continue doing as a team to improve going forward as it relates to the key learning?

RECOMMENDED READING LIST

In the notes section, there is a complete list of books that impacted my writing. Below is a standard reading list I recommend you and your team read.

Toyota Kata by Mike Rother

The culture of Lean Implementation – coaching and problem solving

Creating a Lean Culture by David Mann

Hands-on implementation, management culture

Getting the Right Things Done by Dennis Pascal

Strategic Improvement (Hoshin Kanri)

The Toyota Way by Jeffery K. Liker

14 Management Principles of the world's greatest manufacturer

Smart Leaders, Smarter Team by Roger Schwarz

Team Dynamics and Facilitation Skills (Strategies for Mutual Learning)

The Goal by Eliyahu M. Goldratt

Theory of Constraints

Learning to See by Mike Rother and John Shook

Value Stream Mapping – Business Level Flow

Principle Centered Leadership by Stephen R. Covey

Managerial and Organizational Leadership

Understanding A3 Thinking by Durward K. Sobek II and Art Smalley

A3 Thinking

Lean Lexicon by Lean Enterprise Institute

Glossary of Lean Terms

Good to Great by Jim Collins

Leadership aspect of Continuous Improvement

The 7 Habits of Highly Effective People by Stephen R. Covey

Personal and Interpersonal Leadership

The 21 Irrefutable Laws of Leadership by John Maxwell

Leadership

The 17 Indisputable Laws of Teamwork by John Maxwell

Leading teams

Additional Recommended Authors: W. Edwards Deming, Joseph M. Juran, and Taiichi Ohno

NOTES

About the Author
"Robert Bosch" – Theodor Heuss

Preface
"Accountability: The Key to Driving a High-Performance Culture," -Greg Bustin

Chapter 1 – "Change"
"Managing Strategic Change" – Noel M. Tichy

Chapter 2 – "Leading Change"
"Creating a Lean Culture" – David Mann

"The Machine that Changed the World" - James Womack, Daniel T. Jones, and Daniel Roos

Chapter 3 – "Habit 1: Acting Long-term"
"TRIZ"

"Jumping the S Curve" – Paul Nunes and Time Breen

"How the Mighty Fall" – Jim Collins

"Reasoning Backwards" – Gregg Young

"Seven Habits of Highly Effective People" – Stephen Covey

"Kaizen" – Masaaki Imai

"Training Within Industry"

Chapter 4 – "Habit 2: Valuing the Customer"

"Give Them the Pickle" – Bob Farrell

"Hiring for Attitude" – Mark Murphy

Chapter 5 – "Habit 3: Embracing the Total System"

"Playing to Win" - A.G. Lafley

"The Four Disciplines of Execution" – Sean Covey

"Profit Beyond Measure" – H. Thomas Johnson and Anders Broms

Chapter 6 – "Habit 4: Focusing on the Process"

"Six Sigma – Breakthrough and Beyond" – Joseph A. De Feo and William W. Barnard

"World Class Quality" – Keki R. Bhote

"The Deming Management Method" – Mary Walton

Chapter 7 – "Habit 5: Obsessing Over Quality"

"Ideas are Free" - Alan G. Robinson

"Failure to Learn" – Andrew Hopkins

"Out of the Crisis" – W. Edwards Deming

"FMEA" – Chrysler, Ford, and General Motors

"APQP" – Chrysler, Ford, and General Motors

"The Toyota Way" - Jeffery Liker

Chapter 8 – "Habit 6: Capturing Organizational Learning"

"Understanding A3 Thinking" – Durward Sobek and Art Smally

"Toyota Kata" – Mike Rother

Chapter 9 – "Habit 7: Respecting People"

"The Toyota Way" - Jeffery Liker

"21 Irrefutable Laws of Leadership" – John Maxwell

Chapter 10 – "Getting the Top Right"

"Smart Leaders, Smarter Teams" – Roger Schwarz

"Straight from the Gut" – Jack Welch

"Turning the Flywheel" – Jim Collins

Chapter 11 – "The Journey"

"Getting the Right Things Done" – Pascal Dennis

Conclusion

"Work is a We Thing" – Danny McCall

"The Goal" – Eliyahu Goldratt

"Controlling Design Variants – Modular Product Platforms" by Anna Ericsson and Gunnar Erixson Ph.D.